The Complete Poems of
Paul Laurence Dunbar

The Complete Poems of
Paul Laurence Dunbar

WITH AN INTRODUCTION TO
"LYRICS OF LOWLY LIFE"
BY W. D. HOWELLS

DODD, MEAD & COMPANY
NEW YORK

1 2 3 4 5 6 7 8 9 10

Library of Congress Cataloging in Publication Data

Dunbar, Paul Laurence, 1872-1906.
    The complete poems of Paul Laurence Dunbar.

    I. Title.
PS1556.A1   1980   811'.4   80-16651
ISBN 0-396-07895-8 (pbk.)

DEDICATIONS

LYRICS OF LOWLY LIFE

TO

MY MOTHER

LYRICS OF THE HEARTHSIDE

TO

ALICE

LYRICS OF LOVE AND LAUGHTER

TO

MISS CATHERINE IMPEY

LYRICS OF SUNSHINE AND SHADOW

TO

MRS. FRANK CONOVER
WITH THANKS FOR HER LONG BELIEF

Introduction to Lyrics of Lowly Life

I THINK I should scarcely trouble the reader with a special appeal in behalf of this book, if it had not specially appealed to me for reasons apart from the author's race, origin, and condition. The world is too old now, and I find myself too much of its mood, to care for the work of a poet because he is black, because his father and mother were slaves, because he was, before and after he began to write poems, an elevator-boy. These facts would certainly attract me to him as a man, if I knew him to have a literary ambition, but when it came to his literary art, I must judge it irrespective of these facts, and enjoy or endure it for what it was in itself.

It seems to me that this was my experience with the poetry of Paul Laurence Dunbar when I found it in another form, and in justice to him I cannot wish that it should be otherwise with his readers here. Still, it will legitimately interest those who like to know the causes, or, if these may not be known, the sources, of things, to learn that the father and mother of the first poet of his race in our language were negroes without admixture of white blood. The father escaped from slavery in Kentucky to freedom in Canada, while there was still no hope of freedom otherwise; but the mother was freed by the events of the civil war, and came North to Ohio, where their son was born at Dayton, and grew up with such chances and mischances for mental training as everywhere befall the children of the poor. He has told me that his father picked up the trade of a plasterer, and when he had taught himself to read, loved chiefly to read history. The boy's mother shared his passion for literature, with a special love of poetry, and after the father died she struggled on in more than the poverty she had shared with him. She could value the faculty which her son showed first in prose sketches and attempts at fiction, and she was proud of the praise and kindness they won him among the people of the town, where he has never been without the warmest and kindest friends.

In fact from every part of Ohio and from several cities of the adjoining States, there came letters in cordial appreciation of the critical recognition which it was my pleasure no less than my duty to offer Paul Dunbar's work in another place. It seemed to me a happy omen for him that so many people who had known him, or known of him, were glad of a stranger's good word; and it was gratifying to see that at home he was esteemed for the things he had done rather than because as the son of negro slaves he had done them. If a prophet is often without honor in his own country, it surely is nothing against him when he has it. In this case it deprived me of the glory of a discoverer; but that is sometimes a barren joy, and I am always willing to forego it.

What struck me in reading Mr. Dunbar's poetry was what had already struck his friends in Ohio and Indiana, in Kentucky and Illinois. They had felt, as I felt, that however gifted his race had proven itself in music, in oratory, in several of the other arts, here was the first instance of an American negro who had evinced innate distinction in literature. In my criticism of his book I had alleged Dumas in France, and I had forgetfully failed to allege the far greater Pushkin in Russia; but these were both mulattoes, who might have been supposed to derive their qualities from white blood vastly more artistic than ours, and who were the creatures of an environment more favorable to their literary development. So far as I could remember, Paul Dunbar was the only man of pure African blood and of American civilization to feel the negro life æsthetically and express it lyrically. It seemed to me that this had come to its most modern consciousness in him, and that his brilliant and unique achievement was to have studied the American negro objectively, and to have represented him as he found him to be, with humor, with sympathy, and yet with what the reader must instinctively feel to be entire truthfulness. I said that a race which had come to this effect in any member of it, had attained civilization in him, and I permitted myself the imaginative prophecy that the hostilities and the prejudices which had so long constrained his race were destined to vanish in the arts; that these were to be the final proof that God had made of one blood all nations of men. I thought his merits positive and not comparative; and I held that if his black poems had been written by a white man, I should not have found them less admirable. I accepted them as an evidence of the essential unity of the human race, which does not think or feel black in one and white in another, but humanly in all.

Yet it appeared to me then, and it appears to me now, that there is a precious difference of temperament between the races which it would be a great pity ever to lose, and that this is best preserved and most charmingly suggested by Mr. Dunbar in those pieces of his where he studies the moods and traits of his race in its own accent of our English. We call such pieces dialect pieces for want of some closer phrase, but they are really not dialect so much as delightful personal attempts and failures for the written and spoken language. In nothing is his essentially refined and delicate art so well shown as in these pieces, which, as I ventured to say, described the range between appetite and emotion, with certain lifts far beyond and above it, which is the range of the race. He reveals in these a finely ironical perception of the negro's limitations, with a tenderness for them which I think so very rare as to be almost quite new. I should say, perhaps, that it was this humorous quality which Mr. Dunbar had added to our literature, and it would be this which would most distinguish him, now and hereafter. It is something that one

feels in nearly all the dialect pieces; and I hope that in the present collection he has kept all of these in his earlier volume, and added others to them. But the contents of this book are wholly of his own choosing, and I do not know how much or little he may have preferred the poems in literary English. Some of these I thought very good, and even more than very good, but not distinctively his contribution to the body of American poetry. What I mean is that several people might have written them; but I do not know any one else at present who could quite have written the dialect pieces. These are divinations and reports of what passes in the hearts and minds of a lowly people whose poetry had hitherto been inarticulately expressed in music, but now finds, for the first time in our tongue, literary interpretation of a very artistic completeness.

I say the event is interesting, but how important it shall be can be determined only by Mr. Dunbar's future performance. I cannot undertake to prophesy concerning this; but if he should do nothing more than he has done, I should feel that he had made the strongest claim for the negro in English literature that the negro has yet made. He has at least produced something that, however we may critically disagree about it, we cannot well refuse to enjoy; in more than one piece he has produced a work of art.

W. D. HOWELLS.

Index of Titles

Index of First Lines

xix

Lyrics of Lowly Life

ERE SLEEP COMES DOWN TO SOOTHE THE WEARY EYES

Ere sleep comes down to soothe
   the weary eyes,
    Which all the day with cease-
    less care have sought
The magic gold which from the
   seeker flies;
    Ere dreams put on the gown
    and cap of thought,
And make the waking world a
   world of lies,—
    Of lies most palpable, uncouth,
    forlorn,
That say life's full of aches and
   tears and sighs,—
    Oh, how with more than dreams
    the soul is torn,
Ere sleep comes down to soothe the
   weary eyes.

Ere sleep comes down to soothe the
   weary eyes,
    How all the griefs and heart-
    aches we have known
Come up like pois'nous vapors that
   arise
    From some base witch's caldron,
    when the crone,
To work some potent spell, her
   magic plies.
    The past which held its share of
    bitter pain,

Whose ghost we prayed that Time
   might exorcise,
    Comes up, is lived and suffered
    o'er again,
Ere sleep comes down to soothe the
   weary eyes.

Ere sleep comes down to soothe the
   weary eyes,
    What phantoms fill the dimly
    lighted room;
What ghostly shades in awe-creat-
   ing guise
    Are bodied forth within the
    teeming gloom.
What echoes faint of sad and soul-
   sick cries,
    And pangs of vague inexplicable
    pain
That pay the spirit's ceaseless en-
   terprise,
    Come thronging through the
    chambers of the brain,
Ere sleep comes down to soothe the
   weary eyes.

Ere sleep comes down to soothe the
   weary eyes,
    Where ranges forth the spirit
    far and free?
Through what strange realms and
   unfamiliar skies
    Tends her far course to lands of
    mystery?

To lands unspeakable — beyond
  surmise,
  Where shapes unknowable to
  being spring,
Till, faint of wing, the Fancy fails
  and dies
  Much wearied with the spirit's
  journeying,
Ere sleep comes down to soothe the
  weary eyes.

Ere sleep comes down to soothe the
  weary eyes,
  How questioneth the soul that
  other soul,—
The inner sense which neither
  cheats nor lies,
  But self exposes unto self, a
  scroll
Full writ with all life's acts un-
  wise or wise,
  In characters indelible and
  known;
So, trembling with the shock of
  sad surprise,
  The soul doth view its awful
  self alone,
Ere sleep comes down to soothe
  the weary eyes.

When sleep comes down to seal the
  weary eyes,
  The last deár sleep whose soft
  embrace is balm,
And whom sad sorrow teaches us
  to prize
  For kissing all our passions into
  calm,

Ah, then, no more we heed the sad
  world's cries,
  Or seek to probe th' eternal mys-
  tery,
Or fret our souls at long-withheld
  replies,
  At glooms through which our
  visions cannot see,
When sleep comes down to seal the
  weary eyes.

THE POET AND HIS SONG

A SONG is but a little thing,
And yet what joy it is to sing!
In hours of toil it gives me zest,
And when at eve I long for rest;
When cows come home along the
  bars,
  And in the fold I hear the bell,
As Night, the shepherd, herds his
  stars,
  I sing my song, and all is well.

There are no ears to hear my lays,
No lips to lift a word of praise;
But still, with faith unfaltering,
I live and laugh and love and sing.
What matters yon unheeding
  throng?
  They cannot feel my spirit's
  spell,
Since life is sweet and love is long,
  I sing my song, and all is well.

My days are never days of ease;
I till my ground and prune my
  trees.

When ripened gold is all the plain,
I put my sickle to the grain.
I labor hard, and toil and sweat,
　While others dream within the
　　dell;
But even while my brow is wet,
　I sing my song, and all is well.

Sometimes the sun, unkindly hot,
My garden makes a desert spot;
Sometimes a blight upon the tree
Takes all my fruit away from me;
And then with throes of bitter pain
　Rebellious passions rise and
　　swell;
But — life is more than fruit or
　grain,
　And so I sing, and all is well.

RETORT

" THOU art a fool," said my head
　to my heart,
" Indeed, the greatest of fools thou
　art,
　To be led astray by the trick of
　　a tress,
By a smiling face or a ribbon
　smart;"
　And my heart was in sore dis-
　　tress.

Then Phyllis came by, and her face
　was fair,
The light gleamed soft on her
　raven hair;
　And her lips were blooming a
　rosy red.

Then my heart spoke out with a
　right bold air:
" Thou art worse than a fool, O
　head!"

ACCOUNTABILITY

FOLKS ain't got no right to cen-
　suah othah folks about dey
　habits;
Him dat giv' de squir'ls de bush-
　tails made de bobtails fu' de
　rabbits.
Him dat built de gread big moun-
　tains hollered out de little
　valleys,
Him dat made de streets an' drive-
　ways wasn't shamed to make
　de alleys.

We is all constructed diff'ent,
　d'ain't no two of us de same;
We cain't he'p ouah likes an' dis-
　likes, ef we'se bad we ain't to
　blame.
Ef we 'se good, we need n't show
　off, case you bet it ain't ouah
　doin'
We gits into su'ttain channels dat
　we jes' cain't he'p pu'suin'.

But we all fits into places dat no
　othah ones could fill,
An' we does the things we has to,
　big er little, good er ill.
John cain't tek de place o' Henry,
　Su an' Sally ain't alike;
Bass ain't nuthin' like a suckah,
　chub ain't nuthin' like a pike.

When you come to think about it,
how it's all planned out it's
splendid.
Nuthin's done er evah happens,
'dout hit's somefin' dat's in-
tended;
Don't keer whut you does, you has
to, an' hit sholy beats de
dickens,—
Viney, go put on de kittle, I got
one o' mastah's chickens.

FREDERICK DOUGLASS

A HUSH is over all the teeming
lists,
And there is pause, a breath-
space in the strife;
A spirit brave has passed beyond
the mists
And vapors that obscure the sun
of life.
And Ethiopia, with bosom torn,
Laments the passing of her no-
blest born.

She weeps for him a mother's
burning tears —
She loved him with a mother's
deepest love.
He was her champion thro' direful
years,
And held her weal all other ends
above.
When Bondage held her bleeding
in the dust,

He raised her up and whispered,
"Hope and Trust."

For her his voice, a fearless clarion,
rung
That broke in warning on the
ears of men;
For her the strong bow of his
power he strung,
And sent his arrows to the very
den
Where grim Oppression held his
bloody place
And gloated o'er the mis'ries of a
race.

And he was no soft-tongued apolo-
gist;
He spoke straightforward, fear-
lessly uncowed;
The sunlight of his truth dispelled
the mist,
And set in bold relief each dark
hued cloud;
To sin and crime he gave their
proper hue,
And hurled at evil what was evil's
due.

Through good and ill report he
cleaved his way
Right onward, with his face set
toward the heights,
Nor feared to face the foeman's
dread array,—
The lash of scorn, the sting of
petty spites.

He dared the lightning in the
lightning's track,
And answered thunder with his
thunder back.

When men maligned him, and
their torrent wrath
In furious imprecations o'er him
broke,
He kept his counsel as he kept his
path;
'T was for his race, not for him-
self he spoke.
He knew the import of his Mas-
ter's call,
And felt himself too mighty to be
small.

No miser in the good he held was
he,—
His kindness followed his hori-
zon's rim.
His heart, his talents, and his
hands were free
To all who truly needed aught
of him.
Where poverty and ignorance
were rife,
He gave his bounty as he gave his
life.

The place and cause that first
aroused his might
Still proved its power until his
latest day.
In Freedom's lists and for the aid
of Right

Still in the foremost rank he
waged the fray;
Wrong lived; his occupation was
not gone.
He died in action with his armor
on!

We weep for him, but we have
touched his hand,
And felt the magic of his pres-
ence nigh,
The current that he sent through-
out the land,
The kindling spirit of his battle-
cry.
O'er all that holds us we shall tri-
umph yet,
And place our banner where his
hopes were set!

Oh, Douglass, thou hast passed
beyond the shore,
But still thy voice is ringing o'er
the gale!
Thou 'st taught thy race how high
her hopes may soar,
And bade her seek the heights,
nor faint, nor fail.
She will not fail, she heeds thy
stirring cry,
She knows thy guardian spirit will
be nigh,
And, rising from beneath the
chast'ning rod,
She stretches out her bleeding
hands to God!

LIFE

A CRUST of bread and a corner to
　　sleep in,
A minute to smile and an hour to
　　weep in,
A pint of joy to a peck of trouble,
And never a laugh but the moans
　　come double;
　　　　And that is life!

A crust and a corner that love
　　makes precious,
With a smile to warm and the
　　tears to refresh us;
And joy seems sweeter when cares
　　come after,
And a moan is the finest of foils
　　for laughter;
　　　　And that is life!

THE LESSON

MY cot was down by a cypress
　　grove,
　　And I sat by my window the
　　　　whole night long,
And heard well up from the deep
　　dark wood
　　A　　mocking-bird's　　passionate
　　　　song.

And I thought of myself so sad
　　and lone,
　　And my life's cold winter that
　　　　knew no spring;
Of my mind so weary and sick and
　　wild,
　　Of my heart too sad to sing.

But e'en as I listened the mock-
　　bird's song,
　　A thought stole into my sad-
　　　　dened heart,
And I said, " I can cheer some
　　other soul
　　By a carol's simple art."

For oft from the darkness of
　　hearts and lives
　　Come songs that brim with joy
　　　　and light,
As out of the gloom of the cypress
　　grove
　　The　mocking-bird　sings　at
　　　　night.

So I sang a lay for a brother's ear
　　In a strain to soothe his bleed-
　　　　ing heart,
And he smiled at the sound of my
　　voice and lyre,
　　Though mine was a feeble art.

But at his smile I smiled in turn,
　　And into my soul there came
　　　　a ray:
In trying to soothe another's woes
　　Mine own had passed away.

THE RISING OF THE
STORM

THE lake's dark breast
　　Is all unrest,
It heaves with a sob and a sigh.
Like a tremulous bird,
　　From its slumber stirred,
The moon is a-tilt in the sky.

From the silent deep
The waters sweep,
But faint on the cold white stones,
    And the wavelets fly
    With a plaintive cry
O'er the old earth's bare, bleak
        bones.

And the spray upsprings
    On its ghost-white wings,
And tosses a kiss at the stars;
    While a water-sprite,
    In sea-pearls dight,
Hums a sea-hymn's solemn bars.

Far out in the night,
    On the wavering sight
I see a dark hull loom;
    And its light on high,
    Like a Cyclops' eye,
Shines out through the mist and
        gloom.

Now the winds well up
    From the earth's deep cup,
And fall on the sea and shore,
    And against the pier
    The waters rear
And break with a sullen roar.

Up comes the gale,
    And the mist-wrought veil
Gives way to the lightning's glare,
    And the cloud-drifts fall,
    A sombre pall,
O'er water, earth, and air.

The storm-king flies,
    His whip he plies,
And bellows down the wind.
    The lightning rash
    With blinding flash
Comes pricking on behind.

Rise, waters, rise,
    And taunt the skies
With your swift-flitting form.
    Sweep, wild winds, sweep,
    And tear the deep
To atoms in the storm.

And the waters leapt,
    And the wild winds swept,
And blew out the moon in the sky,
    And I laughed with glee,
    It was joy to me
As the storm went raging by!

SUNSET

THE river sleeps beneath the sky,
    And clasps the shadows to its
        breast;
The crescent moon shines dim on
        high;
    And in the lately radiant west
        The gold is fading into gray.
        Now stills the lark his festive
            lay,
        And mourns with me the
            dying day.

While in the south the first faint
        star
    Lifts to the night its silver face,

And twinkles to the moon afar
  Across the heaven's graying
    space,
Low murmurs reach me from the
    town,
As Day puts on her sombre crown,
And shakes her mantle darkly
    down.

THE OLD APPLE-TREE

THERE's a memory keeps a-run-
    nin'
  Through my weary head to-
    night,
An' I see a picture dancin'
  In the fire-flames' ruddy light;
'Tis the picture of an orchard
  Wrapped in autumn's purple
    haze,
With the tender light about it
  That I loved in other days.
An' a-standin' in a corner
  Once again I seem to see
The verdant leaves an' branches
  Of an old apple-tree.

You perhaps would call it ugly,
  An' I don't know but it's so,
When you look the tree all over
  Unadorned by memory's glow;
For its boughs are gnarled an'
    crooked,
  An' its leaves are gettin' thin,
An' the apples of its bearin'
  Would n't fill so large a bin

As they used to. But I tell you,
  When it comes to pleasin' me,
It's the dearest in the orchard,—
  Is that old apple-tree.

I would hide within its shelter,
  Settlin' in some cosy nook,
Where no calls nor threats could
    stir me
  From the pages o' my book.
Oh, that quiet, sweet seclusion
  In its fulness passeth words!
It was deeper than the deepest
  That my sanctum now affords.
Why, the jaybirds an' the robins,
  They was hand in glove with
    me,
As they winked at me an' warbled
  In that old apple-tree.

It was on its sturdy branches
  That in summers long ago
I would tie my swing an' dangle
  In contentment to an' fro,
Idly dreamin' childish fancies,
  Buildin' castles in the air,
Makin' o' myself a hero
  Of romances rich an' rare.
I kin shet my eyes an' see it
  Jest as plain as plain kin be,
That same old swing a-danglin'
  To the old apple-tree.

There's a rustic seat beneath it
  That I never kin forget.
It's the place where me an'
    Hallie —
  Little sweetheart—used to set,

When we 'd wander to the orchard
So 's no listenin' ones could hear
As I whispered sugared nonsense
    Into her little willin' ear.
Now my gray old wife is Hallie,
    An' I 'm grayer still than she,
But I 'll not forget our courtin'
    'Neath the old apple-tree.

Life for us ain't all been summer,
    But I guess we 've had our share
Of its flittin' joys an' pleasures,
    An' a sprinklin' of its care.
Oft the skies have smiled upon us;
    Then again we 've seen 'em
      frown,
Though our load was ne'er so
      heavy
    That we longed to lay it down.
But when death does come
      a-callin',
    This my last request shall be,—
That they 'll bury me an' Hallie
    'Neath the old apple tree.

A PRAYER

O LORD, the hard-won miles
    Have worn my stumbling feet:
Oh, soothe me with thy smiles,
    And make my life complete.

The thorns were thick and keen
    Where'er I trembling trod;
The way was long between
    My wounded feet and God.

Where healing waters flow
    Do thou my footsteps lead.
My heart is aching so;
    Thy gracious balm I need.

PASSION AND LOVE

A MAIDEN wept and, as a com-
    forter,
Came one who cried, "I love
    thee," and he seized
Her in his arms and kissed her
    with hot breath,
That dried the tears upon her
    flaming cheeks.
While evermore his boldly blaz-
    ing eye
Burned into hers; but she uncom-
    forted
Shrank from his arms and only
    wept the more.

Then one came and gazed mutely
    in her face
With wide and wistful eyes; but
    still aloof
He held himself; as with a rev-
    erent fear,
As one who knows some sacred
    presence nigh.
And as she wept he mingled tear
    with tear,
That cheered her soul like dew a
    dusty flower,—
Until she smiled, approached, and
    touched his hand!

THE SEEDLING

As a quiet little seedling
  Lay within its darksome bed,
To itself it fell a-talking,
  And this is what it said:

"I am not so very robust,
  But I 'll do the best I can;"
And the seedling from that
    moment
  Its work of life began.

So it pushed a little leaflet
  Up into the light of day,
To examine the surroundings
  And show the rest the way.

The leaflet liked the prospect,
  So it called its brother, Stem;
Then two other leaflets heard it,
  And quickly followed them.

To be sure, the haste and hurry
  Made the seedling sweat and
    pant;
But almost before it knew it
  It found itself a plant.

The sunshine poured upon it,
  And the clouds they gave a
    shower;
And the little plant kept growing
  Till it found itself a flower.

Little folks, be like the seedling,
  Always do the best you can;
Every child must share life's
    labor
Just as well as every man.

And the sun and showers will
    help you
  Through the lonesome, strug-
    gling hours,
Till you raise to light and beauty
  Virtue's fair, unfading flowers.

PROMISE

I GREW a rose within a garden
    fair,
And, tending it with more than
    loving care,
I thought how, with the glory of
    its bloom,
I should the darkness of my life
    illume;
And, watching, ever smiled to see
    the lusty bud
Drink freely in the summer sun to
    tinct its blood.

My rose began to open, and its
    hue
Was sweet to me as to it sun and
    dew;
I watched it taking on its ruddy
    flame
Until the day of perfect blooming
    came,
Then hasted I with smiles to find
    it blushing red—
Too late! Some thoughtless child
    had plucked my rose and fled!

FULFILMENT.

I GREW a rose once more to please
    mine eyes.
All things to aid it — dew, sun,
    wind, fair skies —
Were kindly; and to shield it
    from despoil,
I fenced it safely in with grateful
    toil.
No other hand than mine shall
    pluck this flower, said I,
And I was jealous of the bee that
    hovered nigh.
It grew for days; I stood hour
    after hour
To watch the slow unfolding of
    the flower,
And then I did not leave its side
    at all,
Lest some mischance my flower
    should befall.
At last, oh joy! the central petals
    burst apart.
It blossomed—but, alas! a worm
    was at its heart!

SONG

My heart to thy heart,
    My hand to thine;
My lip to thy lips,
    Kisses are wine
Brewed for the lover in sunshine
    and shade;
Let me drink deep, then, my
    African maid.

Lily to lily,
    Rose unto rose;
My love to thy love
    Tenderly grows.
Rend not the oak and the ivy in
    twain,
Nor the swart maid from her
    swarthier swain.

AN ANTE-BELLUM SERMON

We is gathahed hyeah, my
    brothahs,
    In dis howlin' wildaness,
Fu' to speak some words of com-
    fo't
    To each othah in distress.
An' we chooses fu' ouah subjic'
    Dis — we'll 'splain it by an'
    by;
    "An' de Lawd said, 'Moses,
    Moses,'
    An' de man said, 'Hyeah am
    I.'"

Now ole Pher'oh, down in Egypt,
    Was de wuss man evah bo'n,
An' he had de Hebrew chillun
    Down dah wukin' in his co'n;
'T well de Lawd got tiahed o' his
    foolin',
    An' sez he: "I'll let him
    know —
Look hyeah, Moses, go tell
    Pher'oh
    Fu' to let dem chillun go."

"An' ef he refuse to do it,
  I will make him rue de houah,
Fu' I 'll empty down on Egypt
  All de vials of my powah."
Yes, he did — an' Pher'oh's ahmy
  Was n't wuth a ha'f a dime;
Fu' de Lawd will he'p his chillun,
  You kin trust him evah time.

An' yo' enemies may 'sail you
  In de back an' in de front;
But de Lawd is all aroun' you,
  Fu' to ba' de battle's brunt.
Dey kin fo'ge yo' chains an'
    shackles
  F'om de mountains to de sea;
But de Lawd will sen' some
    Moses
  Fu' to set his chillun free.

An' de lan' shall hyeah his thun-
    dah,
  Lak a blas' f'om Gab'el's ho'n,
Fu' de Lawd of hosts is mighty
  When he girds his ahmor on.
But fu' feah some one mistakes
    me,
  I will pause right hyeah to say,
Dat I 'm still a-preachin' ancient,
  I ain't talkin' 'bout to-day.

But I tell you, fellah christuns,
  Things 'll   happen   mighty
    strange;
Now, de Lawd done dis fu' Isrul,
  An' his ways don't nevah
    change,

An' de love he showed to Isrul
  Was n't all on Isrul spent;
Now don't run an' tell yo' mas-
    tahs
  Dat I 's preachin' discontent.

'Cause I is n't; I 'se a-judgin'
  Bible people by deir ac's;
I 'se a-givin' you de Scriptuah,
  I 'se a-handin' you de fac's.
Cose ole Pher'oh b'lieved in
    slav'ry,
  But de Lawd he let him see,
Dat de people he put bref in,—
  Evah mothah's son was free.

An' dahs othahs thinks lak
    Pher'oh,
  But dey calls de Scriptuah liar,
Fu' de Bible says "a servant
  Is a-worthy of his hire."
An' you cain't git roun' nor thoo
    dat,
  An' you cain't git ovah it,
Fu' whatevah place you git in,
  Dis hyeah Bible too 'll fit.

So you see de Lawd's intention,
  Evah sence de worl' began,
Was dat His almighty freedom
  Should belong to evah man,
But I think it would be bettah,
  Ef I 'd pause agin to say,
Dat I 'm talkin' 'bout ouah free-
    dom
  In a Bibleistic way.

But de Moses is a-comin',
  An' he 's comin', suah and fas'

We kin hyeah his feet a-trompin',
  We kin hyeah his trumpit blas'.
But I want to wa'n you people,
  Don't you git too brigity;
An' don't you git to braggin'
  'Bout dese things, you wait an'
    see.

But when Moses wif his powah
  Comes an' sets us chillun free,
We will praise de gracious Mastah
  Dat has gin us liberty;
An' we 'll shout ouah halleluyahs,
  On dat mighty reck'nin' day,
When we 'se reco'nised ez citiz'—
  Huh uh! Chillun, let us pray!

ODE TO ETHIOPIA

O MOTHER RACE! to thee I
    bring
This pledge of faith unwavering,
  This tribute to thy glory.
I know the pangs which thou
    didst feel,
When Slavery crushed thee with
    its heel,
  With thy dear blood all gory.

Sad days were those — ah, sad
    indeed!
But through the land the fruitful
    seed
  Of better times was growing.
The plant of freedom upward
    sprung,

And spread its leaves so fresh and
    young —
  Its blossoms now are blowing.

On every hand in this fair land,
Proud Ethiope's swarthy children
    stand
  Beside their fairer neighbor;
The forests flee before their stroke,
Their hammers ring, their forges
    smoke,—
  They stir in honest labour.

They tread the fields where
    honour calls;
Their voices sound through sen-
    ate halls
  In majesty and power.
To right they cling; the hymns
    they sing
Up to the skies in beauty ring,
  And bolder grow each hour.

Be proud, my Race, in mind and
    soul;
Thy name is writ on Glory's scroll
  In characters of fire.
High 'mid the clouds of Fame's
    bright sky
Thy banner's blazoned folds now
    fly,
  And truth shall lift them
    higher.

Thou hast the right to noble pride,
Whose spotless robes were purified
  By blood's severe baptism.
Upon thy brow the cross was laid,

And labour's painful sweat-beads
made
A consecrating chrism.

No other race, or white or black,
When bound as thou wert, to the
rack,
So seldom stooped to grieving;
No other race, when free again,
Forgot the past and proved them
men
So noble in forgiving.

Go on and up! Our souls and
eyes
Shall follow thy continuous rise;
Our ears shall list thy story
From bards who from thy root
shall spring,
And proudly tune their lyres to
sing
Of Ethiopia's glory.

THE CORN-STALK FIDDLE

WHEN the corn's all cut and the
bright stalks shine
Like the burnished spears of a
field of gold;
When the field-mice rich on the
nubbins dine,
And the frost comes white and
the wind blows cold;
Then it's heigho! fellows and hi-
diddle-diddle,
For the time is ripe for the corn-
stalk fiddle.

And you take a stalk that is
straight and long,
With an expert eye to its
worthy points,
And you think of the bubbling
strains of song
That are bound between its
pithy joints —
Then you cut out strings, with a
bridge in the middle,
With a corn-stalk bow for a corn-
stalk fiddle.

Then the strains that grow as you
draw the bow
O'er the yielding strings with
a practised hand!
And the music's flow never loud
but low
Is the concert note of a fairy
band.
Oh, your dainty songs are a misty
riddle
To the simple sweets of the corn-
stalk fiddle.

When the eve comes on, and our
work is done,
And the sun drops down with a
tender glance,
With their hearts all prime for
the harmless fun,
Come the neighbor girls for
the evening's dance,
And they wait for the well-
known twist and twid-
dle —

More time than tune — from the
corn-stalk fiddle.

Then brother Jabez takes the bow,
  While Ned stands off with Su-
    san Bland,
Then Henry stops by Milly Snow,
  And John takes Nellie Jones's
    hand,
While I pair off with Mandy
    Biddle,
And scrape, scrape, scrape goes
    the corn-stalk fiddle.

" Salute your partners," comes the
    call,
  " All join hands and circle
    round,"
" Grand train back," and " Bal-
    ance all,"
  Footsteps lightly spurn the
    ground.
" Take your lady and balance
    down the middle "
To the merry strains of the corn-
    stalk fiddle.

So the night goes on and the dance
    is o'er,
  And the merry girls are home-
    ward gone,
But I see it all in my sleep once
    more,
  And I dream till the very break
    of dawn
Of an impish dance on a red-hot
    griddle

To the screech and scrape of a
corn-stalk fiddle.

THE MASTER-PLAYER

An old, worn harp that had been
    played
Till all its strings were loose and
    frayed,
Joy, Hate, and Fear, each one
    essayed,
To play. But each in turn had
    found
No sweet responsiveness of sound.

Then Love the Master-Player
    came
With heaving breast and eyes
    aflame;
The Harp he took all undismayed,
Smote on its strings, still strange
    to song,
And brought forth music sweet
    and strong.

THE MYSTERY

I was not; now I am — a few
    days hence
I shall not be; I fain would look
    before
And after, but can neither do;
    some Power
Or lack of power says " no " to all
    I would.
I stand upon a wide and sunless
    plain,

Nor chart nor steel to guide my
    steps aright.
Whene'er, o'ercoming fear, I dare
    to move,
I grope without direction and by
    chance.
Some feign to hear a voice and
    feel a hand
That draws them ever upward
    thro' the gloom.
But I — I hear no voice and touch
    no hand,
Tho' oft thro' silence infinite I
    list,
And strain my hearing to supernal
    sounds;
Tho' oft thro' fateful darkness do
    I reach,
And stretch my hand to find that
    other hand.
I question of th' eternal bending
    skies
That seem to neighbor with the
    novice earth;
But they roll on, and daily shut
    their eyes
On me, as I one day shall do on
    them,
And tell me not the secret that I
    ask.

NOT THEY WHO SOAR

Not they who soar, but they who
    plod
Their rugged way, unhelped, to
    God

Are heroes; they who higher fare,
And, flying, fan the upper air,
Miss all the toil that hugs the sod.
'Tis they whose backs have felt
    the rod,
Whose feet have pressed the path
    unshod,
May smile upon defeated care,
    Not they who soar.

High up there are no thorns to
    prod,
Nor boulders lurking 'neath the
    clod
To turn the keenness of the share,
For flight is ever free and rare;
But heroes they the soil who've
    trod,
    Not they who soar!

WHITTIER

Not o'er thy dust let there be
    spent
The gush of maudlin sentiment;
Such drift as that is not for thee,
Whose life and deeds and songs
    agree,
Sublime in their simplicity.

Nor shall the sorrowing tear be
    shed.
O singer sweet, thou art not
    dead!
In spite of time's malignant chill,
With living fire thy songs shall
    thrill,

And men shall say, " He liveth
   still! "

Great poets never die, for Earth
Doth count their lives of too great
   worth
To lose them from her treasured
   store;
So shalt thou live for evermore —
Though far thy form from mortal
   ken —
Deep in the hearts and minds of
   men.

TWO SONGS

A BEE that was searching for
   sweets one day
Through the gate of a rose garden
   happened to stray.
In the heart of a rose he hid away,
And forgot in his bliss the light of
   day,
As sipping his honey he buzzed in
   song;
Though day was waning, he lin-
   gered long,
   For the rose was sweet, so
     sweet.

A robin sits pluming his ruddy
   breast,
And a madrigal sings to his love
   in her nest:
" Oh, the skies they are blue, the
   fields are green,
And the birds in your nest will
   soon be seen! "

She hangs on his words with a
   thrill of love,
And chirps to him as he sits above
   For the song is sweet, so sweet.

A maiden was out on a summer's
   day
With the winds and the waves
   and the flowers at play;
And she met with a youth of
   gentle air,
With the light of the sunshine on
   his hair.
Together they wandered the flow-
   ers among;
They loved, and loving they lin-
   gered long,
   For to love is sweet, so sweet.

———

BIRD of my lady's bower,
   Sing her a song;
Tell her that every hour,
   All the day long,
Thoughts of her come to me,
   Filling my brain
With the warm ecstasy
   Of love's refrain.

Little bird! happy bird!
   Being so near,
Where e'en her slightest word
   Thou mayest hear,
Seeing her glancing eyes,
   Sheen of her hair,
Thou art in paradise,—
   Would I were there.

I am so far away,
   Thou art so near;
Plead with her, birdling gay,
Plead with my dear.
Rich be thy recompense,
   Fine be thy fee,
If through thine eloquence
   She hearken me.

A BANJO SONG

OH, dere 's lots o' keer an' trouble
   In dis world to swaller down;
An' ol' Sorrer 's purty lively
   In her way o' gittin' roun'.
Yet dere 's times when I furgit
      em,—
   Aches an' pains an' troubles
      all,—
An' it 's when I tek at ebenin'
   My ol' banjo f'om de wall.

'Bout de time dat night is fallin'
   An' my daily wu'k is done,
An' above de shady hilltops
   I kin see de settin' sun;
When de quiet, restful shadders
   Is beginnin' jes' to fall,—
Den I take de little banjo
   F'om its place upon de wall.

Den my fam'ly gadders roun' me
   In de fadin' o' de light,
Ez I strike de strings to try 'em
   Ef dey all is tuned er-right.
An' it seems we 're so nigh heaben
   We kin hyeah de angels sing
When de music o' dat banjo
   Sets my cabin all er-ring.

An' my wife an' all de othahs,—
   Male an' female, small an'
      big,—
Even up to gray-haired granny,
   Seem jes' boun' to do a jig;
'Twell I change de style o' music,
   Change de movement an' de
      time,
An' de ringin' little banjo
   Plays an ol' hea't-feelin' hime.

An' somehow my th'oat gits choky,
   An' a lump keeps tryin' to rise
Lak it wan'ed to ketch de water
   Dat was flowin' to my eyes;
An' I feel dat I could sorter
   Knock de socks clean off o' sin
Ez I hyeah my po' ol' granny
   Wif huh tremblin' voice jine in.

Den we all th'ow in our voices
   Fu' to he'p de chune out too,
Lak a big camp-meetin' choiry
   Tryin' to sing a mou'nah th'oo.
An' our th'oahts let out de music,
   Sweet an' solemn, loud an' free,
'Twell de raftahs o' my cabin
   Echo wif de melody.

Oh, de music o' de banjo,
   Quick an' deb'lish, solemn,
      slow,
Is de greates' joy an' solace
   Dat a weary slave kin know!

So jes' let me hyeah it ringin',
   Dough de chune be po' an'
      rough,
It's a pleasure; an' de pleasures
   O' dis life is few enough.

Now, de blessed little angels
   Up in heaben, we are told,
Don't do nothin' all dere lifetime
   'Ceptin' play on ha'ps o' gold.
Now I think heaben 'd be mo'
      homelike
   Ef we 'd hyeah some music fall
F'om a real ol'-fashioned banjo,
   Like dat one upon de wall.

LONGING

IF you could sit with me beside
   the sea to-day,
And whisper with me sweetest
   dreamings o'er and o'er;
I think I should not find the
   clouds so dim and gray,
And not so loud the waves com-
   plaining at the shore.

If you could sit with me upon the
   shore to-day,
And hold my hand in yours as in
   the days of old,
I think I should not mind the chill
   baptismal spray,
Nor find my hand and heart and
   all the world so cold.

If you could walk with me upon
   the strand to-day,

And tell me that my longing love
   had won your own,
I think all my sad thoughts would
   then be put away,
And I could give back laughter
   for the Ocean's moan!

THE PATH

THERE are no beaten paths to
   Glory's height,
There are no rules to compass
   greatness known;
Each for himself must cleave a
   path alone,
And press his own way forward
   in the fight.
Smooth is the way to ease and
   calm delight,
And soft the road Sloth chooseth
   for her own;
But he who craves the flower of
   life full-blown,
Must struggle up in all his armor
   dight!
What though the burden bear him
   sorely down
And crush to dust the mountain
   of his pride,
Oh, then, with strong heart let
   him still abide;
For rugged is the roadway to
   renown,
Nor may he hope to gain the en-
   vied crown,
Till he hath thrust the looming
   rocks aside.

THE LAWYERS' WAYS

I 'VE been list'nin' to them lawyers
  In the court house up the street,
An' I 've come to the conclusion
  That I'm most completely beat.
Fust one feller riz to argy,
  An' he boldly waded in
As he dressed the tremblin' pris'ner
  In a coat o' deep-dyed sin.

Why, he painted him all over
  In a hue o' blackest crime,
An' he smeared his reputation
    With the thickest kind o'
    grime,
Tell I found myself a-wond'rin',
  In a misty way and dim,
How the Lord had come to fashion
  Sich an awful man as him.

Then the other lawyer started,
    An' with brimmin', tearful
    eyes,
Said his client was a martyr
  That was brought to sacrifice.
An' he give to that same pris'ner
  Every blessed human grace,
Tell I saw the light o' virtue
  Fairly shinin' from his face.

Then I own 'at I was puzzled
    How sich things could rightly
    be;
An' this aggervatin' question
  Seems to keep a-puzzlin' me.
So, will some one please inform
  me,
    An' this mystery unroll —

How an angel an' a devil
  Can persess the self-same soul?

ODE FOR MEMORIAL DAY

DONE are the toils and the weari-
    some marches,
  Done is the summons of bugle
    and drum.
Softly and sweetly the sky over-
    arches,
  Shelt'ring a land where Rebel-
    lion is dumb.
Dark were the days of the coun-
    try's derangement,
  Sad were the hours when the
    conflict was on,
But through the gloom of frater-
    nal estrangement
  God sent his light, and we wel-
    come the dawn.
O'er the expanse of our mighty
    dominions,
  Sweeping away to the uttermost
    parts,
Peace, the wide-flying, on untiring
    pinions,
  Bringeth her message of joy to
    our hearts.

Ah, but this joy which our minds
    cannot measure,
  What did it cost for our fathers
    to gain!
Bought at the price of the heart's
    dearest treasure,
  Born out of travail and sorrow
    and pain;

Born in the battle where fleet
　Death was flying,
　Slaying with sabre-stroke bloody
　　and fell;
Born where the heroes and mar-
　　tyrs were dying,
　Torn by the fury of bullet and
　　shell.
Ah, but the day is past: silent the
　　rattle,
　And the confusion that followed
　　the fight.
Peace to the heroes who died in
　　the battle,
　Martyrs to truth and the crown-
　　ing of Right!

Out of the blood of a conflict fra-
　　ternal,
　Out of the dust and the dimness
　　of death,
Burst into blossoms of glory eter-
　　nal
　Flowers that sweeten the world
　　with their breath.
Flowers of charity, peace, and
　　devotion
　Bloom in the hearts that are
　　empty of strife;
Love that is boundless and broad
　　as the ocean
　Leaps into beauty and fulness
　　of life.
So, with the singing of pæans and
　　chorals,
　And with the flag flashing high
　　in the sun,

Place on the graves of our heroes
　　the laurels
　Which their unfaltering valor
　　has won!

PREMONITION

DEAR heart, good-night!
Nay, list awhile that sweet voice
　　singing
　When the world is all so bright,
And the sound of song sets the
　　heart a-ringing,
　Oh, love, it is not right —
　Not then to say, "Good-
　　night."

Dear heart, good-night!
The late winds in the lake weeds
　　shiver,
　And the spray flies cold and
　　white.
And the voice that sings gives a
　　telltale quiver —
　"Ah, yes, the world is bright,
　But, dearest heart, good-
　　night!"

Dear heart, good-night!
And do not longer seek to hold
　　me!
　For my soul is in affright
As the fearful glooms in their
　　pall enfold me.
　See him who sang how white
　　And still; so, dear, good-
　　night.

Dear heart, good-night!
Thy hand I 'll press no more for-
    ever,
    And mine eyes shall lose the
        light;
For the great white wraith by the
        winding river
    Shall check my steps with
        might.
        So, dear, good-night, good-
            night!

RETROSPECTION

WHEN you and I were young, the
        days
    Were filled with scent of pink
        and rose,
    And full of joy from dawn till
        close,
From morning's mist till evening's
        haze.
    And when the robin sung his
        song
    The verdant woodland ways
        along,
        We whistled louder than he
            sung.
And school was joy, and work was
        sport
For which the hours were all too
        short,
    When you and I were young,
        my boy,
        When you and I were young.

When you and I were young, the
        woods
    Brimmed bravely o'er with every
        joy
    To charm the happy-hearted
        boy.
The quail turned out her timid
        broods;
    The prickly copse, a hostess
        fine,
    Held high black cups of harm-
        less wine;
        And low the laden grape-vine
            swung
With beads of night-kissed ame-
        thyst
Where buzzing lovers held their
        tryst,
    When you and I were young,
        my boy,
        When you and I were young.

When you and I were young, the
        cool
    And fresh wind fanned our
        fevered brows
    When tumbling o'er the scented
        mows,
Or stripping by the dimpling
        pool,
    Sedge-fringed about its shim-
        mering face,
    Save where we 'd worn an en-
        t'ring place.
        How with our shouts the
            calm banks rung!

How flashed the spray as we
    plunged in,—
Pure gems that never caused a
    sin!
    When you and I were young,
        my boy,
        When you and I were young.

When you and I were young, we
    heard
    All sounds of Nature with de-
        light,—
    The whirr of wing in sudden
        flight,
The chirping of the baby-bird.
    The columbine's red bells were
        rung;
    The locust's vested chorus
        sung;
        While every wind his zithern
            strung
To high and holy-sounding keys,
And played sonatas in the trees —
    When you and I were young,
        my boy,
        When you and I were young.

When you and I were young, we
    knew
    To shout and laugh, to work
        and play,
    And night was partner to the
        day
In all our joys. So swift time
    flew
    On silent wings that, ere we
        wist,

The fleeting years had fled **un-**
    missed;
    And from our hearts **this cry**
        was wrung —
To fill with fond regret and **tears**
The days of our remaining years —
    " When you and I were young,
        my boy,
        When you and I were young."

UNEXPRESSED

Deep in my heart that aches with
    the repression,
    And strives with plenitude of
        bitter pain,
There lives a thought that clamors
    for expression,
    And spends its undelivered
        force in vain.

What boots it that some other
    may have thought it?
    The right of thoughts' expres-
        sion is divine;
The price of pain I pay for it has
    bought it,
    I care not who lays claim to it
        —'t is mine!

And yet not mine until it be deliv-
    ered;
    The manner of its birth shall
        prove the test.
Alas, alas, my rock of pride is
    shivered —
    I beat my brow — the thought
        still unexpressed.

SONG OF SUMMER

Dis is gospel weathah sho'—
  Hills is sawt o' hazy.
Meddahs level ez a flo'
  Callin' to de lazy.
Sky all white wif streaks o' blue,
  Sunshine softly gleamin',
D'ain't no wuk hit 's right to do,
  Nothin' 's right but dreamin'.

Dreamin' by de rivah side
  Wif de watahs glist'nin',
Feelin' good an' satisfied
  Ez you lay a-list'nin'
To the little nakid boys
  Splashin' in de watah,
Hollerin' fu' to spress deir joys
  Jes' lak youngsters ought to.

Squir'l a-tippin' on his toes,
  So 's to hide an' view you;
Whole flocks o' camp-meetin'
    crows
  Shoutin' hallelujah.
Peckahwood erpon de tree
  Tappin' lak a hammah;
Jaybird chattin' wif a bee,
  Tryin' to teach him grammah.

Breeze is blowin' wif perfume,
  Jes' enough to tease you;
Hollyhocks is all in bloom,
  Smellin' fu' to please you.
Go 'way, folks, an' let me 'lone,
  Times is gettin' dearah—
Summah's settin' on de th'one,
  An' I 'm a-layin' neah huh!

SPRING SONG

A BLUE-BELL springs upon the
    ledge,
A lark sits singing in the hedge;
Sweet perfumes scent the balmy
    air,
And life is brimming everywhere.
What lark and breeze and blue-
    bird sing,
  Is Spring, Spring, Spring!

No more the air is sharp and cold;
The planter wends across the wold,
And, glad, beneath the shining
    sky
We wander forth, my love and I.
And ever in our hearts doth ring
  This song of Spring, Spring!

For life is life and love is love,
'Twixt maid and man or dove and
    dove.
Life may be short, life may be
    long,
But love will come, and to its
    song
Shall this refrain for ever cling
  Of Spring, Spring, Spring!

TO LOUISE

OH, the poets may sing of their
    Lady Irenes,
And may rave in their rhymes
    about wonderful queens;
But I throw my poetical wings to
    the breeze,

And soar in a song to my Lady
    Louise.
A sweet little maid, who is dearer,
    I ween,
Than any fair duchess, or even a
    queen.
When speaking of her I can't plod
    in my prose,
For she 's the wee lassie who gave
    me a rose.

Since poets, from seeing a lady's
    lip curled,
Have written fair verse that has
    sweetened the world;
Why, then, should not I give the
    space of an hour
To making a song in return for a
    flower?
I have found in my life — it has
    not been so long —
There are too few of flowers — too
    little of song.
So out of that blossom, this lay of
    mine grows,
For the dear little lady who gave
    me the rose.

I thank God for innocence, dearer
    than Art,
That lights on a by-way which
    leads to the heart,
And led by an impulse no less
    than divine,
Walks into the temple and sits at
    the shrine.
I would rather pluck daisies that
    grow in the wild,

Or take one simple rose from the
    hand of a child,
Then to breathe the rich fragrance
    of flowers that bide
In the gardens of luxury, passion,
    and pride.

I know not, my wee one, how
    came you to know
Which way to my heart was the
    right way to go;
Unless in your purity, soul-clean
    and clear,
God whispers his messages into
    your ear.
You have now had my song, let
    me end with a prayer
That your life may be always
    sweet, happy, and fair;
That your joys may be many, and
    absent your woes,
O dear little lady who gave me
    the rose!

THE RIVALS

'T was three an' thirty year ago,
When I was ruther young, you
    know,
I had my last an' only fight
About a gal one summer night.
'T was me an' Zekel Johnson;
    Zeke
'N' me 'd be'n spattin' 'bout a
    week,
Each of us tryin' his best to show
That he was Liza Jones's beau.

We could n't neither prove the
thing,
Fur she was fur too sharp to fling
One over fur the other one
An' by so doin' stop the fun
That we chaps did n't have the
sense
To see she got at our expense,
But that 's the way a feller does,
Fur boys is fools an' allus was.
An' when they 's females in the
game
I reckon men 's about the same.
Well, Zeke an' me went on that
way
An' fussed an' quarrelled day by
day;
While Liza, mindin' not the
fuss,
Jest kep' a-goin' with both of us,
Tell we pore chaps, that 's Zeke
an' me,
Was jest plum mad with jeal-
ousy.
Well, fur a time we kep' our
places,
An' only showed by frownin'
faces
An' looks 'at well our meanin'
boded
How full o' fight we both was
loaded.
At last it come, the thing broke
out,
An' this is how it come about.
One night ('t was fair, you 'll all
agree)

I got Eliza's company,
An' leavin' Zekel in the lurch,
Went trottin' off with her to
church.
An' jest as we had took our seat
(Eliza lookin' fair an' sweet),
Why, I jest could n't help but grin
When Zekel come a-bouncin' in
As furious as the law allows.
He 'd jest be'n up to Liza's house,
To find her gone, then come to
church
To have this end put to his
search.
I guess I laffed that meetin'
through,
An' not a mortal word I knew
Of what the preacher preached er
read
Er what the choir sung er said.
Fur every time I 'd turn my head
I could n't skeercely help but see
'At Zekel had his eye on me.
An' he 'ud sort o' turn an' twist
An' grind his teeth an' shake his
fist.
I laughed, fur la! the hull church
seen us,
An' knowed that suthin' was be-
tween us.
Well, meetin' out, we started
hum,
I sorter feelin' what would come.
We 'd jest got out, when up
stepped Zeke,
An' said, " Scuse me, I 'd like to
speak

To you a minute." " Cert," said
I —
A-nudgin' Liza on the sly
An' laughin' in my sleeve with
glee,
I asked her, please, to pardon me.
We walked away a step er two,
Jest to git out o' Liza's view,
An' then Zeke said, " I want to
know
Ef you think you 're Eliza's beau,
An' 'at I 'm goin' to let her go
Hum with sich a chap as you? "
An' I said bold, " You bet I do."
Then Zekel, sneerin', said 'at he
Did n't want to hender me.
But then he 'lowed the gal was
his
An' 'at he guessed he knowed his
biz,
An' was n't feared o' all my kin
With all my friends an' chums
throwed in.
Some other things he mentioned
there
That no born man could no ways
bear —
Er think o' ca'mly tryin' to stan'
Ef Zeke had be'n the bigges' man
In town, an' not the leanest runt
'At time an' labor ever stunt.
An' so I let my fist go " bim,"
I thought I 'd mos' nigh finished
him.
But Zekel did n't take it so.
He jest ducked down an' dodged
my blow

An' then come back at me so hard,
I guess I must 'a' hurt the yard,
Er spilet the grass plot where I
fell,
An' sakes alive it hurt me / well,
It would n't be'n so bad, you see,
But he jest kep' a-hittin' me.
An' I hit back an' kicked an'
pawed,
But 't seemed 't was mostly air I
clawed,
While Zekel used his science well
A makin' every motion tell.
He punched an' hit, why, good-
ness lands,
Seemed like he had a dozen hands.
Well, afterwhile they stopped the
fuss,
An' some one kindly parted us.
All beat an' cuffed an' clawed an'
scratched,
An' needin' both our faces
patched,
Each started hum a different way;
An' what o' Liza, do you say,
Why, Liza — little humbug —
dern her,
Why, she 'd gone home with
Hiram Turner.

THE LOVER AND THE MOON

A lover whom duty called over
the wave,
With himself communed:
" Will my love be true

If left to herself? Had I bet-
ter not sue
Some friend to watch over her,
good and grave?
But my friend might fail in my
need," he said,
"And I return to find love
dead.
Since friendships fade like the
flow'rs of June,
I will leave her in charge of the
stable moon."

Then he said to the moon: "O
dear old moon,
Who for years and years from
thy thrown above
Hast nurtured and guarded
young lovers and love,
My heart has but come to its
waiting June,
And the promise time of the
budding vine;
Oh, guard thee well this love
of mine."
And he harked him then while
all was still,
And the pale moon answered
and said, "I will."

And he sailed in his ship o'er
many seas,
And he wandered wide o'er
strange far strands:
In isles of the south and in Ori-
ent lands,
Where pestilence lurks in the
breath of the breeze.

But his star was high, so he
braved the main,
And sailed him blithely home
again;
And with joy he bended his
footsteps soon
To learn of his love from the
matron moon.

She sat as of yore, in her olden
place,
Serene as death, in her silver
chair.
A white rose gleamed in her
whiter hair,
And the tint of a blush was on
her face.
At sight of the youth she sadly
bowed
And hid her face 'neath a gra-
cious cloud.
She faltered faint on the night's
dim marge,
But "How," spoke the youth,
"have you kept your
charge?"

The moon was sad at a trust ill-
kept;
The blush went out in her
blanching cheek,
And her voice was timid and
low and weak,
As she made her plea and sighed
and wept.
"Oh, another prayed and an-
other plead,

And I could n't resist," she
answering said;
" But love still grows in the
hearts of men:
Go forth, dear youth, and love
again."

But he turned him away from her
proffered grace.
" Thou art false, O moon, as
the hearts of men,
I will not, will not love again."
And he turned sheer 'round with
a soul-sick face
To the sea, and cried: " Sea,
curse the moon,
Who makes her vows and for-
gets so soon."
And the awful sea with anger
stirred,
And his breast heaved hard as
he lay and heard.

And ever the moon wept down in
rain,
And ever her sighs rose high in
wind;
But the earth and sea were deaf
and blind,
And she wept and sighed her
griefs in vain.
And ever at night, when the
storm is fierce,
The cries of a wraith through
the thunder pierce;
And the waves strain their aw-
ful hands on high

To tear the false moon from the
sky.

CONSCIENCE AND RE-MORSE

" Good-bye," I said to my con-
science —
" Good-bye for aye and aye,"
And I put her hands off harshly,
And turned my face away;
And conscience smitten sorely
Returned not from that day.

But a time came when my spirit
Grew weary of its pace;
And I cried: " Come back, my
conscience;
I long to see thy face."
But conscience cried: " I cannot;
Remorse sits in my place."

IONE

I

Ah, yes, 't is sweet still to remem-
ber,
Though 't were less painful to
forget;
For while my heart glows like an
ember,
Mine eyes with sorrow's drops
are wet,
And, oh, my heart is aching
yet.
It is a law of mortal pain

That old wounds, long accounted well,
Beneath the memory's potent spell,
Will wake to life and bleed again.

So 't is with me; it might be better
If I should turn no look behind,—
If I could curb my heart, and fetter
From reminiscent gaze my mind,
Or let my soul go blind — go blind!
But would I do it if I could?
Nay! ease at such a price were spurned;
For, since my love was once returned,
All that I suffer seemeth good.

I know, I know it is the fashion,
When love has left some heart distressed,
To weight the air with wordful passion;
But I am glad that in my breast
I ever held so dear a guest.
Love does not come at every nod,
Or every voice that calleth "hasten;"
He seeketh out some heart to chasten,
And whips it, wailing, up to God!

Love is no random road wayfarer
Who where he may must sip his glass.
Love is the King, the Purple-Wearer,
Whose guard recks not of tree or grass
To blaze the way that he may pass.
What if my heart be in the blast
That heralds his triumphant way;
Shall I repine, shall I not say:
"Rejoice, my heart, the King has passed!"

In life, each heart holds some sad story —
The saddest ones are never told.
I, too, have dreamed of fame and glory,
And viewed the future bright with gold;
But that is as a tale long told.
Mine eyes have lost their youthful flash,
My cunning hand has lost its art;
I am not old, but in my heart
The ember lies beneath the ash.

I loved! Why not? My heart was youthful,
My mind was filled with healthy thought.
He doubts not whose own self is truthful,

Doubt by dishonesty is taught;
So loved I boldly, fearing
naught.
I did not walk this lowly earth;
Mine was a newer, higher
sphere,
Where youth was long and life
was dear,
And all save love was little worth.

Her likeness! Would that I
might limn it,
As Love did, with enduring
art;
Nor dust of days nor death may
dim it,
Where it lies graven on my
heart,
Of this sad fabric of my life a
part.
I would that I might paint her
now
As I beheld her in that day,
Ere her first bloom had passed
away,
And left the lines upon her brow.

A face serene that, beaming
brightly,
Disarmed the hot sun's glances
bold.
A foot that kissed the ground so
lightly,
He frowned in wrath and
deemed her cold,
But loved her still though he
was old.

A form where every maiden grace
Bloomed to perfection's richest
flower,—
The statued pose of conscious
power,
Like lithe-limbed Dian's of the
chase.

Beneath a brow too fair for frown-
ing,
Like moon-lit deeps that glass
the skies
Till all the hosts above seem
drowning,
Looked forth her steadfast ha-
zel eyes,
With gaze serene and purely
wise.
And over all, her tresses rare,
Which, when, with his desire
grown weak,
The Night bent down to kiss
her cheek,
Entrapped and held him captive
there.

This was Ione; a spirit finer
Ne'er burned to ash its house
of clay;
A soul instinct with fire diviner
Ne'er fled athwart the face of
day,
And tempted Time with earthly
stay.
Her loveliness was not alone
Of face and form and tresses'
hue;

For aye a pure, high soul shone
through
Her every act: this was Ione.

II

'T was in the radiant summer
weather,
    When God looked, smiling,
from the sky;
And we went wand'ring much to-
gether
    By wood and lane, Ione and
I,
    Attracted by the subtle tie
Of common thoughts and com-
mon tastes,
    Of eyes whose vision saw the
same,
    And freely granted beauty's
claim
Where others found but worthless
wastes.

We paused to hear the far bells
ringing
    Across the distance, sweet and
clear.
We listened to the wild bird's
singing
    The song he meant for his
mate's ear,
    And deemed our chance to do
so dear.
We loved to watch the warrior
Sun,
    With flaming shield and flaunt-
ing crest,

Go striding down the gory
West,
When Day's long fight was fought
and won.

And life became a different
story;
    Where'er I looked, I saw new
light.
Earth's self assumed a greater
glory,
    Mine eyes were cleared to
fuller sight.
    Then first I saw the need and
might
Of that fair band, the singing
throng,
    Who, gifted with the skill di-
vine,
    Take up the threads of life,
spun fine,
And weave them into soulful
song.

They sung for me, whose passion
pressing
    My soul, found vent in song
nor line.
They bore the burden of express-
ing
    All that I felt, with art's de-
sign,
    And every word of theirs was
mine.
I read them to Ione, ofttimes,
    By hill and shore, beneath fair
skies,

And she looked deeply in mine
eyes,
And knew my love spoke through
their rhymes.

Her life was like the stream that
floweth,
And mine was like the waiting
sea;
Her love was like the flower that
bloweth,
And mine was like the search-
ing bee —
I found her sweetness all for
me.
God plied him in the mint of
time,
And coined for us a golden day,
And rolled it ringing down
life's way
With love's sweet music in its
chime.

And God unclasped the Book of
Ages,
And laid it open to our sight;
Upon the dimness of its pages,
So long consigned to rayless
night,
He shed the glory of his light.
We read them well, we read them
long,
And ever thrilling did we see
That love ruled all human-
ity,—
The master passion, pure and
strong.

III

To-day my skies are bare and
ashen,
And bend on me without a
beam.
Since love is held the master-pas-
sion,
Its loss must be the pain su-
preme —
And grinning Fate has wrecked
my dream.
But pardon, dear departed Guest,
I will not rant, I will not rail;
For good the grain must feel
the flail;
There are whom love has never
blessed.

I had and have a younger brother,
One whom I loved and love to-
day
As never fond and doting mother
Adored the babe who found its
way
From heavenly scenes into her
day.
Oh, he was full of youth's new
wine,—
A man on life's ascending slope,
Flushed with ambition, full of
hope;
And every wish of his was mine.

A kingly youth; the way before
him
Was thronged with victories to
be won;

So joyous, too, the heavens o'er
him
 Were bright with an unchang-
 ing sun,—
 His days with rhyme were over-
 run.
Toil had not taught him Nature's
prose,
 Tears had not dimmed his bril-
 liant eyes,
 And sorrow had not made him
 wise;
His life was in the budding rose.

I know not how I came to
waken,
 Some instinct pricked my soul
 to sight;
My heart by some vague thrill
was shaken,—
 A thrill so true and yet so
 slight,
 I hardly deemed I read aright.
As when a sleeper, ign'rant why,
 Not knowing what mysterious
 hand
 Has called him out of slumber-
 land,
Starts up to find some danger
nigh.

Love is a guest that comes, un-
bidden,
 But, having come, asserts his
 right;
He will not be repressed nor hid-
den.

And so my brother's dawning
plight
Became uncovered to my sight.
Some sound-mote in his passing
tone
 Caught in the meshes of my
 ear;
 Some little glance, a shade too
 dear,
Betrayed the love he bore Ione.

What could I do? He was my
brother,
 And young, and full of hope
 and trust;
I could not, dared not try to
smother
 His flame, and turn his heart to
 dust.
 I knew how oft life gives a
 crust
To starving men who cry for
bread;
 But he was young, so few his
 days,
 He had not learned the great
 world's ways,
Nor Disappointment's volumes
read.

However fair and rich the booty,
 I could not make his loss my
 gain.
For love is dear, but dearer
duty,
 And here my way was clear and
 plain.

I saw how I could save him pain.
And so, with all my day grown
    dim,
      That this loved brother's sun
        might shine,
      I joined his suit, gave over
        mine,
And sought Ione, to plead for him.

I found her in an eastern bower,
    Where all day long the am'rous
      sun
Lay by to woo a timid flower.
    This day his course was well-
      nigh run,
    But still with lingering art he
      spun
Gold fancies on the shadowed
    wall.
    The vines waved soft and green
      above,
    And there where one might tell
      his love,
I told my griefs — I told her all!

I told her all, and as she heark-
    ened,
    A tear-drop fell upon her dress.
With grief her flushing brow was
    darkened;
    One sob that she could not re-
      press
    Betrayed the depths of her dis-
      tress.
Upon her grief my sorrow fed,
    And I was bowed with unlived
      years,

My heart swelled with a sea of
    tears,
The tears my manhood could not
    shed.

The world is Rome, and Fate is
    Nero,
    Disporting in the hour of
      doom.
God made us men; times make the
    hero —
    But in that awful space of
      gloom
    I gave no thought but sorrow's
      room.
All — all was dim within that
    bower,
    What time the sun divorced the
      day;
    And all the shadows, glooming
      gray,
Proclaimed the sadness of the
    hour.

She could not speak — no word
    was needed;
    Her look, half strength and half
      despair,
Told me I had not vainly pleaded,
    That she would not ignore my
      prayer.
    And so she turned and left me
      there,
And as she went, so passed my
    bliss;
    She loved me, I could not mis-
      take —

But for her own and my love's
sake,
Her womanhood could rise to
this!

My wounded heart fled swift to
cover,
And life at times seemed very
drear.
My brother proved an ardent
lover —
What had so young a man to
fear?
He wed Ione within the year.
No shadow clouds her tranquil
brow,
Men speak her husband's name
with pride,
While she sits honored at his
side —
She is — she must be happy now!

I doubt the course I took no
longer,
Since those I love seem satisfied.
The bond between them will grow
stronger
As they go forward side by
side;
Then will my pains be jus-
fied.
Their joy is mine, and that is
best —
I am not totally bereft;
For I have still the mem'ry
left —
Love stopped with me — a Royal
Guest!

RELIGION

I AM no priest of crooks nor
creeds,
For human wants and human
needs
Are more to me than prophets'
deeds;
And human tears and human
cares
Affect me more than human
prayers.

Go, cease your wail, lugubrious
saint!
You fret high Heaven with your
plaint.
Is this the " Christian's joy " you
paint?
Is this the Christian's boasted
bliss?
Avails your faith no more than
this?

Take up your arms, come out with
me,
Let Heav'n alone; humanity
Needs more and Heaven less from
thee.
With pity for mankind look
'round;
Help them to rise — and Heaven
is found.

DEACON JONES' GRIEV-
ANCE

I 've been watchin' of 'em, par-
son,
　An' I 'm sorry fur to say
'At my mind is not contented
　With the loose an' keerless
　way
'At the young folks treat the mu-
sic;
　'T ain't the proper sort o'
　choir.
Then I don't believe in Chris-
tuns
　A-singin' hymns for hire.

But I never would 'a' mur-
mured
　An' the matter might 'a' gone
Ef it was n't fur the antics
　'At I've seen 'em kerry on;
So I thought it was my dooty
　Fur to come to you an' ask
Ef you would n't sort o' gently
　Take them singin' folks to task.

Fust, the music they 've be'n
singin'
　Will disgrace us mighty soon;
It 's a cross between a opry
　An' a ol' cotillion tune.
With its dashes an' its quavers
　An' its hifalutin style —
Why, it sets my head to swim-
min'
　When I 'm comin' down the
　aisle.

Now it might be almost decent
　Ef it was n't fur the way
'At they git up there an' sing it,
　Hey dum diddle, loud and gay.
Why, it shames the name o'
sacred
　In its brazen wordliness,
An' they 've even got " Ol' Hun-
dred "
　In a bold, new-fangled dress.

You 'll excuse me, Mr. Parson,
　Ef I seem a little sore;
But I 've sung the songs of Isr'el
　For threescore years an' more,
An' it sort o' hurts my feelin's
　Fur to see 'em put away
Fur these harum-scarum ditties
　'At is capturin' the day.

There 's anuther little happ'nin'
　'At I 'll mention while I 'm
　here,
Jes' to show 'at my objections
　All is offered sound and clear.
It was one day they was singin'
　An' was doin' well enough —
Singin' good as people could sing
　Sich an awful mess o' stuff —

When the choir give a holler,
　An' the organ give a groan,
An' they left one weak-voiced fel-
ler
　A-singin' there alone!
But he stuck right to the music,
　Tho' 't was tryin' as could
　be;

An' when I tried to help him,
  Why, the hull church scowled
      at me.

You say that 's so-low singin',
  Well, I pray the Lord that I
Growed up when folks was
      willin'
  To sing their hymns so high.
Why, we never had sich doin's
  In the good ol' Bethel days,
When the folks was all con-
      tented
  With the simple songs of
      praise.

Now I may have spoke too open,
  But 't was too hard to keep
      still,
An' I hope you 'll tell the singers
  'At I bear 'em no ill-will.
'At they all may git to glory
  Is my wish an' my desire,
But they 'll need some extry train-
      in'
  'Fore they jine the heavenly
      choir.

ALICE

KNOW you, winds that blow your
      course
  Down the verdant valleys,
That somewhere you must, per-
      force,
  Kiss the brow of Alice?
When her gentle face you find,
Kiss it softly, naughty wind.

Roses waving fair and sweet
  Thro' the garden alleys,
Grow into a glory meet
  For the eye of Alice;
Let the wind your offering bear
Of sweet perfume, faint and rare.

Lily holding crystal dew
  In your pure white chalice,
Nature kind hath fashioned you
  Like the soul of Alice;
It of purest white is wrought,
Filled with gems of crystal
      thought.

AFTER THE QUARREL

So we, who 've supped the self-
      same cup,
  To-night must lay our friend-
      ship by;
Your wrath has burned your
      judgment up,
  Hot breath has blown the ashes
      high.
You say that you are wronged —
      ah, well,
  I count that friendship poor,
      at best
A bauble, a mere bagatelle,
  That cannot stand so slight a
      test.

I fain would still have been your
      friend,
  And talked and laughed and
      loved with you;

But since it must, why, let it end;
  The false but dies, 't is not the
    true.
So we are favored, you and I,
  Who only want the living
    truth.
It was not good to nurse the lie;
  'T is well it died in harmless
    youth.

I go from you to-night to sleep.
  Why, what 's the odds? why
    should I grieve?
I have no fund of tears to weep
  For happenings that undeceive.
The days shall come, the days
    shall go
  Just as they came and went be-
    fore.
The sun shall shine, the streams
    shall flow
Though you and I are friends no
    more.

And in the volume of my years,
  Where all my thoughts and
    acts shall be,
The page whereon your name
    appears
  Shall be forever sealed to me.
Not that I hate you over-much,
  'T is less of hate than love de-
    fied;
Howe'er, our hands no more shall
    touch,
  We 'll go our ways, the world is
    wide.

BEYOND THE YEARS

I

BEYOND the years the answer lies,
Beyond where brood the grieving
    skies
  And Night drops tears.
Where Faith rod-chastened smiles
    to rise
  And doff its fears,
And carping Sorrow pines and
    dies —
  Beyond the years.

II

Beyond the years the prayer for rest
Shall beat no more within the
    breast;
  The darkness clears,
And Morn perched on the moun-
    tain's crest
  Her form uprears —
The day that is to come is best,
  Beyond the years.

III

Beyond the years the soul shall find
That endless peace for which it
    pined,
  For light appears,
And to the eyes that still were blind
  With blood and tears,
Their sight shall come all uncon-
    fined
  Beyond the years.

AFTER A VISIT

I be'n down in ole Kentucky
  Fur a week er two, an' say,
'T wuz ez hard ez breakin' oxen
  Fur to tear myse'f away.
Allus argerin' 'bout fren'ship
  An' yer hospitality —
Y' ain't no right to talk about it
  Tell you be'n down there to see.

See jest how they give you welcome
  To the best that 's in the land,
Feel the sort o' grip they give you
  When they take you by the hand.
Hear 'em say, "We 're glad to
    have you,
  Better stay a week er two;"
An' the way they treat you makes
    you
  Feel that ev'ry word is true.

Feed you tell you hear the buttons
  Crackin' on yore Sunday vest;
Haul you roun' to see the wonders
  Tell you have to cry for rest.
Drink yer health an' pet an' praise
    you
  Tell you git to feel ez great
Ez the Sheriff o' the county
  Er the Gov'ner o' the State.

Wife, she sez I must be crazy
  'Cause I go on so, an' Nelse
He 'lows, "Goodness gracious!
    daddy,
  Cain't you talk about nuthin'
    else?"

Well, pleg-gone it, I 'm jes' tickled,
  Bein' tickled ain't no sin;
I be'n down in ole Kentucky,
  An' I want o' go ag'in.

CURTAIN

Villain shows his indiscretion,
Villain's partner makes confession.
Juvenile, with golden tresses,
Finds her pa and dons long dresses.
Scapegrace comes home money-
    laden,
Hero comforts tearful maiden,
Soubrette marries loyal chappie,
Villain skips, and all are happy.

THE SPELLIN'-BEE

I never shall furgit that night
  when father hitched up Dob-
  bin,
An' all us youngsters clambered in
  an' down the road went bob-
  bin'
To school where we was kep'
  at work in every kind o'
  weather,
But where that night a spellin'-
  bee was callin' us together.
'Twas one o' Heaven's banner
  nights, the stars was all a
  glitter,
The moon was shinin' like the
  hand o' God had jest then lit
  her.

The ground was white with spotless snow, the blast was sort o' stingin';

But underneath our round-abouts, you bet our hearts was singin'.

That spellin'-bee had be'n the talk o' many a precious moment,

The youngsters all was wild to see jes' what the precious show meant,

An' we whose years was in their teens was little less desirous

O' gittin' to the meetin' so 's our sweethearts could admire us.

So on we went so anxious fur to satisfy our mission

That father had to box our ears, to smother our ambition.

But boxin' ears was too short work to hinder our arrivin',

He jest turned roun' an' smacked us all, an' kep' right on a-drivin'.

Well, soon the schoolhouse hove in sight, the winders beamin' brightly;

The sound o' talkin' reached our ears, and voices laffin' lightly.

It puffed us up so full an' big 'at I 'll jest bet a dollar,

There wa'n't a feller there but felt the strain upon his collar.

So down we jumped an' in we went ez sprightly ez you make 'em,

But somethin' grabbed us by the knees an' straight began to shake 'em.

Fur once within that lighted room, our feelin's took a canter,

An' scurried to the zero mark ez quick ez Tam O'Shanter.

'Cause there was crowds o' people there, both sexes an' all stations;

It looked like all the town had come an' brought all their relations.

The first I saw was Nettie Gray, I thought that girl was dearer

'N' gold; an' when I got a chance, you bet I aidged up near her.

An' Farmer Dobbs's girl was there, the one 'at Jim was sweet on,

An' Cyrus Jones an' Mandy Smith an' Faith an' Patience Deaton.

Then Parson Brown an' Lawyer Jones were present — all attention,

An' piles on piles of other folks too numerous to mention.

The master rose an' briefly said: "Good friends, dear brother Crawford,

To spur the pupils' minds along, a little prize has offered.

To him who spells the best to-

night — or 't may be 'her'—
no tellin'—
He offers ez a jest reward, this
precious work on spellin'."
A little blue-backed spellin'-book
with fancy scarlet trimmin';
We boys devoured it with our
eyes — so did the girls an'
women.
He held it up where all could see,
then on the table set it,
An' ev'ry speller in the house felt
mortal bound to get it.
At his command we fell in line,
prepared to do our dooty,
Outspell the rest an' set 'em down,
an' carry home the booty.
'T was then the merry times be-
gan, the blunders, an' the
laffin',
The nudges an' the nods an' winks
an' stale good-natured chaf-
fin'.
Ole Uncle Hiram Dane was there,
the clostest man a-livin',
Whose only bugbear seemed to be
the dreadful fear o' givin'.
His beard was long, his hair un-
cut, his clothes all bare an'
dingy;
It was n't 'cause the man was
pore, but jest so mortal
stingy;
An' there he sot by Sally Riggs
a-smilin' an' a-smirkin',
An' all his children lef' to home a
diggin' an' a-workin'.

A widower he was, an' Sal was
thinkin' 'at she 'd wing him;
I reckon he was wond'rin' what
them rings o' hern would
bring him.
An' when the spellin'-test com-
menced, he up an' took his
station,
A-spellin' with the best o' them
to beat the very nation.
An' when he 'd spell some young-
ster down, he 'd turn to look
at Sally,
An' say: "The teachin' nowadays
can't be o' no great vally."
But true enough the adage says,
"Pride walks in slipp'ry
places,"
Fur soon a thing occurred that
put a smile on all our faces.
The laffter jest kep' ripplin' 'roun'
an' teacher could n't quell it,
Fur when he give out "charity"
ole Hiram could n't spell it.
But laffin' 's ketchin' an' it
throwed some others off their
bases,
An' folks 'u'd miss the very word
that seemed to fit their cases.
Why, fickle little Jessie Lee come
near the house upsettin'
By puttin' in a double "kay" to
spell the word "coquettin'."
An' when it come to Cyrus Jones,
it tickled me all over —
Him settin' up to Mandy Smith
an' got sot down on "lover."

But Lawyer Jones of all gone men
  did shorely look the gonest,
When he found out that he 'd fur-
  got to put the " h " in " hon-
  est."
An' Parson Brown, whose ser-
  mons were too long fur tol-
  eration,
Caused lots o' smiles by missin'
  when they give out " con-
  densation."
So one by one they giv' it up —
  the big words kep' a-landin',
Till me an' Nettie Gray was left,
  the only ones a-standin',
An' then my inward strife began
  — I guess my mind was
  petty —
I did so want that spellin'-book;
  but then to spell down Net-
  tie
Jest sort o' went ag'in my grain —
  I somehow could n't do it,
An' when I git a notion fixed,
  I 'm great on stickin' to it.
So when they giv' the next word
  out — I had n't orter tell
  it,
But then 't was all fur Nettie's
  sake — I missed so 's she
  could spell it.
She spelt the word, then looked at
  me so lovin'-like an' mello',
I tell you 't sent a hunderd pins
  a shootin' through a fello'.

O' course I had to stand the jokes
  an' chaffin' of the fello's,
But when they handed her the
  book I vow I was n't jealous.
We sung a hymn, an' Parson
  Brown dismissed us like he
  orter,
Fur, la! he 'd learned a thing er
  two an' made his blessin'
  shorter.
'T was late an' cold when we got
  out, but Nettie liked cold
  weather,
An' so did I, so we agreed we 'd
  jest walk home together.
We both wuz silent, fur of words
  we nuther had a surplus,
'Till she spoke out quite sudden
  like, " You missed that word
  on purpose."
Well, I declare it frightened me;
  at first I tried denyin',
But Nettie, she jest smiled an'
  smiled, she knowed that I
  was lyin'.
Sez she: " That book is yourn by
  right;" sez I: " It never
  could be —
I — I — you — ah —" an' there
  I stuck, an' well she under-
  stood me.
So we agreed that later on when
  age had giv' us tether,
We 'd jine our lots an' settle down
  to own that book together.

KEEP A-PLUGGIN' AWAY

I 've a humble little motto
That is homely, though it 's
　　true,—
　Keep a-pluggin' away.
It 's a thing when I 've an object
That I always try to do,—
　Keep a-pluggin' away.
When you 've rising storms to
　quell,
When opposing waters swell,
It will never fail to tell,—
　Keep a-pluggin' away.

If the hills are high before
And the paths are hard to climb,
　Keep a-pluggin' away.
And remember that successes
Come to him who bides his
　time,—
　Keep a-pluggin' away.
From the greatest to the least,
None are from the rule released.
Be thou toiler, poet, priest,
　Keep a-pluggin' away.

Delve away beneath the surface,
There is treasure farther down,—
　Keep a-pluggin' away.
Let the rain come down in tor-
　rents,
Let the threat'ning heavens frown,
　Keep a-pluggin' away.
When the clouds have rolled
　away,

There will come a brighter day
All your labor to repay,—
　Keep a-pluggin' away.

There 'll be lots of sneers to swal-
　low,
There 'll be lots of pain to bear,—
　Keep a-pluggin' away.
If you 've got your eye on heaven,
Some bright day you 'll wake up
　there,—
　Keep a-pluggin' away.
Perseverance still is king;
Time its sure reward will bring;
Work and wait unwearying,—
　Keep a-pluggin' away.

NIGHT OF LOVE

THE moon has left the sky, love,
　The stars arc hiding now,
And frowning on the world, love,
　Night bares her sable brow.
The snow is on the ground, love,
　And cold and keen the air is.
I 'm singing here to you, love;
　You 're dreaming there in Paris.

But this is Nature's law, love,
　Though just it may not seem,
That men should wake to sing,
　love,
　While maidens sleep and dream.
Them care may not molest, love,
　Nor stir them from their slum-
　bers,

Though midnight find the swain,
  love,
Still halting o'er his numbers.

I watch the rosy dawn, love,
  Come stealing up the east,
While all things round rejoice,
  love,
  That Night her reign has
  ceased.
The lark will soon be heard, love,
  And on his way be winging;
When Nature's poets wake, love,
  Why should a man be singing?

COLUMBIAN ODE

I

FOUR hundred years ago a tangled
  waste
  Lay sleeping on the west At-
  lantic's side;
Their devious ways the Old
  World's millions traced
  Content, and loved, and la-
  bored, dared and died,
While students still believed the
  charts they conned,
  And revelled in their thriftless
  ignorance,
Nor dreamed of other lands that
  lay beyond
  Old Ocean's dense, indefinite
  expanse.

II

But deep within her heart old Na-
  ture knew
  That she had once arrayed, at
  Earth's behest,
Another offspring, fine and fair
  to view,—
  The chosen suckling of the
  mother's breast.
The child was wrapped in vest-
  ments soft and fine,
  Each fold a work of Nature's
  matchless art;
The mother looked on it with love
  divine,
  And strained the loved one
  closely to her heart.
And there it lay, and with the
  warmth grew strong
  And hearty, by the salt sea
  breezes fanned,
Till Time with mellowing touches
  passed along,
  And changed the infant to a
  mighty land.

III

But men knew naught of this, till
  there arose
  That mighty mariner, the
  Genoese,
Who dared to try, in spite of fears
  and foes,
  The unknown fortunes of un-
  sounded seas.
O noblest of Italia's sons, thy
  bark

Went not alone into that shroud-
ing night!
O dauntless darer of the rayless
dark,
The world sailed with thee to
eternal light!
The deer-haunts that with game
were crowded then
To-day are tilled and cultivated
lands;
The schoolhouse tow'rs where
Bruin had his den,
And where the wigwam stood
the chapel stands;
The place that nurtured men of
savage mien
Now teems with men of Na-
ture's noblest types;
Where moved the forest-foliage
banner green,
Now flutters in the breeze the
stars and stripes!

A BORDER BALLAD

OH, I have n't got long to live, for
we all
Die soon, e'en those who live
longest;
And the poorest and weakest are
taking their chance
Along with the richest and
strongest.
So it 's heigho for a glass and a
song,
And a bright eye over the table,

And a dog for the hunt when the
game is flush,
And the pick of a gentleman's
stable.

There is Dimmock o' Dune, he
was here yester-night,
But he 's rotting to-day on Glen
Arragh;
'T was the hand o' MacPherson
that gave him the blow,
And the vultures shall feast on
his marrow.
But it 's heigho for a brave old
song
And a glass while we are able;
Here 's a health to death and an-
other cup
To the bright eye over the table.

I can show a broad back and a
jolly deep chest,
But who argues now on ap-
pearance?
A blow or a thrust or a stumble
at best
May send me to-day to my
clearance.
Then it 's heigho for the things I
love,
My mother 'll be soon wearing
sable,
But give me my horse and my dog
and my glass,
And a bright eye over the table.

AN EASY-GOIN' FELLER

Ther' ain't no use in all this
strife,
An' hurryin', pell-mell, right thro'
life.
I don't believe in goin' too fast
To see what kind o' road you 've
passed.
It ain't no mortal kind o' good,
'N' I would n't hurry ef I could.
I like to jest go joggin' 'long,
To limber up my soul with song;
To stop awhile 'n' chat the men,
'N' drink some cider now an'
then.
Do' want no boss a-standin' by
To see me work; I allus try
To do my dooty right straight up,
An' earn what fills my plate an'
cup.
An' ez fur boss, I 'll be my own,
I like to jest be let alone,
To plough my strip an' tend my
bees,
An' do jest like I doggoned please.
My head 's all right, an' my
heart 's meller,
But I 'm a easy-goin' feller.

A NEGRO LOVE SONG

Seen my lady home las' night,
 Jump back, honey, jump back.
Hel' huh han' an' sque'z it tight,
 Jump back, honey, jump back.
Hyeahd huh sigh a little sigh,

Seen a light gleam f'om huh eye,
An' a smile go flittin' by —
 Jump back, honey, jump back.

Hyeahd de win' blow thoo de
pine,
 Jump back, honey, jump back.
Mockin'-bird was singin' fine,
 Jump back, honey, jump back.
An' my hea't was beatin' so,
When I reached my lady's do',
Dat I could n't ba' to go —
 Jump back, honey, jump back.

Put my ahm aroun' huh wais',
 Jump back, honey, jump back.
Raised huh lips an' took a tase,
 Jump back, honey, jump back.
Love me, honey, love me true?
Love me well ez I love you?
An' she answe'd, " 'Cose I do "—
 Jump back, honey, jump back.

THE DILETTANTE: A MODERN TYPE

He scribbles some in prose and
verse,
 And now and then he prints it;
He paints a little,— gathers some
 Of Nature's gold and mints it.

He plays a little, sings a song,
 Acts tragic rôles, or funny;
He does, because his love is strong,
 But not, oh, not for money!

He studies almost everything
   From social art to science;
A thirsty mind, a flowing spring,
   Demand and swift compliance.

He looms above the sordid
      crowd —
   At least through friendly lenses;
While his mamma looks pleased
      and proud,
   And kindly pays expenses.

BY THE STREAM

By the stream I dream in calm
      delight, and watch as in a
      glass,
How the clouds like crowds of
      snowy-hued and white-robed
      maidens pass,
And the water into ripples breaks
      and sparkles as it spreads,
Like a host of armored knights
      with silver helmets on their
      heads.
And I deem the stream an emblem
      fit of human life may go,
For I find a mind may sparkle
      much and yet but shallows
      show,
And a soul may glow with myriad
      lights and wondrous mys-
      teries,
When it only lies a dormant thing
      and mirrors what it sees.

THE COLORED SOLDIERS

If the muse were mine to tempt it
   And my feeble voice were
      strong,
If my tongue were trained to
      measures,
   I would sing a stirring song.
I would sing a song heroic
   Of those noble sons of Ham,
Of the gallant colored soldiers
   Who fought for Uncle Sam!

In the early days you scorned
      them,
   And with many a flip and flout
Said " These battles are the white
      man's,
   And the whites will fight them
      out."
Up the hills you fought and fal-
      tered,
   In the vales you strove and bled,
While your ears still heard the
      thunder
   Of the foes' advancing tread.

Then distress fell on the nation,
   And the flag was drooping low;
Should the dust pollute your ban-
      ner?
   No! the nation shouted, No!
So when War, in savage triumph,
   Spread abroad his funeral
      pall —
Then you called the colored sol-
      diers,
   And they answered to your call.

And like hounds unleashed and
  eager
For the life blood of the prey,
Sprung they forth and bore them
  bravely
In the thickest of the fray.
And where'er the fight was hot-
  test,
Where the bullets fastest fell,
There they pressed unblanched
  and fearless
At the very mouth of hell.

Ah, they rallied to the standard
  To uphold it by their might;
None were stronger in the labors,
  None were braver in the fight.
From the blazing breach of Wag-
  ner
  To the plains of Olustee,
They were foremost in the fight
  Of the battles of the free.

And at Pillow! God have mercy
  On the deeds committed there,
And the souls of those poor vic-
  tims
  Sent to Thee without a prayer.
Let the fulness of Thy pity
  O'er the hot wrought spirits
  sway
Of the gallant colored soldiers
  Who fell fighting on that day!

Yes, the Blacks enjoy their free-
  dom,
  And they won it dearly, too;

For the life blood of their thou-
  sands
Did the southern fields bedew.
In the darkness of their bondage,
  In the depths of slavery's night,
Their muskets flashed the dawn-
  ing,
  And they fought their way to
  light.

They were comrades then and
  brothers,
  Are they more or less to-day?
They were good to stop a bullet
  And to front the fearful fray.
They were citizens and soldiers,
  When rebellion raised its head;
And the traits that made them
  worthy, —
  Ah! those virtues are not dead.

They have shared your nightly
  vigils,
  They have shared your daily
  toil;
And their blood with yours com-
  mingling
  Has enriched the Southern soil.

They have slept and marched and
  suffered
  'Neath the same dark skies as
  you,
They have met as fierce a foe-
  man,
  And have been as brave and
  true.

And their deeds shall find a record
  In the registry of Fame;
For their blood has cleansed com-
    pletely
  Every blot of Slavery's shame.
So all honor and all glory
  To those noble sons of Ham—
The gallant colored soldiers
  Who fought for Uncle Sam!

NATURE AND ART

TO MY FRIEND CHARLES BOOTH NETTLETON

I

THE young queen Nature, ever
    sweet and fair,
  Once on a time fell upon evil
    days.
  From hearing oft herself dis-
    cussed with praise,
There grew within her heart the
    longing rare
To see herself; and every passing
    air
  The warm desire fanned into
    lusty blaze.
  Full oft she sought this end by
    devious ways,
But sought in vain, so fell she in
    despair.
For none within her train nor by
    her side
  Could solve the task or give the
    envied boon.
  So day and night, beneath the
    sun and moon,

She wandered to and fro unsatis-
    fied,
  Till Art came by, a blithe in-
    ventive elf,
  And made a glass wherein she
    saw herself.

II

Enrapt, the queen gazed on her
    glorious self,
  Then trembling with the thrill
    of sudden thought,
  Commanded that the skilful
    wight be brought
That she might dower him with
    lands and pelf.
Then out upon the silent sea-lapt
    shelf
  And up the hills and on the
    downs they sought
  Him who so well and won-
    drously had wrought;
And with much search found and
    brought home the elf.
  But he put by all gifts with sad
    replies,
And from his lips these words
    flowed forth like wine:
  "O queen, I want no gift but
    thee," he said.
She heard and looked on him with
    love-lit eyes,
Gave him her hand, low murmur-
    ing, "I am thine,"
  And at the morrow's dawning
    they were wed.

AFTER WHILE

A POEM OF FAITH

I THINK that though the clouds
be dark,
That though the waves dash o'er
the bark,
Yet after while the light will
come,
And in calm waters safe at home
The bark will anchor.
Weep not, my sad-eyed, gray-
robed maid,
Because your fairest blossoms
fade,
That sorrow still o'erruns your
cup,
And even though you root them
up,
The weeds grow ranker.

For after while your tears shall
cease,
And sorrow shall give way to
peace;
The flowers shall bloom, the
weeds shall die,
And in that faith seen, by and by
Thy woes shall perish.
Smile at old Fortune's adverse
tide,
Smile when the scoffers sneer and
chide.
Oh, not for you the gems that
pale,
And not for you the flowers that
fail;
Let this thought cherish:

That after while the clouds will
part,
And then with joy the waiting
heart
Shall feel the light come stealing
in,
That drives away the cloud of sin
And breaks its power.
And you shall burst your chrysa-
lis,
And wing away to realms of
bliss,
Untrammelled, pure, divinely
free,
Above all earth's anxiety
From that same hour.

THE OL' TUNES

You kin talk about yer anthems
An' yer arias an' sich,
An' yer modern choir-singin'
That you think so awful rich;
But you orter heerd us youngsters
In the times now far away,
A-singin' o' the ol' tunes
In the ol'-fashioned way.

There was some of us sung treble
An' a few of us growled bass,
An' the tide o' song flowed
smoothly
With its 'comp'niment o' grace;
There was spirit in that music,
An' a kind o' solemn sway,
A-singin' o' the ol' tunes
In the ol'-fashioned way.

I remember oft o' standin'
　In my homespun pantaloons —
On my face the bronze an' freckles
　O' the suns o' youthful Junes —
Thinkin' that no mortal minstrel
　Ever chanted sich a lay
As the ol' tunes we was singin'
　In the ol'-fashioned way.

The boys 'ud always lead us,
　An' the girls 'ud all chime in
Till the sweetness o' the singin'
　Robbed the list'nin' soul o' sin;
An' I used to tell the parson
　'T was as good to sing as pray,
When the people sung the ol'
　　tunes
　In the ol'-fashioned way.

How I long ag'in to hear 'em
　Pourin' forth from soul to soul,
With the treble high an' meller,
　An' the bass's mighty roll;
But the times is very diff'rent,
　An' the music heerd to-day
Ain't the singin' o' the ol' tunes
　In the ol'-fashioned way.

Little screechin' by a woman,
　Little squawkin' by a man,
Then the organ's twiddle-twaddle,
　Jest the empty space to span, —
An' ef you should even think it,
　'T is n't proper fur to say
That you want to hear the ol'
　　tunes
　In the ol'-fashioned way.

But I think that some bright
　　mornin',
　When the toils of life air o'er,
An' the sun o' heaven arisin'
　Glads with light the happy
　　shore,
I shall hear the angel chorus,
　In the realms of endless day,
A-singin' o' the ol' tunes
　In the ol'-fashioned way.

MELANCHOLIA

SILENTLY without my window,
　Tapping gently at the pane,
　Falls the rain.
Through the trees sighs the breeze
　Like a soul in pain.
Here alone I sit and weep;
Thought hath banished sleep.

Wearily I sit and listen
　To the water's ceaseless drip.
　To my lip
Fate turns up the bitter cup,
　Forcing me to sip;
'T is a bitter, bitter drink,
Thus I sit and think, —

Thinking things unknown and
　　awful,
　Thoughts on wild, uncanny
　　themes,
　Waking dreams.
Spectres dark, corpses stark,
　Show the gaping seams
Whence the cold and cruel knife
Stole away their life.

Bloodshot eyes all strained and
   staring,
   Gazing ghastly into mine;
   Blood like wine
On the brow — clotted now—
   Shows death's dreadful sign.
Lonely vigil still I keep;
Would that I might sleep!

Still, oh, still, my brain is whirl-
   ing!
   Still runs on my stream of
   thought;
   I am caught
In the net fate hath set.
   Mind and soul are brought
To destruction's very brink;
Yet I can but think!

Eyes that look into the future,—
   Peeping forth from out my
   mind,
   They will find
Some new weight, soon or late,
   On my soul to bind,
   Crushing all its courage out,—
Heavier than doubt.

Dawn, the Eastern monarch's
   daughter,
   Rising from her dewy bed,
   Lays her head
'Gainst the clouds' sombre
   shrouds
   Now half fringed with red.
O'er the land she 'gins to peep;
Come, O gentle Sleep!

Hark! the morning cock is crow-
   ing;
   Dreams, like ghosts, must hie
   away;
   'Tis the day.
Rosy morn now is born;
   Dark thoughts may not stay.
Day my brain from foes will keep;
Now, my soul, I sleep.

THE WOOING

A YOUTH went faring up and
   down,
   Alack and well-a-day.
He fared him to the market town,
   Alack and well-a-day.
And there he met a maiden fair,
With hazel eyes and auburn hair;
His heart went from him then and
   there,
   Alack and well-a-day.

She posies sold right merrily,
   Alack and well-a-day;
But not a flower was fair as she,
   Alack and well-a-day.
He bought a rose and sighed a
   sigh,
" Ah, dearest maiden, would that I
Might dare the seller too to buy! "
   Alack and well-a-day.

She tossed her head, the coy co-
   quette,
   Alack and well-a-day.

" I'm not, sir, in the market yet,"
    Alack and well-a-day.
" Your love must cool upon a
        shelf;
Tho' much I sell for gold and
        pelf,
I 'm yet too young to sell myself,"
    Alack and well-a-day.

The youth was filled with sorrow
        sore,
    Alack and well-a-day.
And looked he at the maid once
        more,
    Alack and well-a-day.
Then loud he cried, " Fair maid-
        en, if
Too young to sell, now as I live,
You're not too young yourself to
        give,"
    Alack and well-a-day.

The little maid cast down her
        eyes,
    Alack and well-a-day.
And many a flush began to rise,
    Alack and well-a-day.
" Why, since you are so bold," she
        said,
" I doubt not you are highly bred,
So take me! " and the twain were
        wed,
    Alack and well-a-day.

MERRY AUTUMN

It's all a farce,— these tales they
        tell
    About the breezes sighing,
And moans astir o'er field and
        dell,
    Because the year is dying.

Such principles are most absurd,—
    I care not who first taught
        'em;
There 's nothing known to beast
        or bird
    To make a solemn autumn.

In solemn times, when grief holds
        sway
    With countenance distressing,
You'll note the more of black and
        gray
    Will then be used in dressing.

Now purple tints are all around;
    The sky is blue and mellow;
And e'en the grasses turn the
        ground
    From modest green to yellow.

The seed burrs all with laughter
        crack
    On featherweed and jimson;
And leaves that should be dressed
        in black
    Are all decked out in crimson.

A butterfly goes winging by;
    A singing bird comes after;

And Nature, all from earth to
  sky,
  Is bubbling o'er with laughter.

The ripples wimple on the rills,
  Like sparkling little lasses;
The sunlight runs along the hills,
  And laughs among the grasses.

The earth is just so full of fun
  It really can't contain it;
And streams of mirth so freely
  run
  The heavens seem to rain it.

Don't talk to me of solemn days
  In autumn's time of splendor,
Because the sun shows fewer rays,
  And these grow slant and slen-
  der.

Why, it's the climax of the
  year, —
  The highest time of living! —
Till naturally its bursting cheer
  Just melts into thanksgiving.

WHEN DE CO'N PONE'S
HOT

DEY is times in life when Nature
  Seems to slip a cog an' go,
Jes' a-rattlin' down creation,
  Lak an ocean's overflow;
When de worl' jes' stahts a-spin-
  nin'
  Lak a picaninny's top,

An' yo' cup o' joy is brimmin'
  'Twell it seems about to slop,
An' you feel jes' lak a racah,
  Dat is trainin' fu' to trot —
When yo' mammy says de blessin'
  An' de co'n pone 's hot.

When you set down at de table,
  Kin' o' weary lak an' sad,
An' you 'se jes' a little tiahed
  An' purhaps a little mad;
How yo' gloom tu'ns into glad-
  ness,
  How yo' joy drives out de
  doubt
When de oven do' is opened,
  An' de smell comes po'in' out;
Why, de 'lectric light o' Heaven
  Seems to settle on de spot,
When yo' mammy says de blessin'
  An' de co'n pone 's hot.

When de cabbage pot is steamin'
  An' de bacon good an' fat,
When de chittlins is a-sputter'n'
  So 's to show you whah dey 's
  at;
Tek away yo' sody biscuit,
  Tek away yo' cake an' pie,
Fu' de glory time is comin',
  An' it 's 'proachin' mighty
  nigh,
An' you want to jump an' hollah,
  Dough you know you 'd bettah
  not,
When yo' mammy says de blessin'
  An' de co'n pone 's hot.

I have hyeahd o' lots o' sermons,
  An' I 've hyeahd o' lots o'
    prayers,
An' I've listened to some singin'
  Dat has tuck me up de stairs
Of de Glory-Lan' an' set me
  Jes' below de Mastah's th'one,
An' have lef' my hea't a-singin'
  In a happy aftah tone;
But dem wu'ds so sweetly mur-
    mured
  Seem to tech de softes' spot,
When my mammy says de blessin',
  An' de co'n pone 's hot.

BALLAD

I KNOW my love is true,
  And oh the day is fair.
The sky is clear and blue,
The flowers are rich of hue,
  The air I breathe is rare,
  I have no grief or care;
For my own love is true,
  And oh the day is fair.

My love is false I find,
  And oh the day is dark.
Blows sadly down the wind,
While sorrow holds my mind;
  I do not hear the lark,
  For quenched is life's dear
    spark,—
My love is false I find,
  And oh the day is dark!

For love doth make the day
  Or dark or doubly bright;
Her beams along the way
Dispel the gloom and gray.
  She lives and all is bright,
  She dies and life is night.
For love doth make the day,
  Or dark or doubly bright.

THE CHANGE HAS COME

THE change has come, and Helen
    sleeps —
Not sleeps; but wakes to greater
    deeps
  Of wisdom, glory, truth, and
    light,
  Than ever blessed her seeking
    sight,
  In this low, long, lethargic
    night,
    Worn out with strife
    Which men call life.

The change has come, and who
    would say
"I would it were not come to-
    day"?
  What were the respite till to-
    morrow?
  Postponement of a certain sor-
    row,
  From which each passing day
    would borrow!
    Let grief be dumb,
    The change has come.

COMPARISON

THE sky of brightest gray seems
    dark
    To one whose sky was ever
    white.
To one who never knew a spark,
    Thro' all his life, of love or
    light,
    The grayest cloud seems over-
    bright.

The robin sounds a beggar's note
    Where one the nightingale has
    heard,
But he for whom no silver throat
    Its liquid music ever stirred,
    Deems robin still the sweetest
    bird.

A CORN-SONG

ON the wide veranda white,
    In the purple failing light,
Sits the master while the sun is
    lowly burning;
And his dreamy thoughts are
    drowned
In the softly flowing sound
Of the corn-songs of the field-
    hands slow returning.

>   Oh, we hoe de co'n
>   Since de ehly mo'n;
>   Now de sinkin' sun
>   Says de day is done.

O'er the fields with heavy tread,
Light of heart and high of head,

Though the halting steps be la-
    bored, slow, and weary;
Still the spirits brave and strong
Find a comforter in song,
And their corn-song rises ever
    loud and cheery.

>   Oh, we hoe de co'n
>   Since de ehly mo'n;
>   Now de sinkin' sun
>   Says de day is done.

To the master in his seat,
Comes the burden, full and sweet,
Of the mellow minor music grow-
    ing clearer,
As the toilers raise the hymn,
Thro' the silence dusk and dim,
To the cabin's restful shelter
    drawing nearer.

>   Oh, we hoe de co'n
>   Since de ehly mo'n;
>   Now de sinkin' sun
>   Says de day is done.

And a tear is in the eye
Of the master sitting by,
As he listens to the echoes low-
    replying
To the music's fading calls
As it faints away and falls
Into silence, deep within the cabin
    dying.

>   Oh, we hoe de co'n
>   Since de ehly mo'n;
>   Now de sinkin' sun
>   Says de day is done.

DISCOVERED

SEEN you down at chu'ch las'
    night,
    Nevah min', Miss Lucy.
What I mean? oh, dat's all right,
    Nevah min', Miss Lucy.
You was sma't ez sma't could be,
But you could n't hide f'om me.
Ain't I got two eyes to see!
    Nevah min', Miss Lucy.

Guess you thought you 's awful
    keen;
    Nevah min', Miss Lucy.
Evahthing you done, I seen;
    Nevah min', Miss Lucy.
Seen him tek yo' ahm jes' so,
When he got outside de do' —
Oh, I know dat man 's yo' beau!
    Nevah min', Miss Lucy.

Say now, honey, wha 'd he say? —
    Nevah min', Miss Lucy!
Keep   yo'   secrets — dat's   yo'
    way —
    Nevah min', Miss Lucy.
Won't tell me an' I'm yo' pal —
I'm gwine tell his othah gal, —
Know huh, too, huh name is Sal;
    Nevah min', Miss Lucy!

DISAPPOINTED

AN old man planted and dug and
    tended,

Toiling in joy from dew to
    dew;
The sun was kind, and the rain
    befriended;
    Fine grew his orchard and fair
    to view.
Then he said: "I will quiet my
    thrifty fears,
For here is fruit for my failing
    years."

But even then the storm-clouds
    gathered,
    Swallowing up the azure sky;
The sweeping winds into white
    foam lathered
    The placid breast of the bay,
    hard by;
Then the spirits that raged in the
    darkened air
Swept o'er his orchard and left it
    bare.

The old man stood in the rain, un-
    caring,
    Viewing the place the storm had
    swept;
And then with a cry from his soul
    despairing,
    He bowed him down to the
    earth and wept.
But a voice cried aloud from the
    driving rain;
"Arise, old man, and plant
    again!"

INVITATION TO LOVE

COME when the nights are bright
    with stars
Or when the moon is mellow;
Come when the sun his golden
    bars
Drops on the hay-field yellow.
Come in the twilight soft and
    gray,
Come in the night or come in the
    day,
Come, O love, whene'er you may,
    And you are welcome, welcome.

You are sweet, O Love, dear
    Love,
You are soft as the nesting dove.
Come to my heart and bring it rest
As the bird flies home to its wel-
    come nest.

Come when my heart is full of
    grief
Or when my heart is merry;
Come with the falling of the leaf
Or with the redd'ning cherry.
Come when the year's first blos-
    som blows,
Come when the summer gleams
    and glows,
Come with the winter's drifting
    snows,
    And you are welcome, welcome.

HE HAD HIS DREAM

HE had his dream, and all
    through life,
Worked up to it through toil and
    strife.
Afloat fore'er before his eyes,
It colored for him all his skies:
    The storm-cloud dark
    Above his bark,
The calm and listless vault of blue
Took on its hopeful hue,
It tinctured every passing beam —
    He had his dream.

He labored hard and failed at last,
His sails too weak to bear the
    blast,
The raging tempests tore away
And sent his beating bark astray.
    But what cared he
    For wind or sea!
He said, "The tempest will be
    short,
My bark will come to port."
He saw through every cloud a
    gleam —
    He had his dream.

GOOD-NIGHT

THE lark is silent in his nest,
    The breeze is sighing in its
        flight,
Sleep, Love, and peaceful be thy
    rest.
    Good-night, my love, good-
        night, good-night.

Sweet dreams attend thee in thy
    sleep,
  To soothe thy rest till morn-
    ing's light,
And angels round thee vigil keep.
  Good-night, my love, good-
    night, good-night.

Sleep well, my love, on night's
    dark breast,
  And ease thy soul with slumber
    bright;
Be joy but thine and I am blest.
  Good-night, my love, good-
    night, good-night.

A COQUETTE CON-
QUERED

YES, my ha't 's ez ha'd ez stone —
Go 'way, Sam, an' lemme 'lone.
No; I ain't gwine change my
    min' —
Ain't gwine ma'y you — nuffin' de
    kin'.

Phiny loves you true an' deah?
Go ma'y Phiny; whut I keer?
Oh, you need n't mou'n an' cry —
I don't keer how soon you die.

Got a present! Whut you got?
Somef'n fu' de pan er pot!
Huh! yo' sass do sholy beat —
Think I don't git 'nough to eat?

Whut 's dat un'neaf yo' coat?
Looks des lak a little shoat.

'T ain't no possum! Bless de
    Lamb!
Yes, it is, you rascal, Sam!

Gin it to me; whut you say?
Ain't you sma't now! Oh, go
    'way!
Possum do look mighty nice,
But you ax too big a price.

Tell me, is you talkin' true,
Dat 's de gal's whut ma'ies you?
Come back, Sam; now whah 's
    you gwine?
Co'se you knows dat possum's
    mine!

NORA: A SERENADE

AH, Nora, my Nora, the light
    fades away,
  While Night like a spirit steals
    up o'er the hills;
The thrush from his tree where he
    chanted all day,
  No longer his music in ecstasy
    trills.
Then, Nora, be near me; thy pres-
    ence doth cheer me,
  Thine eye hath a gleam that is
    truer than gold.

I cannot but love thee; so do not
    reprove me,
  If the strength of my passion
    should make me too bold.

Nora, pride of my heart —
  Rosy cheeks, cherry lips, spar-
    kling with glee,—
Wake from thy slumbers, wher-
    ever thou art;
  Wake from thy slumbers to
    me.

Ah, Nora, my Nora, there's love
    in the air,—
  It stirs in the numbers that
    thrill in my brain;
Oh, sweet, sweet is love with its
    mingling of care,
  Though joy travels only a step
    before pain.
Be roused from thy slumbers and
    list to my numbers;
My heart is poured out in this
    song unto thee.
Oh, be thou not cruel, thou treas-
    ure, thou jewel;
  Turn thine ear to my pleading
    and hearken to me.

OCTOBER

October is the treasurer of the
    year,
  And all the months pay bounty
    to her store;
The fields and orchards still their
    tribute bear,
  And fill her brimming coffers
    more and more.
But she, with youthful lavishness,

Spends all her wealth in gaudy
    dress,
  And decks herself in garments
    bold
  Of scarlet, purple, red, and
    gold.

She heedeth not how swift the
    hours fly,
  But smiles and sings her happy
    life along;
She only sees above a shining sky;
  She only hears the breezes' voice
    in song.
Her garments trail the woodlands
    through,
And gather pearls of early dew
  That sparkle, till the roguish
    Sun
  Creeps up and steals them every
    one.

But what cares she that jewels
    should be lost,
  When all of Nature's bounte-
    ous wealth is hers?
Though princely fortunes may
    have been their cost,
  Not one regret her calm de-
    meanor stirs.
Whole-hearted, happy, careless,
    free,
She lives her life out joyously,
  Nor cares when Frost stalks o'er
    her way
  Aud turns her auburn locks to
    gray.

A SUMMER'S NIGHT

THE night is dewy as a maiden's
mouth,
  The skies are bright as are a
  maiden's eyes,
  Soft as a maiden's breath the
  wind that flies
Up from the perfumed bosom of
the South.
Like sentinels, the pines stand in
the park;
  And hither hastening, like rakes
  that roam,
  With lamps to light their way-
  ward footsteps home,
The fireflies come stagg'ring down
the dark.

SHIPS THAT PASS IN THE NIGHT

OUT in the sky the great dark
clouds are massing;
  I look far out into the pregnant
  night,
Where I can hear a solemn boom-
ing gun
  And catch the gleaming of a
  random light,
That tells me that the ship I seek
is passing, passing.

My tearful eyes my soul's deep
hurt are glassing;
  For I would hail and check that
  ship of ships.

I stretch my hands imploring, cry
aloud,
  My voice falls dead a foot from
  mine own lips,
And but its ghost doth reach that
vessel, passing, passing.

O Earth, O Sky, O Ocean, both
surpassing,
  O heart of mine, O soul that
  dreads the dark!
Is there no hope for me?   Is there
no way
  That I may sight and check that
  speeding bark
Which out of sight and sound is
passing, passing?

THE DELINQUENT

Goo'-BY, Jinks, I got to hump,
Got to mek dis pony jump;
See dat sun a-goin' down
'N' me a-foolin' hyeah in town!
  Git up, Suke — go long!

Guess Mirandy 'll think I's tight,
Me not home an' comin' on night.
What 's dat stan'in' by de fence?
Pshaw! why don't I lu'n some
sense?
  Git up, Suke — go long!

Guess I spent down dah at Jinks'
Mos' a dollah fur de drinks.
Bless yo'r soul, you see dat star?
Lawd, but won't Mirandy rar?
  Git up, Suke — go long!

Went dis mo'nin', hyeah it 's night,
Dah 's de cabin dah in sight.
Who 's dat stan'in' in de do'?
Dat must be Mirandy, sho',
    Git up, Suke — go long!

Got de close-stick in huh han',
Dat look funny, goodness lan',
Sakes alibe, but she look glum!
Hyeah, Mirandy, hyeah I come!
    Git up, Suke — go long!

    Ef 't had n't a' b'en fur you, you
slow ole fool, I 'd a' be'n home
long fo' now!

DAWN

An angel, robed in spotless white,
Bent down and kissed the sleeping
    Night.
Night woke to blush; the sprite
    was gone.
Men saw the blush and called it
    Dawn.

A DROWSY DAY

The air is dark, the sky is gray,
    The misty shadows come and
    go,
And here within my dusky room
Each chair looks ghostly in the
    gloom.
    Outside the rain falls cold and
    slow —

Half-stinging drops, half-blinding
    spray.

Each slightest sound is magnified,
    For drowsy quiet holds her
    reign;
The burnt stick in the fireplace
    breaks,
The nodding cat with start
    awakes,
    And then to sleep drops off
    again,
Unheeding Towser at her side.

I look far out across the lawn,
    Where huddled stand the silly
    sheep;
My work lies idle at my hands,
My thoughts fly out like scattered
    strands
    Of thread, and on the verge of
    sleep —
Still half awake — I dream and
    yawn.

What spirits rise before my eyes!
    How various of kind and form!
Sweet memories of days long past,
The dreams of youth that could
    not last,
    Each smiling calm, each raging
    storm,
That swept across my early skies.

Half seen, the bare, gaunt-fingered
    boughs
    Before my window sweep and
    sway,
And chafe in tortures of unrest.

My chin sinks down upon my
   breast;
I cannot work on such a day,
But only sit and dream and
   drowse.

DIRGE

PLACE this bunch of mignonette
   In her cold, dead hand;
When the golden sun is set,
   Where the poplars stand,
Bury her from sun and day,
Lay my little love away
   From my sight.

She was like a modest flower
   Blown in sunny June,
Warm as sun at noon's high hour,
   Chaster than the moon.
Ah, her day was brief and bright,
Earth has lost a star of light;
   She is dead.

Softly breathe her name to me,—
   Ah, I loved her so.
Gentle let your tribute be;
   None may better know
Her true worth than I who weep
O'er her as she lies asleep —
   Soft asleep.

Lay these lilies on her breast,
   They are not more white
Than the soul of her, at rest
   'Neath their petals bright.
Chant your aves soft and low,

Solemn be your tread and slow,—
   She is dead.

Lay her here beneath the grass,
   Cool and green and sweet,
Where the gentle brook may pass
   Crooning at her feet.
Nature's bards shall come and
   sing,
And the fairest flowers shall spring
   Where she lies.

Safe above the water's swirl,
   She has crossed the bar;
Earth has lost a precious pearl,
   Heaven has gained a star,
That shall ever sing and shine,
Till it quells this grief of mine
   For my love.

HYMN

WHEN storms arise
And dark'ning skies
   About me threat'ning lower,
To thee, O Lord, I raise mine
   eyes,
To thee my tortured spirit flies
   For solace in that hour.

The mighty arm
Will let no harm
   Come near me nor befall me;
Thy voice shall quiet my alarm,
When life's great battle waxeth
   warm —
   No foeman shall appall me.

Upon thy breast
Secure I rest,
　From sorrow and vexation;
No more by sinful cares oppressed,
But in thy presence ever blest,
　O God of my salvation.

PREPARATION

THE little bird sits in the nest and
　sings
　A shy, soft song to the morning
　light;
And it flutters a little and prunes
　its wings.
　　The song is halting and poor
　　and brief,
　　And the fluttering wings scarce
　　stir a leaf;
But the note is a prelude to
　sweeter things,
　　And the busy bill and the flutter
　　slight
　　Are proving the wings for a
　　bolder flight!

THE DESERTED PLAN-
TATION

OH, de grubbin'-hoe 's a-rustin' in
　de co'nah,
　An' de plow 's a-tumblin' down
　in de fiel',
While de whippo'will 's a-wailin'
　lak a mou'nah
　When his stubbo'n hea't is try-
　in' ha'd to yiel'.

In de furrers whah de co'n was
　allus wavin',
　Now de weeds is growin' green
　an' rank an' tall;
An' de swallers roun' de whole
　place is a-bravin'
　Lak dey thought deir folks had
　allus owned it all.

An' de big house stan's all quiet
　lak an' solemn,
　Not a blessed soul in pa'lor,
　po'ch, er lawn;
Not a guest, ner not a ca'iage lef'
　to haul 'em,
　Fu' de ones dat tu'ned de latch-
　string out air gone.

An' de banjo's voice is silent in de
　qua'ters,
　D' ain't a hymn ner co'n-song
　ringin' in de air;
But de murmur of a branch's pass-
　in' waters
　Is de only soun' dat breks 'de
　stillness dere.

Whah 's de da'kies, dem dat used
　to be a-dancin'
　Evry night befo' de ole cabin
　do'?
Whah 's de chillun, dem dat used
　to be a-prancin'
　Er a-rollin' in de san' er on de
　flo'?

Whah 's ole Uncle Mordecai an'
　Uncle Aaron?

Whah 's Aunt Doshy, Sam, an'
　　Kit, an' all de res'?
Whah 's ole Tom de da'ky fiddlah,
　　how 's he farin'?
　Whah 's de gals dat used to sing
　　an' dance de bes'?

Gone! not one o' dem is lef' to tell
　　de story;
　Dey have lef' de deah ole place
　　to fall away.
Could n't one o' dem dat seed it in
　　its glory
　Stay to watch it in de hour of
　　decay?

Dey have lef' de ole plantation to
　　de swallers,
　But it hol's in me a lover till de
　　las';
Fu' I fin' hyeah in de memory dat
　　follers
　All dat loved me an' dat I loved
　　in de pas'.

So I 'll stay an' watch de deah ole
　　place an' tend it
　Ez I used to in de happy days
　　gone by.
'Twell de othah Mastah thinks
　　it 's time to end it,
　An' calls me to my qua'ters in
　　de sky.

THE SECRET

WHAT says the wind to the wav-
　　ing trees?
　What says the wave to the
　　river?
What means the sigh in the passing
　　breeze?
　Why do the rushes quiver?
Have you not heard the fainting
　　cry
Of the flowers that said " Good-
　　bye, good-bye "?

List how the gray dove moans and
　　grieves
　Under the woodland cover;
List to the drift of the falling
　　leaves,
　List to the wail of the lover.
Have you not caught the message
　　heard
Already by wave and breeze and
　　bird?

Come, come away to the river's
　　bank,
　Come in the early morning;
Come when the grass with dew is
　　dank,
　There you will find the warn-
　　ing —
A hint in the kiss of the quicken-
　　ing air
Of the secret that birds and
　　breezes bear.

THE WIND AND THE SEA

I STOOD by the shore at the death
     of day,
  As the sun sank flaming red;
And the face of the waters that
     spread away
  Was as gray as the face of the
     dead.

And I heard the cry of the wan-
     ton sea
  And the moan of the wailing
     wind;
For love's sweet pain in his heart
     had he,
  But the gray old sea had sinned.

The wind was young and the sea
     was old,
  But their cries went up to-
     gether;
The wind was warm and the sea
     was cold,
  For age makes wintry weather.

So they cried aloud and they wept
     amain,
  Till the sky grew dark to hear
     it;
And out of its folds crept the misty
     rain,
  In its shroud, like a troubled
     spirit.

For the wind was wild with a
     hopeless love,
  And the sea was sad at heart

At many a crime that he wot of,
  Wherein he had played his part.

He thought of the gallant ships
     gone down
  By the will of his wicked waves;
And he thought how the church-
     yard in the town
  Held the sea-made widows'
     graves.

The wild wind thought of the love
     he had left
  Afar in an Eastern land,
And he longed, as long the much
     bereft,
  For the touch of her perfumed
     hand.

In his winding wail and his deep-
     heaved sigh
  His aching grief found vent;
While the sea looked up at the
     bending sky
  And murmured: " I repent."

But e'en as he spoke, a ship came
     by,
  That bravely ploughed the
     main,
And a light came into the sea's
     green eye,
  And his heart grew hard again.

Then he spoke to the wind:
     " Friend, seest thou not
  Yon vessel is eastward bound?
Pray speed with it to the happy
     spot

Where thy loved one may be
  found."

And the wind rose up in a dear
  delight,
  And after the good ship sped;
But the crafty sea by his wicked
  might
  Kept the vessel ever ahead.

Till the wind grew fierce in his
  despair,
  And white on the brow and lip.
He tore his garments and tore his
  hair,
  And fell on the flying ship.

And the ship went down, for a
  rock was there,
  And the sailless sea loomed
    black;
While burdened again with dole
  and care,
  The wind came moaning back.

And still he moans from his bosom
  hot
  Where his raging grief lies pent,
And ever when the ships come not,
  The sea says: " I repent."

RIDING TO TOWN

WHEN labor is light and the
  morning is fair,
I find it a pleasure beyond all
  compare

To hitch up my nag and go hur-
  rying down
And take Katie May for a ride
  into town;
  For bumpety-bump goes the
    wagon,
    But tra-la-la-la our lay.
There's joy in a song as we rattle
  along
  In the light of the glorious day.

A coach would be fine, but a
  spring wagon's good;
My jeans are a match for Kate's
  gingham and hood;
The hills take us up and the vales
  take us down,
But what matters that? we are
  riding to town,
  And bumpety-bump goes the
    wagon,
    But tra-la-la-la sing we.
There's never a care may live in
  the air
  That is filled with the breath
    of our glee.

And after we've started, there's
  naught can repress
The thrill of our hearts in their
  wild happiness;
The heavens may smile or the
  heavens may frown,
And it's all one to us when we're
  riding to town.
  For bumpety-bump goes the
    wagon,
    But tra-la-la-la we shout,

For our hearts they are clear and
there's nothing to fear,
And we've never a pain nor a
doubt.

The wagon is weak and the road-
way is rough,
And tho' it is long it is not long
enough,
For mid all my ecstasies this is the
crown
To sit beside Katie and ride into
town,
When bumpety-bump goes the
wagon,
But tra-la-la-la our song;
And if I had my way, I'd be will-
ing to pay
If the road could be made twice
as long.

WE WEAR THE MASK

WE wear the mask that grins and
lies,
It hides our cheeks and shades our
eyes,—
This debt we pay to human guile;
With torn and bleeding hearts we
smile,
And mouth with myriad subtle-
ties.

Why should the world be over-
wise,
In counting all our tears and
sighs?

Nay, let them only see us, while
We wear the mask.

We smile, but, O great Christ,
our cries
To thee from tortured souls arise.
We sing, but oh the clay is vile
Beneath our feet, and long the
mile;
But let the world dream other-
wise,
We wear the mask!

THE MEADOW LARK

THOUGH the winds be dank,
And the sky be sober,
And the grieving Day
In a mantle gray
Hath let her waiting maiden
robe her,—
All the fields along
I can hear the song
Of the meadow lark,
As she flits and flutters,
And laughs at the thunder
when it mutters.
O happy bird, of heart most
gay
To sing when skies are gray!

When the clouds are full,
And the tempest master
Lets the loud winds sweep
From his bosom deep
Like heralds of some dire disas-
ter,

Then the heart alone
To itself makes moan;
And the songs come slow,
While the tears fall fleeter,
And silence than song by far
seems sweeter.
Oh, few are they along the
way
Who sing when skies are
gray!

ONE LIFE

OH, I am hurt to death, my
Love;
The shafts of Fate have pierced
my striving heart,
And I am sick and weary of
The endless pain and smart.
My soul is weary of the strife,
And chafes at life, and chafes at
life.

Time mocks me with fair prom-
ises;
A blooming future grows a bar-
ren past,
Like rain my fair full-blossomed
trees
Unburden in the blast.
The harvest fails on grain and
tree,
Nor comes to me, nor comes to
me.

The stream that bears my hopes
abreast

Turns ever from my way its
pregnant tide.
My laden boat, torn from its rest,
Drifts to the other side.
So all my hopes are set astray,
And drift away, and drift away.

The lark sings to me at the morn,
And near me wings her sky-
ward-soaring flight;
But pleasure dies as soon as born,
The owl takes up the night,
And night seems long and doubly
dark;
I miss the lark, I miss the lark.

Let others labor as they may,
I'll sing and sigh alone, and
write my line.
Their fate is theirs, or grave or
gay,
And mine shall still be mine.
I know the world holds joy and
glee,
But not for me,—'t is not for me.

CHANGING TIME

THE cloud looked in at the win-
dow,
And said to the day, " Be dark!"
And the roguish rain tapped hard
on the pane,
To stifle the song of the lark.

The wind sprang up in the tree
tops

And shrieked with a voice of
death,
But the rough-voiced breeze, that
shook the trees,
Was touched with a violet's
breath.

DEAD

A KNOCK is at her door, but she
is weak;
Strange dews have washed the
paint streaks from her
cheek;
She does not rise, but, ah, this
friend is known,
And knows that he will find her
all alone.
So opens he the door, and with
soft tread
Goes straightway to the richly
curtained bed.
His soft hand on her dewy head
he lays.
A strange white light she gives
him for his gaze.
Then, looking on the glory of her
charms,
He crushes her resistless in his
arms.

Stand back! look not upon this
bold embrace,
Nor view the calmness of the
wanton's face;
With joy unspeakable and 'bated
breath,

She keeps her last, long liaison
with death!

A CONFIDENCE

UNCLE JOHN, he makes me tired;
Thinks 'at he's jest so all-fired
Smart, 'at he kin pick up, so,
Ever'thing he wants to know.
Tried to ketch me up last night,
But you bet I would n't bite.
I jest kep' the smoothes' face,
But I led him sich a chase,
Could n't corner me, you bet—
I skipped all the traps he set.
Makin' out he wan'ed to know
Who was this an' that girl's beau;
So 's he 'd find out, don't you see,
Who was goin' 'long with me.
But I answers jest ez sly,
An' I never winks my eye,
Tell he hollers with a whirl,
" Look here, ain't you got a girl? "
Y' ought 'o seen me spread my
eyes,
Like he 'd took me by surprise,
An' I said, " Oh, Uncle John,
Never thought o' havin' one."
An' somehow that seemed to tickle
Him an' he shelled out a nickel.
Then you ought to seen me leave
Jest a-laffin' in my sleeve.
Fool him — well, I guess I did;
He ain't on to this here kid.
Got a girl! well, I guess yes,
Got a dozen more or less,
But I got one reely one,

Not no foolin' ner no fun;
Fur I 'm sweet on her, you see,
An' I ruther guess 'at she
Must be kinder sweet on me,
So we 're keepin' company.
Honest Injun! this is true,
Ever' word I 'm tellin' you!
But you won't be sich a scab
Ez to run aroun' an' blab.
Mebbe 't ain't the way with you,
But you know some fellers do.
Spoils a girl to let her know
'At you talk about her so.
Don't you know her? her name 's
    Liz,
Nicest girl in town she is.
Purty? ah, git out, you gilly —
Liz 'ud purt 'nigh knock you silly.
Y' ought 'o see her when she 's
    dressed
All up in her Sunday best,
All the fellers nudgin' me,
An' a-whisperin', gemunee!
Betcher life 'at I feel proud
When she passes by the crowd.
'T 's kinder nice to be a-goin'
With a girl 'at makes some show-
    in'—
One you know 'at hain't no snide,
Makes you feel so satisfied.
An' I 'll tell you she 's a trump,
Never even seen her jump
Like some silly girls 'ud do,
When I 'd hide and holler " Boo! "
She 'd jest laff an' say " Git out!
What you hollerin' about? "
When some girls 'ud have a fit

That 'un don't git skeered a bit,
Never makes a bit o' row
When she sees a worm er cow.
Them kind 's few an' far between;
Bravest girl I ever seen.
Tell you 'nuther thing she 'll do,
Mebbe you won't think it 's true,
But if she 's jest got a dime
She 'll go halvers ever' time.
Ah, you goose, you need n't laff;
That 's the kinder girl to have.
If you knowed her like I do,
Guess you 'd kinder like her too.
Tell you somep'n' if you 'll swear
You won't tell it anywhere.
Oh, you got to cross yer heart
Earnest, truly, 'fore I start.
Well, one day I kissed her cheek;
Gee, but I felt cheap an' weak,
'Cause at first she kinder flared,
'N', gracious goodness! I was
    scared.
But I need n't been, fer la!
Why, she never told her ma.
That 's what I call grit, don't
    you?
Sich a girl 's worth stickin' to.

PHYLLIS

PHYLLIS, ah, Phyllis, my life is a
    gray day,
    Few are my years, but my griefs
    are not few,
Ever to youth should each day be
    a May-day,

Warm wind and rose-breath and
  diamonded dew —
Phyllis, ah, Phyllis, my life is a
  gray day.

Oh for the sunlight that shines on
  a May-day!
  Only the cloud hangeth over
    my life.
Love that should bring me youth's
  happiest heyday
  Brings me but seasons of sor-
    row and strife;
Phyllis, ah, Phyllis, my life is a
  gray day.

Sunshine or shadow, or gold day
  or gray day,
  Life must be lived as our des-
    tinies rule;
Leisure or labor or work day or
  play day —
  Feasts for the famous and fun
    for the fool;
Phyllis, ah, Phyllis, my life is a
  gray day.

RIGHT'S SECURITY

WHAT if the wind do howl with-
  out,
And turn the creaking weather-
  vane;
What if the arrows of the rain
Do beat against the window-pane?
Art thou not armored strong and
  fast

Against the sallies of the blast?
Art thou not sheltered safe and
  well
Against the flood's insistent swell?

What boots it, that thou stand'st
  alone,
And laughest in the battle's face
When all the weak have fled the
  place
And let their feet and fears keep
  pace?
Thou wavest still thine ensign,
  high,
And shoutest thy loud battle-cry;
Higher than e'er the tempest
  roared,
It cleaves the silence like a sword.

Right arms and armors, too, that
  man
Who will not compromise with
  wrong;
Though single, he must front the
  throng,
And wage the battle hard and
  long.
Minorities, since time began,
Have shown the better side of
  man;
And often in the lists of Time
One man has made a cause sub-
  lime!

IF

IF life were but a dream, my Love,
  And death the waking time;

If day had not a beam, my Love,
  And night had not a rhyme,—
    A barren, barren world were
      this
    Without one saving gleam;
    I'd only ask that with a kiss
    You'd wake me from the
      dream.

If dreaming were the sum of
    days,
  And loving were the bane;
If battling for a wreath of bays
    Could soothe a heart in pain,—
    I'd scorn the meed of battle's
      might,
    All other aims above
    I'd choose the human's higher
      right,
    To suffer and to love!

THE SONG

My soul, lost in the music's mist,
Roamed, rapt, 'neath skies of ame-
  thyst.
The cheerless streets grew summer
  meads,
The Son of Phœbus spurred his
  steeds,
And, wand'ring down the mazy
  tune,
December lost its way in June,
While from a verdant vale I
  heard
The piping of a love-lorn bird.

A something in the tender strain
Revived an old, long-conquered
  pain,
And as in depths of many seas,
My heart was drowned in mem-
  ories.
The tears came welling to my
  eyes,
Nor could I ask it otherwise;
For, oh! a sweetness seems to
  last
Amid the dregs of sorrows past.

It stirred a chord that here of
  late
I'd grown to think could not vi-
  brate.
It brought me back the trust of
  youth,
The world again was joy and
  truth.
And Avice, blooming like a
  bride,
Once more stood trusting at my
  side.
But still, with bosom desolate,
The 'lorn bird sang to find his
  mate.

Then there are trees, and lights
  and stars,
The silv'ry tinkle of guitars;
And throbs again as throbbed that
  waltz,
Before I knew that hearts were
  false.
Then like a cold wave on a shore,

Comes silence and she sings no
    more.
I wake, I breathe, I think again,
And walk the sordid ways of men.

SIGNS OF THE TIMES

Air a-gittin' cool an' coolah,
    Frost a-comin' in de night,
Hicka' nuts an' wa'nuts fallin',
    Possum keepin' out o' sight.
Tu'key struttin' in de ba'nya'd,
    Nary step so proud ez his;
Keep on struttin', Mistah Tu'key,
    Yo' do' know whut time it is.

Cidah press commence a-squeakin'
    Eatin' apples sto'ed away,
Chillun swa'min' 'roun' lak ho'-
    nets,
    Huntin' aigs ermung de hay.
Mistah Tu'key keep on gobblin'
    At de geese a-flyin' souf,
Oomph! dat bird do' know whut's
    comin';
    Ef he did he'd shet his mouf.

Pumpkin gittin' good an' yallah
    Mek me open up my eyes;
Seems lak it's a-lookin' at me
    Jes' a-la'in' dah sayin' " Pies."
Tu'key gobbler gwine 'roun' blow-
    in',
    Gwine 'roun' gibbin' sass an'
    slack;
Keep on talkin', Mistah Tu'key,
    You ain't seed no almanac.

Fa'mer walkin' th'oo de ba'nya'd
    Seein' how things is comin' on,
Sees ef all de fowls is fatt'nin' —
    Good times comin' sho's you
    bo'n.
Hyeahs dat tu'key gobbler brag-
    gin',
    Den his face break in a smile —
Nebbah min', you sassy rascal,
    He's gwine nab you atter while.

Choppin' suet in de kitchen,
    Stonin' raisins in de hall,
Beef a-cookin' fu' de mince meat,
    Spices groun' — I smell 'em all.
Look hyeah, Tu'key, stop dat
    gobblin',
    You ain' luned de sense ob
    feah,
You ol' fool, yo' naik's in dangah,
    Do' you know Thanksgibbin's
    hyeah?

WHY FADES A DREAM?

Why fades a dream?
    An iridescent ray
Flecked in between the tryst
    Of night and day.
    Why fades a dream? —
Of consciousness the shade
Wrought out by lack of light and
    made
    Upon life's stream.
    Why fades a dream?

That thought may thrive,
    So fades the fleshless dream;

Lest men should learn to trust
 The things that seem.
 So fades a dream,
That living thought may grow
And like a waxing star-beam glow
 Upon life's stream —
 So fades a dream.

THE SPARROW

A LITTLE bird, with plumage
 brown,
Beside my window flutters down,
A moment chirps its little strain,
Ten taps upon my window-pane,
And chirps again, and hops along,
To call my notice to its song;
But I work on, nor heed its lay,
Till, in neglect, it flies away.

So birds of peace and hope and
 love
Come fluttering earthward from
 above,
To settle on life's window-sills,
And ease our load of earthly ills;
But we, in traffic's rush and din
Too deep engaged to let them in,
With deadened heart and sense
 plod on,
Nor know our loss till they are
 gone.

SPEAKIN' O' CHRISTMAS

BREEZES blowin' middlin' brisk,
Snow-flakes thro' the air a-whisk,
Fallin' kind o' soft an' light,

Not enough to make things white,
But jest sorter siftin' down
So 's to cover up the brown
Of the dark world's rugged ways
'N' make things look like holidays.
Not smoothed over, but jest
 specked,
Sorter strainin' fur effect,
An' not quite a-gittin' through
What it started in to do.
Mercy sakes! it does seem queer
Christmas day is 'most nigh here.
Somehow it don't seem to me
Christmas like it used to be,—
Christmas with its ice an' snow,
Christmas of the long ago.
You could feel its stir an' hum
Weeks an' weeks before it come;
Somethin' in the atmosphere
Told you when the day was near,
Did n't need no almanacs;
That was one o' Nature's fac's.
Every cottage decked out gay —
Cedar wreaths an' holly spray —
An' the stores, how they were
 drest,
Tinsel tell you could n't rest;
Every winder fixed up pat,
Candy canes, an' things like that;
Noah's arks, an' guns, an' dolls,
An' all kinds o' fol-de-rols.
Then with frosty bells a-chime,
Slidin' down the hills o' time,
Right amidst the fun an' din
Christmas come a-bustlin' in,
Raised his cheery voice to call
Out a welcome to us all;

Hale and hearty, strong an' bluff,
That was Christmas, sure enough.
Snow knee-deep an' coastin' fine,
Frozen mill-ponds all ashine,
Seemin' jest to lay in wait,
Beggin' you to come an' skate.
An' you 'd git your gal an' go
Stumpin' cheerily thro' the snow,
Feelin' pleased an' skeert an'
    warm
'Cause she had a-holt yore arm.
Why, when Christmas come in,
    we
Spent the whole glad day in glee,
Havin' fun an' feastin' high
An' some courtin' on the sly.
Bustin' in some neighbor's door
An' then suddenly, before
He could give his voice a lift,
Yellin' at him, " Christmas gift."
Now sich things are never heard,
" Merry Christmas " is the word.
But it 's only change o' name,
An' means givin' jest the same.
There 's too many new-styled ways
Now about the holidays.
I 'd jest like once more to see
Christmas like it used to be!

LONESOME

MOTHER 's gone a-visitin' to spend
    a month er two,
An', oh, the house is lonesome ez a
    nest whose birds has flew
To other trees to build ag'in; the
    rooms seem jest so bare

That the echoes run like sperrits
    from the kitchen to the
    stair.
The shetters flap more lazy-like
    'n what they used to do,
Sence mother 's gone a-visitin' to
    spend a month er two.

We 've killed the fattest chicken
    an' we've cooked her to a
    turn;
We 've made the richest gravy,
    but I jest don't give a durn
Fur nothin' 'at I drink er eat, er
    nothin' 'at I see.
The food ain't got the pleasant
    taste it used to have to me.
They 's somep'n' stickin' in my
    throat ez tight ez hardened
    glue,
Sence mother 's gone a-visitin' to
    spend a month er two.

The hollyhocks air jest ez pink,
    they 're double ones at that,
An' I wuz prouder of 'em than a
    baby of a cat.
But now I don't go near 'em,
    though they nod an' blush at
    me,
Fur they 's somep'n' seems to gall
    me in their keerless sort o'
    glee
An' all their fren'ly noddin' an'
    their blushin' seems to say:
" You 're purty lonesome, John,
    old boy, sence mother 's gone
    away."

The neighbors ain't so fren'ly ez it
　　seems they 'd ort to be;
They seem to be a-lookin' kinder
　　sideways like at me,
A-kinder feared they 'd tech me
　　off ez ef I wuz a match,
An' all because 'at mother 's gone
　　an' I 'm a-keepin' batch!
I 'm shore I don't do nothin'
　　worse 'n what I used to do
'Fore mother went a-visitin' to
　　spend a month er two.

The sparrers ac's more fearsome
　　like an' won't hop quite so
　　near,
The cricket's chirp is sadder, an'
　　the sky ain't ha'f so clear;
When ev'nin' comes, I set an'
　　smoke tell my eyes begin to
　　swim,
An' things aroun' commence to
　　look all blurred an' faint an'
　　dim.
Well, I guess I 'll have to own up
　　'at I 'm feelin' purty blue
Sence mother 's gone a-visitin' to
　　spend a month er two.

GROWIN' GRAY

HELLO, ole man, you 're a-gittin'
　　gray,
An' it beats ole Ned to see the
　　way
'At the crow's feet 's a-getherin'
　　aroun' yore eyes;

Tho' it ought n't to cause me no
　　su'prise,
Fur there 's many a sun 'at you 've
　　seen rise
An' many a one you 've seen go
　　down
Sence yore step was light an' yore
　　hair was brown,
An' storms an' snows have had
　　their way —
Hello, ole man, you 're a-gittin'
　　gray.

Hello, ole man, you 're a-gittin'
　　gray,
An' the youthful pranks 'at you
　　used to play
Are dreams of a far past long ago
That lie in a heart where the fires
　　burn low —
That has lost the flame though it
　　kept the glow,
An' spite of drivin' snow an' storm,
Beats bravely on forever warm.
December holds the place of
　　May —
Hello, ole man, you 're a-gittin'
　　gray.

Hello, ole man, you 're a-gittin'
　　gray —
Who cares what the carpin' young-
　　sters say?
For, after all, when the tale is told,
Love proves if a man is young or
　　old!
Old age can't make the heart grow
　　cold

When it does the will of an honest
  mind;
When it beats with love fur all
  mankind;
Then the night but leads to a fairer
  day —
Hello, ole man, you 're a-gittin'
  gray!

TO THE MEMORY OF
MARY YOUNG

God has his plans, and what if we
With our sight be too blind to see
Their full fruition; cannot he,
Who made it, solve the mystery?
One whom we loved has fall'n
  asleep,
Not died; although her calm be
  deep,
Some new, unknown, and strange
  surprise
In Heaven holds enrapt her eyes.

And can you blame her that her
  gaze
Is turned away from earthly ways,
When to her eyes God's light and
  love
Have giv'n the view of things
  above?
A gentle spirit sweetly good,
The pearl of precious womanhood;
Who heard the voice of duty
  clear,
And found her mission soon and
  near.

She loved all nature, flowers fair,
The warmth of sun, the kiss of air,
The birds that filled the sky with
  song,
The stream that laughed its way
  along.
Her home to her was shrine and
  throne,
But one love held her not alone;
She sought out poverty and grief,
Who touched her robe and found
  relief.

So sped she in her Master's
  work,
Too busy and too brave to shirk,
When through the silence, dusk
  and dim,
God called her and she fled to him.
We wonder at the early call,
And tears of sorrow can but fall
For her o'er whom we spread the
  pall;
But faith, sweet faith, is over
  all.

The house is dust, the voice is
  dumb,
But through undying years to
  come,
The spark that glowed within her
  soul
Shall light our footsteps to the
  goal.
She went her way; but oh, she
  trod
The path that led her straight to
  God.

Such lives as this put death to
    scorn;
They lose our day to find God's
    morn.

WHEN MALINDY SINGS

G'way an' quit dat noise, Miss
    Lucy —
Put dat music book away;
What 's de use to keep on tryin'?
    Ef you practise twell you 're
    gray,
You cain't sta't no notes a-flyin'
    Lak de ones dat rants and rings
F'om de kitchen to be big woods
    When Malindy sings.

You ain't got de nachel o'gans
    Fu' to make de soun' come right,
You ain't got de tu'ns an' twistin's
    Fu' to make it sweet an' light.
Tell you one thing now, Miss
    Lucy,
    An' I 'm tellin' you fu' true,
When hit comes to raal right
    singin',
    'T ain't no easy thing to do.

Easy 'nough fu' folks to hollah,
    Lookin' at de lines an' dots,
When dey ain't no one kin sence it,
    An' de chune comes in, in spots;
But fu' real melojous music,
    Dat jes' strikes yo' hea't and
    clings,
Jes' you stan' an' listen wif me
    When Malindy sings.

Ain't you nevah hyeahd Malindy?
    Blessed soul, tek up de cross!
Look hyeah, ain't you jokin',
    honey?
    Well, you don't know whut you
    los'.
Y' ought to hyeah dat gal a-wa'b-
    lin',
    Robins, la'ks, an' all dem things,
Heish dey moufs an' hides dey
    face,
    When Malindy sings.

Fiddlin' man jes' stop his fiddlin',
    Lay his fiddle on de she'f;
Mockin'-bird quit tryin' to whistle,
    'Cause he jes' so shamed hisse'f.
Folks a-playin' on de banjo
    Draps dey fingahs on de
    strings —
Bless yo' soul — fu'gits to move
    em,
    When Malindy sings.

She jes' spreads huh mouf and hol-
    lahs,
    " Come to Jesus," twell you
    hyeah
Sinnahs' tremblin' steps and voices
    Timid-lak a-drawin' neah;
Den she tu'ns to " Rock of Ages,'
    Simply to de cross she clings,
An' you fin' yo' teahs a-drappin'
    When Malindy sings.

Who dat says dat humble praises
    Wif de Master nevah counts?

Heish yo' mouf, I hyeah dat music,
    Ez hit rises up an' mounts —
Floatin' by de hills an' valleys,
    Way above dis buryin' sod,
Ez hit makes its way in glory
    To de very gates of God!

Oh, hit 's sweetah dan de music
    Of an edicated band;
An' hit 's dearah dan de battle's
    Song o' triumph in de lan'.
It seems holier dan evenin'
    When de solemn chu'ch bell
        rings,
Ez I sit an' ca'mly listen
    While Malindy sings.

Towsah, stop dat ba'kin', hyeah
        me!
    Mandy, mek dat chile keep still;
Don't you hyeah de echoes callin'
    F'om de valley to de hill?
Let me listen, I can hyeah it,
    Th'oo de bresh of angels' wings,
Sof' an' sweet, " Swing Low,
        Sweet Chariot,"
    Ez Malindy sings.

THE PARTY

Dey had a gread big pahty
    down to Tom's de othah
    night;
Was I dah? You bet! I nevah
    in my life see sich a sight;
All de folks f'om fou' plantations
    was invited, an' dey come,

Dey come troopin' thick ez chillun
    when dey hyeahs a fife an'
    drum.
Evahbody dressed deir fines'—
    Heish yo' mouf an' git
    away,
Ain't seen no sich fancy dressin'
    sence las' quah'tly meetin'
    day;
Gals all dressed in silks an' satins,
    not a wrinkle ner a crease,
Eyes a-battin', teeth a-shinin', haih
    breshed back ez slick ez
    grease;
Sku'ts all tucked an' puffed an'
    ruffled, evah blessed seam an'
    stitch;
Ef you 'd seen 'em wif deir mistus,
    could n't swahed to which
    was which.
Men all dressed up in Prince Al-
    berts, swaller-tails 'u'd tek yo'
    bref!
I cain't tell you nothin' 'bout it,
    y' ought to seen it fu' yo'se'f.
Who was dah? Now who you
    askin'? How you 'spect I
    gwine to know?
You mus' think I stood an'
    counted evahbody at de do.'
Ole man Babah's house-boy Isaac,
    brung dat gal, Malindy Jane,
Huh a-hangin' to his elbow, him
    a-struttin' wif a cane;
My, but Hahvey Jones was jeal-
    ous! seemed to stick him lak
    a tho'n;

But he laughed with Viney Cah-
　　teh, tryin' ha'd to not let on,
But a pusson would 'a' noticed
　　f'om de d'rection of his look,
Dat he was watchin' ev'ry step dat
　　Ike an' Lindy took.
Ike he foun' a cheer an' asked huh:
　　" Won't you set down?" wif
　　a smile,
An' she answe'd up a-bowin',
　　" Oh, I reckon 't ain't wuth
　　while."
Dat was jes' fu' style, I reckon,
　　'cause she sot down jes' de
　　same,
An' she stayed dah 'twell he
　　fetched huh fu' to jine some
　　so't o' game;
Den I hyeahd huh sayin' propah,
　　ez she riz to go away,
" Oh, you raly mus' excuse me,
　　fu' I hardly keers to play."
But I seen huh in a minute wif de
　　othahs on de flo',
An' dah wasn't any one o' dem
　　a-playin' any mo';
Comin' down de flo' a-bowin' an'
　　a-swayin' an' a-swingin',
Puttin' on huh high-toned man-
　　nahs all de time dat she was
　　singin':
" Oh, swing Johnny up an' down,
　　swing him all aroun',
Swing Johnny up an' down, swing
　　him all aroun',
Oh, swing Johnny up an' down,
　　swing him all aroun'

Fa' you well, my dahlin'."
Had to laff at ole man Johnson,
　　he's a caution now, you bet —
Hittin' clost onto a hunderd, but
　　he's spry an' nimble yet;
He 'lowed how a-so't o' gigglin',
　　" I ain't ole, I 'll let you see,
D'ain't no use in gittin' feeble, now
　　you youngstahs jes' watch
　　me,"
An' he grabbed ole Aunt Marier
　　— weighs th'ee hunderd mo'
　　er less,
An' he spun huh 'roun' de cabin
　　swingin' Johnny lak de res'.
Evahbody laffed an' hollahed:
　　" Go it! Swing huh, Uncle
　　Jim!"
An' he swung huh too, I reckon,
　　lak a youngstah, who but
　　him.
Dat was bettah 'n young Scott
　　Thomas, tryin' to be so awful
　　smaht.
You know when dey gits to singin'
　　an' dey comes to dat ere paht:
　　" In some lady's new brick
　　house,
　　In some lady's gyahden.
　　　Ef you don't let me out, I
　　　will jump out,
　　So fa' you well, my dahlin'."
Den dey's got a circle 'roun' you,
　　an' you's got to break de
　　line;
Well, dat dahky was so anxious,
　　lak to bust hisse'f a-tryin';

Kep' on blund'rin' 'roun' an'
     foolin' 'twell he giv' one
     gread big jump,
Broke de line, an lit head-fo'most
     in de fiah-place right plump;
Hit 'ad fiah in it, mind you; well,
     I thought my soul I 'd bust,
Tried my best to keep f'om laffin',
     but hit seemed like die I
     must!
Y' ought to seen dat man a-scram-
     blin' f'om de ashes an' de
     grime.
Did it bu'n him! Sich a question,
     why he did n't give it time;
Th'ow'd dem ashes and dem cin-
     dahs evah which-a-way I
     guess,
An' you nevah did, I reckon, clap
     yo' eyes on sich a mess;
Fu' he sholy made a picter an' a
     funny one to boot,
Wif his clothes all full o' ashes
     an' his face all full o' soot.
Well, hit laked to stopped de
     pahty, an' I reckon lak ez
     not
Dat it would ef Tom's wife,
     Mandy, had n't happened on
     de spot,
To invite us out to suppah — well,
     we scrambled to de table,
An' I 'd lak to tell you 'bout it —
     what we had — but I ain't
     able,
Mention jes' a few things, dough
     I know I had n't orter,

Fu' I know 't will staht a hank'rin'
     an' yo' mouf 'll 'mence to
     worter.
We had wheat bread white ez cot-
     ton an' a egg pone jes like
     gol',
Hog jole, bilin' hot an' steamin'
     roasted shoat an' ham sliced
     cold —
Look out! What 's de mattah wif
     you? Don't be fallin' on de
     flo';
Ef it 's go'n' to 'fect you dat way,
     I won't tell you nothin'
     mo'.
Dah now — well, we had hot
     chittlin's — now you 's tryin'
     ag'in to fall,
Cain't you stan' to hyeah about it?
     S'pose you'd been an' seed it
     all;
Seed dem gread big sweet pertaters,
     layin' by de possum's side,
Seed dat coon in all his gravy,
     reckon den you 'd up and
     died!
Mandy 'lowed "you all mus'
     'scuse me, d' wa'n't much
     upon my she'ves,
But I 's done my bes' to suit you,
     so set down an' he'p
     yo'se'ves."
Tom, he 'lowed: "I don't b'lieve
     in 'pologisin' an' perfessin',
Let 'em tek it lak dey ketch it.
     Eldah Thompson, ask de
     blessin'."

Wish you'd seed dat colo'ed
    preachah cleah his th'oat an'
    bow his head;
One eye shet, an' one eye open,—
    dis is evah wud he said:
" Lawd, look down in tendah
    mussy on sich generous hea'ts
    ez dese;
Make us truly thankful, amen.
    Pass dat possum, ef you
    please!"
Well, we eat and drunk ouah
    po'tion, 'twell dah was n't
    nothin' lef,
An' we felt jes' like new sausage,
    we was mos' nigh stuffed to
    def!
Tom, he knowed how we'd be
    feelin', so he had de fiddlah
    'roun',
An' he made us cleah de cabin
    fu' to dance dat suppah
    down.
Jim, de fiddlah, chuned his fiddle,
    put some rosum on his
    bow,
Set a pine box on de table, mounted
    it an' let huh go!
He's a fiddlah, now I tell you, an'
    he made dat fiddle ring,
'Twell de ol'est an' de lamest had
    to give deir feet a fling.

Jigs, cotillions, reels an' break-
    downs, cordrills an' a waltz
    er two;
Bless yo' soul, dat music winged
    'em an' dem people lak to
    flew.
Cripple Joe, de old rheumatic,
    danced dat flo' f'om side to
    middle,
Th'owed away his crutch an'
    hopped it; what's rheumatics
    'ginst a fiddle?
Eldah Thompson got so tickled
    dat he lak to los' his grace,
Had to tek bofe feet an' hol' dem
    so 's to keep 'em in deir place.
An' de Christuns an' de sinnahs
    got so mixed up on dat flo',
Dat I don't see how dey'd pahted
    ef de trump had chanced to
    blow.
Well, we danced dat way an' ca-
    pahed in de mos' redic'lous
    way,
'Twell de roostahs in de bahnyard
    cleahed deir th'oats an' crowed
    fu' day.
Y' ought to been dah, fu' I tell
    you evahthing was rich an'
    prime,
An' dey ain't no use in talkin', we
    jes had one scrumptious time!

Lyrics of
the Heartside

LOVE'S APOTHEOSIS

Love me. I care not what the
circling years
To me may do.
If, but in spite of time and tears,
You prove but true.

Love me — albeit grief shall dim
mine eyes,
And tears bedew,
I shall not e'en complain, for then
my skies
Shall still be blue.

Love me, and though the winter
snow shall pile,
And leave me chill,
Thy passion's warmth shall make
for me, meanwhile,
A sun-kissed hill.

And when the days have length-
ened into years,
And I grow old,
Oh, spite of pains and griefs and
cares and fears,
Grow thou not cold.

Then hand and hand we shall pass
up the hill,
I say not down;
That twain go up, of love, who 've
loved their fill,—
To gain love's crown.

Love me, and let my life take up
thine own,
As sun the dew.
Come, sit, my queen, for in my
heart a throne
Awaits for you!

THE PARADOX

I AM the mother of sorrows,
I am the ender of grief;
I am the bud and the blossom,
I am the late-falling leaf.

I am thy priest and thy poet,
I am thy serf and thy king;
I cure the tears of the heartsick,
When I come near they shall
sing.

White are my hands as the snow-
drop;
Swart are my fingers as clay;
Dark is my frown as the mid-
night,
Fair is my brow as the day.

Battle and war are my minions,
Doing my will as divine;
I am the calmer of passions,
Peace is a nursling of mine.

Speak to me gently or curse me,
Seek me or fly from my sight;
I am thy fool in the morning,
Thou art my slave in the night.

Down to the grave will I take
    thee,
  Out from the noise of the
    strife;
Then shalt thou see me and know
    me —
  Death, then, no longer, but life.

Then shalt thou sing at my com-
    ing,
  Kiss me with passionate breath,
Clasp me and smile to have
    thought me
  Aught save the foeman of
    Death.

Come to me, brother, when weary,
  Come when thy lonely heart
    swells;
I 'll guide thy footsteps and lead
    thee
  Down where the Dream Wom-
    an dwells.

OVER THE HILLS

OVER the hills and the valleys of
    dreaming
  Slowly I take my way.
Life is the night with its dream-
    visions teeming,
  Death is the waking at day.

Down thro' the dales and the bow-
    ers of loving,
  Singing, I roam afar.

Daytime or night-time, I con-
    stantly roving,—
  Dearest one, thou art my star.

WITH THE LARK

NIGHT is for sorrow and dawn is
    for joy,
Chasing the troubles that fret and
    annoy;
Darkness for sighing and daylight
    for song,—
Cheery and chaste the strain,
    heartfelt and strong.
All the night through, though I
    moan in the dark,
I wake in the morning to sing
    with the lark.

Deep in the midnight the rain
    whips the leaves,
Softly and sadly the wood-spirit
    grieves.
But when the first hue of dawn
    tints the sky,
I shall shake out my wings like
    the birds and be dry;
And though, like the rain-drops, I
    grieved through the dark,
I shall wake in the morning to
    sing with the lark.

On the high hills of heaven, some
    morning to be,
Where the rain shall not grieve
    thro' the leaves of the tree,

There my heart will be glad for
the pain I have known,
For my hand will be clasped in the
hand of mine own;
And though life has been hard and
death's pathway been dark,
I shall wake in the morning to
sing with the lark.

IN SUMMER

Oh, summer has clothed the earth
In a cloak from the loom of
the sun!
And a mantle, too, of the skies'
soft blue,
And a belt where the rivers run.

And now for the kiss of the wind,
And the touch of the air's soft
hands,
With the rest from strife and the
heat of life,
With the freedom of lakes and
lands.

I envy the farmer's boy
Who sings as he follows the
plow;
While the shining green of the
young blades lean
To the breezes that cool his
brow.

He sings to the dewy morn,
No thought of another's ear;

But the song he sings is a chant
for kings
And the whole wide world to
hear.

He sings of the joys of life,
Of the pleasures of work and
rest,
From an o'erfull heart, without
aim or art;
'T is a song of the merriest.

O ye who toil in the town,
And ye who moil in the mart,
Hear the artless song, and your
faith made strong
Shall renew your joy of heart.

Oh, poor were the worth of the
world
If never a song were heard,—
If the sting of grief had no re-
lief,
And never a heart were stirred.

So, long as the streams run down,
And as long as the robins trill,
Let us taunt old Care with a
merry air,
And sing in the face of ill.

THE MYSTIC SEA

The smell of the sea in my nos-
trils,
The sound of the sea in mine
ears;

The touch of the spray on my
burning face,
  Like the mist of reluctant tears.

The blue of the sky above me,
  The green of the waves be-
  neath;
The sun flashing down on a gray-
  white sail
  Like a scimitar from its sheath.

And ever the breaking billows,
  And ever the rocks' disdain;
And ever a thrill in mine inmost
  heart
That my reason cannot explain.

So I say to my heart, " Be silent,
  The mystery of time is here;
Death's way will be plain when
  we fathom the main,
  And the secret of life be clear."

A SAILOR'S SONG

OH for the breath of the briny
  deep,
And the tug of the bellying sail,
With the sea-gull's cry across the
  sky
And a passing boatman's hail.
For, be she fierce or be she gay,
The sea is a famous friend alway.

Ho! for the plains where the
  dolphins play,
And the bend of the mast and
  spars,

And a fight at night with the wild
  sea-sprite
When the foam has drowned the
  stars.
And, pray, what joy can the lands-
  man feel
Like the rise and fall of a sliding
  keel?

Fair is the mead; the lawn is fair
And the birds sing sweet on the
  lea;
But the echo soft of a song aloft
Is the strain that pleases me;
And swish of rope and ring of
  chain
Are music to men who sail the
  main.

Then, if you love me, let me sail
While a vessel dares the deep;
For the ship's my wife, and the
  breath of life
Are the raging gales that sweep;
And when I'm done with calm
  and blast,
A slide o'er the side, and rest at
  last.

THE BOHEMIAN

BRING me the livery of no other
  man.
  I am my own to robe me at my
  pleasure.
  Accepted rules to me disclose no
  treasure:

What is the chief who shall my
  garments plan?
  No garb conventional but I 'll
    attack it.
  (Come, why not don my span-
    gled jacket?)

ABSENCE

GOOD-NIGHT, my love, for I have
  dreamed of thee
In waking dreams, until my soul
  is lost —
Is lost in passion's wide and shore-
  less sea,
Where, like a ship, unruddered, it
  is tost
Hither and thither at the wild
  waves' will.
There is no potent Master's voice
  to still
This newer, more tempestuous
  Galilee!

The stormy petrels of my fancy
  fly
In warning course across the
  darkening green,
And, like a frightened bird, my
  heart doth cry
And seek to find some rock of rest
  between
The threatening sky and the re-
  lentless wave.
It is not length of life that grief
  doth crave,
But only calm and peace in which
  to die.

Here let me rest upon this single
  hope,
For oh, my wings are weary of the
  wind,
And with its stress no more may
  strive or cope.
One cry has dulled mine ears,
  mine eyes are blind,—
Would that o'er all the interven-
  ing space,
I might fly forth and see thee face
  to face.
I fly; I search, but, love, in gloom
  I grope.

Fly home, far bird, unto thy wait-
  ing nest;
Spread thy strong wings above the
  wind-swept sea.
Beat the grim breeze with thy un-
  ruffled breast
Until thou sittest wing to wing
  with me.
Then, let the past bring up its
  tales of wrong;
We shall chant low our sweet con-
  nubial song,
Till storm and doubt and past no
  more shall be!

HER THOUGHT AND HIS

THE gray of the sea, and the gray
  of the sky,
A glimpse of the moon like a half-
  closed eye.
The gleam on the waves and the
  light on the land,

A thrill in my heart,— and — my
  sweetheart's hand.

She turned from the sea with a
  woman's grace,
And the light fell soft on her
  upturned face,
And I thought of the flood-tide of
  infinite bliss
That would flow to my heart from
  a single kiss.

But my sweetheart was shy, so I
  dared not ask
For the boon, so bravely I wore
  the mask.
But into her face there came a
  flame: —
I wonder could she have been
  thinking the same?

THE RIGHT TO DIE

I HAVE no fancy for that ancient
  cant
That makes us masters of our des-
  tinies,
And not our lives, to hold or give
  them up
As will directs; I cannot, will not
  think
That men, the subtle worms, who
  plot and plan
And scheme and calculate with
  such shrewd wit,
Are such great blund'ring fools as
  not to know

When they have lived enough.
                    Men court not death
When there are sweets still left in
  life to taste.
Nor will a brave man choose to
  live when he,
Full deeply drunk of life, has
  reached the dregs,
And knows that now but bitter-
  ness remains.
He is the coward who, outfaced
  in this,
Fears the false goblins of another
  life.
I honor him who being much
  harassed
Drinks of sweet courage until
  drunk of it,—
Then seizing Death, reluctant, by
  the hand,
Leaps with him, fearless, to eter-
  nal peace!

BEHIND THE ARRAS

As in some dim baronial hall re-
  strained,
A prisoner sits, engirt by secret
  doors
And waving tapestries that argue
  forth
Strange passages into the outer
  air;
So in this dimmer room which we
  call life,
Thus sits the soul and marks with
  eye intent

That mystic curtain o'er the por-
tal death;
Still deeming that behind the
arras lies
The lambent way that leads to
lasting light.
Poor fooled and foolish soul!
Know now that death
Is but a blind, false door that no-
where leads,
And gives no hope of exit final,
free.

WHEN THE OLD MAN
SMOKES

In the forenoon's restful quiet,
When the boys are off at school,
When the window lights are
shaded
And the chimney-corner cool,
Then the old man seeks his arm-
chair,
Lights his pipe and settles back;
Falls a-dreaming as he draws it
Till the smoke-wreaths gather
black.

And the tear-drops come a-trick-
ling
Down his cheeks, a silver
flow —
Smoke or memories you wonder,
But you never ask him,— no;
For there's something almost sa-
cred
To the other family folks

In those moods of silent dream-
ing
When the old man smokes.

Ah, perhaps he sits there dream-
ing
Of the love of other days
And of how he used to lead her
Through the merry dance's
maze;
How he called her "little prin-
cess,"
And, to please her, used to
twine
Tender wreaths to crown her
tresses,
From the "matrimony vine."

Then before his mental vision
Comes, perhaps, a sadder day,
When they left his little princess
Sleeping with her fellow clay.
How his young heart throbbed,
and pained him!
Why, the memory of it chokes!
Is it of these things he's thinking
When the old man smokes?

But some brighter thoughts pos-
sess him,
For the tears are dried the
while.
And the old, worn face is wrin-
kled
In a reminiscent smile,
From the middle of the forehead
To the feebly trembling lip,

At some ancient prank remem-
    bered
  Or some long unheard-of quip.

Then the lips relax their tension
  And the pipe begins to slide,
Till in little clouds of ashes,
  It falls softly at his side;
And his head bends low and lower
  Till his chin lies on his breast,
And he sits in peaceful slumber
  Like a little child at rest.

Dear old man, there's something
    sad'ning,
  In these dreamy moods of yours,
Since the present proves so fleet-
    ing,
  All the past for you endures.
Weeping at forgotten sorrows,
  Smiling at forgotten jokes;
Life epitomized in minutes,
  When the old man smokes.

THE GARRET

WITHIN a London garret high,
Above the roofs and near the sky,
My ill-rewarding pen I ply
    To win me bread.
This little chamber, six by four,
Is castle, study, den, and more,—
Altho' no carpet decks the floor,
    Nor down, the bed.

My room is rather bleak and bare;
I only have one broken chair,
But then, there's plenty of fresh
    air,—
    Some light, beside.
What tho' I cannot ask my friends
To share with me my odds and
    ends,
A liberty my aerie lends,
    To most denied.

The bore who falters at the stair
No more shall be my curse and
    care,
And duns shall fail to find my lair
    With beastly bills.
When debts have grown and
    funds are short,
I find it rather pleasant sport
To live " above the common sort "
    With all their ills.

I write my rhymes and sing away,
And dawn may come or dusk or
    day:
Tho' fare be poor, my heart is
    gay,
    And full of glee.
Though chimney-pots be all my
    views;
'T is nearer for the winging
    Muse,
So I am sure she 'll not refuse
    To visit me.

TO E. H. K.

ON THE RECEIPT OF A FAMILIAR
POEM

To me, like hauntings of a va-
grant breath
From some far forest which I
once have known,
The perfume of this flower of
verse is blown.
Tho' seemingly soul-blossoms faint
to death,
Naught that with joy she bears
e'er withereth.
So, tho' the pregnant years have
come and flown,
Lives come and gone and al-
tered like mine own,
This poem comes to me a shib-
boleth:
Brings sound of past communings
to my ear,
Turns round the tide of time
and bears me back
Along an old and long un-
traversed way;
Makes me forget this is a later
year,
Makes me tread o'er a reminis-
cent track,
Half sad, half glad, to one
forgotten day!

A BRIDAL MEASURE

COME, essay a sprightly measure,
Tuned to some light song of
pleasure.
Maidens, let your brows be
crowned
As we foot this merry round.

From the ground a voice is sing-
ing,
From the sod a soul is springing.
Who shall say 't is but a clod
Quick'ning upward toward its
God?

Who shall say it? Who may
know it,
That the clod is not a poet
Waiting but a gleam to waken
In a spirit music-shaken?

Phyllis, Phyllis, why be waiting?
In the woods the birds are mating.
From the tree beside the wall,
Hear the am'rous robin call.

Listen to yon thrush's trilling;
Phyllis, Phyllis, are you willing,
When love speaks from cave
and tree,
Only we should silent be?

When the year, itself renewing,
All the world with flowers is
strewing,
Then through Youth's Arcadian
land,
Love and song go hand in hand.

Come, unfold your vocal treasure,
Sing with me a nuptial measure,—
Let this springtime gambol be
Bridal dance for you and me.

VENGEANCE IS SWEET

WHEN I was young I longed for
    Love,
And held his glory far above
All other earthly things. I cried:
" Come, Love, dear Love, with me
    abide ; "
And with my subtlest art I wooed,
And eagerly the wight pursued.
But Love was gay and Love was
    shy,
He laughed at me and passed me
    by.

Well, I grew old and I grew gray,
When Wealth came wending
    down my way.
I took his golden hand with glee,
And comrades from that day were
    we.
Then Love came back with dole-
    ful face,
And prayed that I would give him
    place.
But, though his eyes with tears
    were dim,
I turned my back and laughed at
    him.

A HYMN

AFTER READING " LEAD, KINDLY LIGHT."

LEAD gently, Lord, and slow,
    For oh, my steps are weak,
And ever as I go,
    Some soothing sentence speak;

That I may turn my face
    Through doubt's obscurity
Toward thine abiding-place,
    E'en tho' I cannot see.

For lo, the way is dark;
    Through mist and cloud I grope,
Save for that fitful spark,
    The little flame of hope.

Lead gently, Lord, and slow,
    For fear that I may fall;
I know not where to go
    Unless I hear thy call.

My fainting soul doth yearn
    For thy green hills afar;
So let thy mercy burn —
    My greater, guiding star!

JUST WHISTLE A BIT

JUST whistle a bit, if the day be
    dark,
    And the sky be overcast:
If mute be the voice of the piping
    lark,
    Why, pipe your own small blast.

And it's wonderful how o'er the
    gray sky-track
The truant warbler comes steal-
    ing back.
But why need he come? for your
    soul's at rest,
And the song in the heart,— ah
    that is best.

Just whistle a bit, if the night be
    drear
And the stars refuse to shine:
And a gleam that mocks the star-
    light clear
Within you glows benign.

Till the dearth of light in the
    glooming skies
Is lost to the sight of your soul-lit
    eyes.
What matters the absence of moon
    or star?
The light within is the best by far.

Just whistle a bit, if there's work
    to do,
With the mind or in the soil.
And your note will turn out a
    talisman true
To exorcise grim Toil.

It will lighten your burden and
    make you feel
That there's nothing like work as
    a sauce for a meal.
And with song in your heart and
    the meal in — its place,
There'll be joy in your bosom and
    light in your face.

Just whistle a bit, if your heart
    be sore;
'Tis a wonderful balm for pain.
Just pipe some old melody o'er
    and o'er
Till it soothes like summer rain.

And perhaps 't would be best in a
    later day,
When Death comes stalking down
    the way,
To knock at your bosom and see
    if you 're fit,
Then, as you wait calmly, just
    whistle a bit.

THE BARRIER

The Midnight wooed the Morn-
    ing-Star,
    And prayed her: "Love come
      nearer;
Your swinging coldly there afar
    To me but makes you dearer!"

The Morning-Star was pale with
    dole
    As said she, low replying:
"Oh, lover mine, soul of my soul,
    For you I too am sighing.

"But One ordained when we
    were born,
    In spite of Love's insistence,
That Night might only view the
    Morn
    Adoring at a distance."

But as she spoke the jealous Sun
    Across the heavens panted.
"Oh, whining fools," he cried,
    "have done;
    Your wishes shall be granted!"

He hurled his flaming lances far;
  The twain stood unaffrighted —
And Midnight and the Morning-
    Star
  Lay down in death united!

DREAMS

DREAM on, for dreams are sweet:
  Do not awaken!
Dream on, and at thy feet
  Pomegranates shall be shaken.

Who likeneth the youth
  Of life to morning?
'Tis like the night in truth,
  Rose-coloured dreams adorning.

The wind is soft above,
  The shadows umber.
(There is a dream called Love.)
  Take thou the fullest slumber!

In Lethe's soothing stream,
  Thy thirst thou slakest.
Sleep, sleep; 't is sweet to dream.
  Oh, weep when thou awakest!

THE DREAMER

TEMPLES he built and palaces of
    air,
  And, with the artist's parent-
    pride aglow,
  His fancy saw his vague ideals
    grow
Into creations marvellously fair;

He set his foot upon Fame's
    nether stair.
  But ah, his dream,— it had
    entranced him so
  He could not move. He could
    no farther go;
But paused in joy that he was even
    there!

He did not wake until one day
    there gleamed
  Thro' his dark consciousness a
    light that racked
His being till he rose, alert to act.
But lo! what he had dreamed, the
    while he dreamed,
  Another, wedding action unto
    thought,
  Into the living, pulsing world
    had brought.

WAITING

THE sun has slipped his tether
  And galloped down the west.
(Oh, it 's weary, weary waiting,
    love.)
The little bird is sleeping
  In the softness of its nest.
Night follows day, day follows
    dawn,
And so the time has come and
    gone:
  And it 's weary, weary waiting,
    love.

The cruel wind is rising
  With a whistle and a wail.

(And it's weary, weary waiting,
    love.)
My eyes are seaward straining
    For the coming of a sail;
But void the sea, and void the
    beach
Far and beyond where gaze can
    reach!
    And it's weary, weary waiting,
      love.

I heard the bell-buoy ringing —
    How long ago it seems!
(Oh, it's weary, weary waiting,
    love.)
And ever still, its knelling
    Crashes in upon my dreams.
The banns were read, my frock
    was sewn;
Since then two seasons' winds
    have blown —
    And it's weary, weary waiting,
      love.

The stretches of the ocean
    Are bare and bleak to-day.
(Oh, it's weary, weary waiting,
    love.)
My eyes are growing dimmer —
    Is it tears, or age, or spray?
But I will stay till you come home.
Strange ships come in across the
    foam!
    But it's weary, weary waiting,
      love.

THE END OF THE CHAPTER

AH, yes, the chapter ends to-day;
We even lay the book away;
But oh, how sweet the moments
    sped
Before the final page was read!

We tried to read between the lines
The Author's deep-concealed de-
    signs;
But scant reward such search se-
    cures;
You saw my heart and I saw
    yours.

The Master, — He who penned
    the page
And bade us read it, — He is sage:
And what he orders, you and I
Can but obey, nor question why.

We read together and forgot
The world about us. Time was
    not.
Unheeded and unfelt, it fled.
We read and hardly knew we
    read.

Until beneath a sadder sun,
We came to know the book was
    done.
Then, as our minds were but new
    lit,
It dawned upon us what was writ;

And we were startled. In our
    eyes,

Looked forth the light of great
  surprise.
Then as a deep-toned tocsin tolls,
A voice spoke forth: " Behold
  your souls! "

I do, I do. I cannot look
Into your eyes: so close the book.
But brought it grief or brought it
  bliss,
No other page shall read like this!

SYMPATHY

I KNOW what the caged bird feels,
  alas!
  When the sun is bright on the
    upland slopes;
When the wind stirs soft through
  the springing grass,
And the river flows like a stream
  of glass;
  When the first bird sings and
    the first bud opes,
And the faint perfume from its
  chalice steals —
I know what the caged bird feels!

I know why the caged bird beats
  his wing
  Till its blood is red on the cruel
    bars;
For he must fly back to his perch
  and cling
When he fain would be on the
  bough a-swing;
  And a pain still throbs in the
    old, old scars

And they pulse again with a keener
  sting —
I know why he beats his wing!

I know why the caged bird sings,
  ah me,
  When his wing is bruised and
    his bosom sore,—
When he beats his bars and he
  would be free;
It is not a carol of joy or glee,
  But a prayer that he sends from
    his heart's deep core,
But a plea, that upward to Heaven
  he flings —
I know why the caged bird sings!

LOVE AND GRIEF

OUT of my heart, one treach'rous
  winter's day,
I locked young Love and threw
  the key away.
Grief, wandering widely, found
  the key,
And hastened with it, straight-
  way, back to me,
With Love beside him. He un-
  locked the door
And bade Love enter with him
  there and stay.
And so the twain abide for ever-
  more.

LOVE'S CHASTENING

Once Love grew bold and arro-
  gant of air,

Proud of the youth that made him
    fresh and fair;
So unto Grief he spake, " What
    right hast thou
To part or parcel of this heart?"
    Grief's brow
Was darkened with the storm of
    inward strife;
Thrice smote he Love as only he
    might dare,
And Love, pride purged, was chas-
    tened all his life.

MORTALITY

ASHES to ashes, dust unto dust,
What of his loving, what of his
    lust?
What of his passion, what of his
    pain?
What of his poverty, what of his
    pride?
Earth, the great mother, has called
    him again:
Deeply he sleeps, the world's ver-
    dict defied.
Shall he be tried again? Shall he
    go free?
Who shall the court convene?
    Where shall it be?
No answer on the land, none from
    the sea.
Only we know that as he did, we
    must:
You with your theories, you with
    your trust,—
Ashes to ashes, dust unto dust!

LOVE

A LIFE was mine full of the close
    concern
  Of many-voiced affairs. The
    world sped fast;
  Behind me, ever rolled a preg-
    nant past.
A present came equipped with lore
    to learn.
Art, science, letters, in their turn,
  Each one allured me with its
    treasures vast;
  And I staked all for wisdom,
    till at last
Thou cam'st and taught my soul
    anew to yearn.
  I had not dreamed that I could
    turn away
From all that men with brush
    and pen had wrought;
  But ever since that memorable
    day
When to my heart the truth of
    love was brought,
  I have been wholly yielded to
    its sway,
And had no room for any other
    thought.

SHE GAVE ME A ROSE

SHE gave a rose,
  And I kissed it and pressed it.
I love her, she knows,
  And my action confessed it.
She gave me a rose,
  And I kissed it and pressed it

Ah, how my heart glows,
  Could I ever have guessed it?
It is fair to suppose
  That I might have repressed it:
She gave me a rose,
  And I kissed it and pressed it.

'T was a rhyme in life's prose
  That uplifted and blest it.
Man's nature, who knows
  Until love comes to test it?
She gave me a rose,
  And I kissed it and pressed it.

Be thy far home by mountain,
  vale, or sea.
My yearning heart may never find
  its rest
Until thou liest rapt upon my
  breast.
The wind may bring its perfume
  from the south,
Is it so sweet as breath from my
  love's mouth?
Oh, naught that surely is, and
  naught that seems
May turn me from the lady of my
  dreams.

DREAM SONG I

LONG years ago, within a distant
  clime,
Ere Love had touched me with
  his wand sublime,
I dreamed of one to make my life's
  calm May
The panting passion of a sum-
  mer's day.
And ever since, in almost sad sus-
  pense,
I have been waiting with a soul
  intense
To greet and take unto myself
  the beams,
Of her, my star, the lady of my
  dreams.

O Love, still longed and looked
  for, come to me,

DREAM SONG II

PRAY, what can dreams avail
  To make love or to mar?
The child within the cradle rail
  Lies dreaming of the star.
But is the star by this beguiled
To leave its place and seek the
  child?

The poor plucked rose within its
  glass
  Still dreameth of the bee;
But, tho' the lagging moments
  pass,
  Her Love she may not see.
If dream of child and flower fail,
Why should a maiden's dreams
  prevail?

CHRISTMAS IN THE HEART

THE snow lies deep upon the
ground,
And winter's brightness all around
Decks bravely out the forest sere,
With jewels of the brave old year.
The coasting crowd upon the hill
With some new spirit seems to
thrill;
And all the temple bells achime.
Ring out the glee of Christmas
time.

In happy homes the brown oak-
bough
Vies with the red-gemmed holly
now;
And here and there, like pearls,
there show
The berries of the mistletoe.
A sprig upon the chandelier
Says to the maidens, "Come not
here!"
Even the pauper of the earth
Some kindly gift has cheered to
mirth!

Within his chamber, dim and cold,
There sits a grasping miser old.
He has no thought save one of
gain,—
To grind and gather and grasp
and drain.
A peal of bells, a merry shout
Assail his ear: he gazes out
Upon a world to him all gray,
And snarls, "Why, this is Christ-
mas Day!"

No, man of ice,— for shame, for
shame!
For "Christmas Day" is no mere
name.
No, not for you this ringing cheer,
This festal season of the year.
And not for you the chime of bells
From holy temple rolls and swells.
In day and deed he has no part —
Who holds not Christmas in his
heart!

THE KING IS DEAD

AYE, lay him in his grave, the old
dead year!
His life is lived — fulfilled his
destiny.
Have you for him no sad, regret-
ful tear
To drop beside the cold, unfol-
lowed bier?
Can you not pay the tribute of a
sigh?

Was he not kind to you, this dead
old year?
Did he not give enough of earthly
store?
Enough of love, and laughter, and
good cheer?
Have not the skies you scanned
sometimes been clear?

How, then, of him who dies, could
  you ask more?

It is not well to hate him for the
  pain
He brought you, and the sorrows
  manifold.
To pardon him these hurts still I
  am fain;
For in the panting period of his
  reign,
He brought me new wounds, but
  he healed the old.

One little sigh for thee, my poor,
  dead friend —
One little sigh while my com-
  panions sing.
Thou art so soon forgotten in the
  end;
We cry e'en as thy footsteps down-
  ward tend:
" The king is dead! long live the
  king!"

THEOLOGY

THERE is a heaven, for ever, day
  by day,
The upward longing of my soul
  doth tell me so.
There is a hell, I 'm quite as sure;
  for pray,
If there were not, where would
  my neighbours go?

RESIGNATION

LONG had I grieved at what I
  deemed abuse;
  But now I am as grain within
    the mill.
If so be thou must crush me for
  thy use,
  Grind on, O potent God, and
    do thy will!

LOVE'S HUMILITY

As some rapt gazer on the lowly
  earth,
  Looks up to radiant planets,
    ranging far,
So I, whose soul doth know thy
  wondrous worth
  Look longing up to thee as to a
    star.

PRECEDENT

THE poor man went to the rich
  man's doors,
" I come as Lazarus came," he
  said.
The rich man turned with humble
  head,—
" I will send my dogs to lick your
  sores!"

SHE TOLD HER BEADS

SHE told her beads with down-
  cast eyes,
  Within the ancient chapel dim;
  And ever as her fingers slim

Slipt o'er th' insensate ivories,
My rapt soul followed, spaniel-
    wise.
Ah, many were the beads she wore;
    But as she told them o'er and
      o'er,
They did not number all my sighs.
My heart was filled with unvoiced
    cries
    And prayers and pleadings un-
      expressed;
    But while I burned with Love's
      unrest,
She told her beads with down-
    cast eyes.

LITTLE LUCY LANDMAN

OH, the day has set me dreaming
    In a strange, half solemn way
Of the feelings I experienced
    On another long past day,—
Of the way my heart made music
    When the buds began to blow,
And o' little Lucy Landman
    Whom I loved long years ago.

It's in spring, the poet tells us,
    That we turn to thoughts of
      love,
And our hearts go out a-wooing
    With the lapwing and the dove.
But whene'er the soul goes seeking
    Its twin-soul, upon the wing,
I've a notion, backed by mem'ry,
    That it's love that makes the
    spring.

I have heard a robin singing
    When the boughs were brown
      and bare,
And the chilling hand of winter
Scattered jewels through the air.
And in spite of dates and seasons,
    It was always spring, I know,
When I loved Lucy Landman
    In the days of long ago.

Ah, my little Lucy Landman,
    I remember you as well
As if 't were only yesterday
    I strove your thoughts to tell,—
When I tilted back your bonnet,
    Looked into your eyes so true,
Just to see if you were loving
    Me as I was loving you.

Ah, my little Lucy Landman
    It is true it was denied
You should see a fuller summer
    And an autumn by my side.
But the glance of love's sweet sun-
    light
    Which your eyes that morning
    gave
Has kept spring within my bosom,
    Though you lie within the
    grave.

THE GOURD

IN the heavy earth the miner
    Toiled and laboured day by day,
Wrenching from the miser moun-
    tain
    Brilliant treasure where it lay.

And the artist worn and weary
  Wrought with labour manifold
That the king might drink his
    nectar
From a goblet made of gold.

On the prince's groaning table
  Mid the silver gleaming bright
Mirroring the happy faces
  Giving back the flaming light,
Shine the cups of priceless crystal
  Chased with many a lovely line,
Glowing now with warmer colour,
  Crimsoned by the ruby wine.

In a valley sweet with sunlight,
  Fertile with the dew and rain,
Without miner's daily labour,
  Without artist's nightly pain,
There there grows the cup I drink
    from,
  Summer's sweetness in it stored,
And my lips pronounce a blessing
  As they touch an old brown
    gourd.

Why, the miracle at Cana
  In the land of Galilee,
Tho' it puzzles all the scholars,
  Is no longer strange to me.
For the poorest and the humblest
  Could a priceless wine afford,
If they 'd only dip up water
  With a sunlight-seasoned gourd.

So a health to my old comrade,
  And a song of praise to sing

When he rests inviting kisses
  In his place beside the spring.
Give the king his golden goblets,
  Give the prince his crystal
    hoard;
But for me the sparkling water
  From a brown and brimming
    gourd!

THE KNIGHT

Our good knight, Ted, girds his
    broadsword on
  (And he wields it well, I
    ween);
He 's on his steed, and away has
    gone
  To the fight for king and queen.
What tho' no edge the broadsword
    hath?
What tho' the blade be made of
    lath?
  'T is a valiant hand
  That wields the brand,
So, foeman, clear the path!

He prances off at a goodly pace;
  'T is a noble steed he rides,
That bears as well in the speedy
    race
  As he bears in battle-tides.
What tho' 't is but a rocking-chair
That prances with this stately air?
  'T is a warrior bold
  The reins doth hold,
Who bids all foes beware!

THOU ART MY LUTE

THOU art my lute, by thee I
  sing,—
My being is attuned to thee.
Thou settest all my words a-wing,
And meltest me to melody.

Thou art my life, by thee I live,
  From thee proceed the joys I
    know;
Sweetheart, thy hand has power
    to give
  The meed of love — the cup of
    woe.

Thou art my love, by thee I lead
  My soul the paths of light along,
From vale to vale, from mead to
    mead,
  And home it in the hills of song.

My song, my soul, my life, my all,
  Why need I pray or make my
    plea,
Since my petition cannot fall;
  For I 'm already one with thee!

THE PHANTOM KISS

ONE night in my room, still and
    beamless,
  With will and with thought in
    eclipse,
I rested in sleep that was dream-
    less;
  When softly there fell on my
    lips

A touch, as of lips that were press-
    ing
  Mine own with the message of
    bliss —
A sudden, soft, fleeting caressing,
  A breath like a maiden's first
    kiss.

I woke — and the scoffer may
    doubt me —
  I peered in surprise through the
    gloom;
But nothing and none were about
    me,
  And I was alone in my room.

Perhaps 't was the wind that
    caressed me
  And touched me with dew-laden
    breath;
Or, maybe, close-sweeping, there
    passed me
  The low-winging Angel of
    Death.

Some sceptic may choose to dis-
    dain it,
  Or one feign to read it aright;
Or wisdom may seek to explain
    it —
  This mystical kiss in the night.

But rather let fancy thus clear it:
  That, thinking of me here alone,
The miles were made naught, and,
    in spirit,
  Thy lips, love, were laid on
    mine own.

COMMUNION

In the silence of my heart,
  I will spend an hour with thee,
When my love shall rend apart
  All the veil of mystery:

All that dim and misty veil
  That shut in between our souls
When Death cried, " Ho, maiden,
    hail! "
  And your barque sped on the
    shoals.

On the shoals? Nay, wrongly
    said.
  On the breeze of Death that
    sweeps
Far from life, thy soul has sped
  Out into unsounded deeps.

I shall take an hour.and come
  Sailing, darling, to thy side.
Wind nor sea may keep me from
  Soft communings with my bride.

I shall rest my head on thee
  As I did long days of yore,
When a calm, untroubled sea
  Rocked thy vessel at the shore.

I shall take thy hand in mine,
  And live o'er the olden days
When thy smile to me was wine,—
  Golden wine thy word of praise,

For the carols I had wrought
  In my soul's simplicity;

For the petty beads of thought
  Which thine eyes alone could
    see.

Ah, those eyes, love-blind, but keen
  For my welfare and my weal!
Tho' the grave-door shut between,
  Still their love-lights o'er me
    steal.

I can see thee thro' my tears,
  As thro' rain we see the sun.
What tho' cold and cooling years
  Shall their bitter courses run,—

I shall see thee still and be
  Thy true lover evermore,
And thy face shall be to me
  Dear and helpful as before.

Death may vaunt and Death may
    boast,
  But we laugh his pow'r to
    scorn;
He is but a slave at most,—
  Night that heralds coming morn.

I shall spend an hour with thee
  Day by day, my little bride.
True love laughs at mystery,
  Crying, " Doors of Death, fly
    wide."

MARE RUBRUM

In Life's Red Sea with faith I
    plant my feet,
  And wait the sound of that sus-
    taining word

Which long ago the men of
 Israel heard,
When Pharaoh's host behind them,
 fierce and fleet,
Raged on, consuming with re-
 vengeful heat.
  Why are the barrier waters
  still unstirred? —
  That struggling faith may die
  of hope deferred?
Is God not sitting in His ancient
 seat?

The billows swirl above my trem-
 bling limbs,
  And almost chill my anxious
  heart to doubt
  And disbelief, long conquered
  and defied.
But tho' the music of my hopeful
 hymns
  Is drowned by curses of the rag-
  ing rout,
   No voice yet bids th' opposing
   waves divide!

IN AN ENGLISH GARDEN

In this old garden, fair, I walk
 to-day
  Heart-charmed with all the
  beauty of the scene:
  The rich, luxuriant grasses'
  cooling green,
The wall's environ, ivy-decked and
 gray,

The waving branches with the
 wind at play,
  The slight and tremulous
  blooms that show between,
  Sweet all: and yet my yearning
  heart doth lean
Toward Love's Egyptian flesh-
 pots far away.

Beside the wall, the slim Labur-
 num grows
  And flings its golden flow'rs to
  every breeze.
  But e'en among such soothing
  sights as these,
I pant and nurse my soul-devour-
 ing woes.
Of all the longings that our
 hearts wot of,
There is no hunger like the want
 of love!

THE CRISIS

A MAN of low degree was sore op-
 pressed,
  Fate held him under iron-handed
  sway,
And ever, those who saw him
 thus distressed
  Would bid him bend his stub-
  born will and pray.
But he, strong in himself and ob-
 durate,
  Waged, prayerless, on his losing
  fight with Fate.

Friends gave his proffered hand
their coldest clasp,
Or took it not at all; and Pov-
erty,
That bruised his body with relent-
less grasp,
Grinned, taunting, when he
struggled to be free.
But though with helpless hands he
beat the air,
His need extreme yet found no
voice in prayer.

Then he prevailed; and forthwith
snobbish Fate,
Like some whipped cur, came
fawning at his feet;
Those who had scorned forgave
and called him great —
His friends found out that
friendship still was sweet.
But he, once obdurate, now bowed
his head
In prayer, and trembling with its
import, said:

" Mere human strength may stand
ill-fortune's frown;
So I prevailed, for human
strength was mine;
But from the killing pow'r of
great renown,
Naught may protect me save a
strength divine.
Help me, O Lord, in this my
trembling cause;
I scorn men's curses, but I dread
applause!"

THE CONQUERORS

THE BLACK TROOPS IN CUBA

ROUND the wide earth, from the
red field your valour has won,
Blown with the breath of the far-
speaking gun,
Goes the word.
Bravely you spoke through the bat-
tle cloud heavy and dun,
Tossed though the speech toward
the mist-hidden sun,
The world heard.

Hell would have shrunk from you
seeking it fresh from the fray,
Grim with the dust of the battle,
and gray
From the fight.
Heaven would have crowned you,
with crowns not of gold but
of bay,
Owning you fit for the light of
her day,
Men of night.

Far through the cycle of years and
of lives that shall come,
There shall speak voices long muf-
fled and dumb,
Out of fear.
And through the noises of trade
and the turbulent hum,
Truth shall rise over the militant
drum,
Loud and clear.

Then on the cheek of the honester
nation that grows,

All for their love of you, not for
    your woes,
      There shall lie
Tears that shall be to your souls as
    the dew to the rose;
Afterward thanks, that the pres-
    ent yet knows
      Not to ply!

ALEXANDER CRUMMELL — DEAD

BACK to the breast of thy mother,
Child of the earth!
E'en her caress can not smother
What thou hast done.
Follow the trail of the westering
    sun
Over the earth.
Thy light and his were as one —
Sun, in thy worth.
Unto a nation whose sky was as
    night,
Camest thou, holily, bearing thy
    light:
And the dawn came,
In it thy fame
Flashed up in a flame.

Back to the breast of thy mother —
To rest.
Long hast thou striven;
Dared where the hills by the light-
    ning of heaven were riven;
Go now, pure shriven.
Who shall come after thee, out of
    the clay —

Learned one and leader to show
    us the way?
Who shall rise up when the world
    gives the test?
Think thou no more of this —
Rest!

WHEN ALL IS DONE

WHEN all is done, and my last
    word is said,
And ye who loved me murmur,
    " He is dead,"
Let no one weep, for fear that I
    should know,
And sorrow too that ye should
    sorrow so.

When all is done and in the ooz-
    ing clay,
Ye lay this cast-off hull of mine
    away,
Pray not for me, for, after long
    despair,
The quiet of the grave will be a
    prayer.

For I have suffered loss and
    grievous pain,
The hurts of hatred and the
    world's disdain,
And wounds so deep that love,
    well-tried and pure,
Had not the pow'r to ease them
    or to cure.

When all is done, say not my day
    is o'er,

And that thro' night I seek a dim-
    mer shore:
Say rather that my morn has just
    begun,—
I greet the dawn and not a setting
    sun,
        When all is done.

THE POET AND THE
BABY

How's a man to write a sonnet,
    can you tell,—
How's he going to weave the dim,
    poetic spell,—
    When a-toddling on the floor
    Is the muse he must adore,
And this muse he loves, not
    wisely, but too well?

Now, to write a sonnet, every one
    allows,
One must always be as quiet as a
    mouse;
    But to write one seems to me
    Quite superfluous to be,
When you've got a little sonnet
    in the house.

Just a dainty little poem, true and
    fine,
That is full of love and life in
    every line,
    Earnest, delicate, and sweet,
    Altogether so complete

That I wonder what's the use of
    writing mine.

DISTINCTION

" I am but clay," the sinner plead,
    Who fed each vain desire.
" Not only clay," another said,
    " But worse, for thou art mire."

THE SUM

A little dreaming by the way,
A little toiling day by day;
A little pain, a little strife,
A little joy,— and that is life.

A   little   short-lived   summer's
    morn,
When joy seems all so newly born,
When one day's sky is blue above,
And one bird sings,— and that is
    love.

A little sickening of the years,
The tribute of a few hot tears
Two folded hands, the failing
    breath,
And peace at last,— and that is
    death.

Just dreaming, loving, dying so,
The actors in the drama go —
A flitting picture on a wall,
Love, Death, the themes; but is
    that all?

SONNET

ON AN OLD BOOK WITH UNCUT LEAVES

EMBLEM of blasted hope and lost desire,
   No finger ever traced thy yellow page
   Save Time's. Thou hast not wrought to noble rage
The hearts thou wouldst have stirred. Not any fire
Save sad flames set to light a funeral pyre
   Dost thou suggest. Nay,— impotent in age,
   Unsought, thou holdst a corner of the stage
And ceasest even dumbly to aspire.

How different was the thought of him that writ.
   What promised he to love of ease and wealth,
When men should read and kindle at his wit.
   But here decay eats up the book by stealth,
While it, like some old maiden, solemnly,
Hugs its incongruous virginity!

ON THE SEA WALL

I SIT upon the old sea wall,
   And watch the shimmering sea,
Where soft and white the moonbeams fall,
   Till, in a fantasy,
Some pure white maiden's funeral pall
   The strange light seems to me.

The waters break upon the shore
   And shiver at my feet,
While I dream old dreams o'er and o'er,
   And dim old scenes repeat;
Tho' all have dreamed the same before,
   They still seem new and sweet.

The waves still sing the same old song
   That knew an elder time;
The breakers' beat is not more strong,
   Their music more sublime;
And poets thro' the ages long
   Have set these notes to rhyme.

But this shall not deter my lyre,
   Nor check my simple strain;
If I have not the old-time fire,
   I know the ancient pain:
The hurt of unfulfilled desire,—
   The ember quenched by rain.

I know the softly shining sea
   That rolls this gentle swell
Has snarled and licked its tongues at me
   And bared its fangs as well;
That 'neath its smile so heavenly,
   There lurks the scowl of hell!

But what of that? I strike my string
  (For songs in youth are sweet);
I'll wait and hear the waters bring
  Their loud resounding beat;
Then, in her own bold numbers sing
  The Ocean's dear deceit!

But far and strange, thou still dost make them fair.

Now thou dost sing, and I am lost in thee
  As one who drowns
In floods of melody.
  Still in thy art
  Give me this part,
Till perfect love, the love of loving crowns.

TO A LADY PLAYING THE HARP

THY tones are silver melted into sound,
  And as I dream
I see no walls around,
  But seem to hear
  A gondolier
Sing sweetly down some slow Venetian stream.

Italian skies — that I have never seen —
  I see above.
(Ah, play again, my queen;
  Thy fingers white
  Fly swift and light
And weave for me the golden mesh of love.)

Oh, thou dusk sorceress of the dusky eyes
  And soft dark hair,
T is thou that mak'st my skies
  So swift to change
  To far and strange;

CONFESSIONAL

SEARCH thou my heart;
  If there be guile,
It shall depart
  Before thy smile.

Search thou my soul;
  Be there deceit,
'T will vanish whole
  Before thee, sweet.

Upon my mind
  Turn thy pure lens;
Naught shalt thou find
  Thou canst not cleanse.

If I should pray,
  I scarcely know
In just what way
  My prayers would go.

So strong in me
  I feel love's leaven,
I'd bow to thee
  As soon as Heaven!

MISAPPREHENSION

OUT of my heart, one day, I
    wrote a song,
  With my heart's blood imbued,
Instinct with passion, tremulously
    strong,
  With grief subdued;
  Breathing a fortitude
  Pain-bought.
And one who claimed much love
    for what I wrought,
  Read and considered it,
  And spoke:
" Ay, brother,—'t is well writ,
  But where 's the joke? "

PROMETHEUS

PROMETHEUS stole from Heaven
    the sacred fire
  And swept to earth with it o'er
    land and sea.
  He lit the vestal flames of poesy,
Content, for this, to brave celes-
    tial ire.

Wroth were the gods, and with
    eternal hate
  Pursued the fearless one who
    ravished Heaven
  That earth might hold in fee
    the perfect leaven
To lift men's souls above their
    low estate.

But judge you now, when poets
    wield the pen,

Think you not well the wrong
    has been repaired?
'T was all in vain that ill Pro-
    metheus fared:
The fire has been returned to
    Heaven again!

We have no singers like the ones
    whose note
  Gave challenge to the noblest
    warbler's song.
  We have no voice so mellow,
    sweet, and strong
As that which broke from Shelley's
    golden throat.

The measure of our songs is our
    desires:
  We tinkle where old poets used
    to storm.
  We lack their substance tho' we
    keep their form:
We strum our banjo-strings and
    call them lyres.

LOVE'S PHASES

LOVE hath the wings of the but-
    terfly,
  Oh, clasp him but gently,
Pausing and dipping and flutter-
    ing by
  Inconsequently.
Stir not his poise with the breath
    of a sigh;
Love hath the wings of the but-
    terfly.

Love hath the wings of the eagle
    bold,
  Cling to him strongly —
What if the look of the world be
    cold,
  And life go wrongly?
Rest on his pinions, for broad is
    their fold;
Love hath the wings of the eagle
    bold.

Love hath the voice of the nightin-
    gale,
  Hearken his trilling —
List to his song when the moon-
    light is pale,—
  Passionate, thrilling.
Cherish the lay, ere the lilt of it
    fail;
Love hath the voice of the nightin-
    gale.

Love hath the voice of the storm
    at night,
  Wildly defiant.
Hear him and yield up your soul
    to his might,
  Tenderly pliant.
None shall regret him who heed
    him aright;
Love hath the voice of the storm
    at night.

FOR THE MAN WHO FAILS

THE world is a snob, and the man
  who wins
Is the chap for its money's
    worth:
And the lust for success causes
    half of the sins
  That are cursing this brave old
    earth.
For it's fine to go up, and the
    world's applause
  Is sweet to the mortal ear;
But the man who fails in a noble
    cause
  Is a hero that's no less dear.

'T is true enough that the laurel
    crown
  Twines but for the victor's
    brow;
For many a hero has lain him
    down
  With naught but the cypress
    bough.
There are gallant men in the los-
    ing fight,
  And as gallant deeds are done
As ever graced the captured
    height
  Or the battle grandly won.

We sit at life's board with our
    nerves highstrung,
  And we play for the stake of
    Fame,
And our odes are sung and our
    banners hung
  For the man who wins the
    game.
But I have a song of another kind

Than breathes in these fame-
    wrought gales,—
An ode to the noble heart and
    mind
Of the gallant man who fails!

The man who is strong to fight his
    fight,
    And whose will no front can
      daunt,
If the truth be truth and the right
    be right,
    Is the man that the ages want.
Tho' he fail and die in grim de-
    feat,
    Yet he has not fled the strife,
And the house of Earth will seem
    more sweet
    For the perfume of his life.

HARRIET BEECHER STOWE

SHE told the story, and the whole
    world wept
    At wrongs and cruelties it had
      not known
    But for this fearless woman's
      voice alone.
    She spoke to consciences that
      long had slept:
Her message, Freedom's clear
    reveille, swept
    From heedless hovel to compla-
      cent throne.
    Command and prophecy were
      in the tone

And from its sheath the sword
    of justice leapt.
Around two peoples swelled a
    fiery wave,
    But both came forth transfig-
      ured from the flame.
Blest be the hand that dared be
    strong to save,
    And blest be she who in our
      weakness came —
Prophet and priestess! At one
    stroke she gave
A race to freedom and herself
    to fame.

VAGRANTS

LONG time ago, we two set out,
    My soul and I.
    I know not why,
For all our way was dim with
    doubt.
    I know not where
    We two may fare:
Though still with every changing
    weather,
We wander, groping on together.

We do not love, we are not
    friends,
    My soul and I.
    He lives a lie;
Untruth lines every way he wends.
    A scoffer he
    Who jeers at me:

And so, my comrade and my
    brother,
We wander on and hate each
    other.

Ay, there be taverns and to spare,
    Beside the road;
    But some strange goad
Lets me not stop to taste their
    fare.
    Knew I the goal
    Toward which my soul
And I made way, hope made life
    fragrant:
But no.   We wander, aimless, va-
    grant!

A WINTER'S DAY

Across the hills and down the
    narrow ways,
    And up the valley where the
    free winds sweep,
    The earth is folded in an er-
    mined sleep
That mocks the melting mirth of
    myriad Mays.
Departed her disheartening duns
    and grays,
    And all her crusty black is cov-
    ered deep.
    Dark streams are locked in
    Winter's donjon-keep,
And made to shine with keen, un-
    wonted rays.

O icy mantle, and deceitful snow!
    What world-old liars in your
    hearts ye are!
    Are there not still the darkened
    seam and scar
Beneath the brightness that you
    fain would show?
Come from the cover with thy
    blot and blur,
O reeking Earth, thou whited
    sepulchre!

MY LITTLE MARCH
GIRL

Come to the pane, draw the cur-
    tain apart,
There she is passing, the girl of
    my heart;
See where she walks like a queen
    in the street,
Weather-defying, calm, placid and
    sweet.
Tripping along with impetuous
    grace,
Joy of her life beaming out of her
    face,
Tresses all truant-like, curl upon
    curl,
Wind-blown and rosy, my little
    March girl.

Hint of the violet's delicate
    bloom,
Hint of the rose's pervading per-
    fume!

How can the wind help from kiss-
ing her face,—
Wrapping her round in his stormy
embrace?
But still serenely she laughs at his
rout,
She is the victor who wins in the
bout.
So may life's passions about her
soul swirl,
Leaving it placid,—my little
March girl.

What self-possession looks out of
her eyes!
What are the wild winds, and
what are the skies,
Frowning and glooming when,
brimming with life,
Cometh the little maid ripe for the
strife?
Ah! Wind, and bah! Wind, what
might have you now?
What can you do with that inno-
cent brow?
Blow, Wind, and grow, Wind,
and eddy and swirl,
But bring her to me, Wind,—my
little March girl.

REMEMBERED

SHE sang, and I listened the
whole song thro'.
(It was sweet, so sweet, the
singing.)

The stars were out and the moon
it grew
From a wee soft glimmer way out
in the blue
To a bird thro' the heavens
winging.

She sang, and the song trembled
down to my breast,—
(It was sweet, so sweet the
singing.)
As a dove just out of its fledgling
nest,
And, putting its wings to the first
sweet test,
Flutters homeward so wearily
winging.

She sang and I said to my heart
" That song,
That was sweet, so sweet i' the
singing,
Shall live with us and inspire us
long,
And thou, my heart, shalt be brave
and strong
For the sake of those words
a-winging.

The woman died and the song
was still.
(It was sweet, so sweet, the
singing.)
But ever I hear the same low
trill,
Of the song that shakes my heart
with a thrill,
And goes forever winging.

LOVE DESPOILED

As lone I sat one summer's day,
  With mien dejected, Love
      came by;
His face distraught, his locks
      astray,
  So slow his gait, so sad his eye,
  I hailed him with a pitying cry:

" Pray, Love, what has disturbed
      thee so? "
  Said I, amazed. " Thou seem'st
      bereft;
And see thy quiver hanging
      low,—
  What, not a single arrow left?
  Pray, who is guilty of this
      theft? "

Poor Love looked in my face and
      cried:
  " No thief were ever yet so bold
To rob my quiver at my side.
  But Time, who rules, gave ear
      to Gold,
  And all my goodly shafts are
      sold."

THE LAPSE

THIS poem must be done to-day;
  Then, I 'll e'en to it.
I must not dream my time away,—
  I 'm sure to rue it.
The day is rather bright, I know
  The Muse will pardon

My half-defection, if I go
  Into the garden.
It must be better working
      there,—
  I 'm sure it 's sweeter:
And something in the balmy air
  May clear my metre.

[*In the Garden.*]

Ah this is noble, what a sky!
  What breezes blowing!
The very clouds, I know not why,
  Call one to rowing.
The stream will be a paradise
  To-day, I 'll warrant.
I know the tide that 's on the rise
  Will seem a torrent;
I know just how the leafy boughs
  Are all a-quiver;
I know how many skiffs and scows
  Are on the river.
I think I 'll just go out awhile
  Before I write it;
When Nature shows us such a
      smile,
  We should n't slight it.
For Nature always makes desire
  By giving pleasure;
And so 't will help me put more
      fire
  Into my measure.

[*On the River.*]

The river 's fine, I 'm glad I came
  That poem 's teasing;
But health is better far than fame
  Though cheques are pleasing.

I don't know what I did it for,—
This air 's a poppy.
I 'm sorry for my editor,—
He 'll get no copy!

THE WARRIOR'S PRAYER

LONG since, in sore distress, I
heard one pray,
" Lord, who prevailest with re-
sistless might,
Ever from war and strife keep me
away,
My battles fight! "

I know not if I play the Pharisee,
And if my brother after all be
right;
But mine shall be the warrior's
plea to thee —
Strength for the fight.

I do not ask that thou shalt front
the fray,
And drive the warring foeman
from my sight;
I only ask, O Lord, by night, by
day,
Strength for the fight!

When foes upon me press, let me
not quail
Nor think to turn me into
coward flight.
I only ask, to make mine arms
prevail,
Strength for the fight!

Still let mine eyes look ever on the
foe,
Still let mine armor case me
strong and bright;
And grant me, as I deal each right-
eous blow,
Strength for the fight!

And when, at eventide, the fray
is done,
My soul to Death's bedchamber
do thou light,
And give me, be the field or lost
or won,
Rest from the fight!

FAREWELL TO ARCADY

WITH sombre mien, the Evening
gray
Comes nagging at the heels of
Day,
And driven faster and still faster
Before the dusky-mantled Master,
The light fades from her fearful
eyes,
She hastens, stumbles, falls, and
dies.

Beside me Amaryllis weeps;
The swelling tears obscure the
deeps
Of her dark eyes, as, mistily,
The rushing rain conceals the sea.
Here, lay my tuneless reed away,—
I have no heart to tempt a lay.

I scent the perfume of the rose
Which by my crystal fountain
    grows.
In this sad time, are roses blow-
    ing?
And thou, my fountain, art thou
    flowing,

While I who watched thy waters
    spring
Am all too sad to smile or sing?
Nay, give me back my pipe again,
It yet shall breathe this single
    strain:
        Farewell to Arcady!

THE VOICE OF THE BANJO

In a small and lonely cabin out
    of noisy traffic's way,
Sat an old man, bent and feeble,
    dusk of face, and hair of gray,
And beside him on the table, bat-
    tered, old, and worn as he,
Lay a banjo, droning forth this
    reminiscent melody:

"Night is closing in upon us,
    friend of mine, but don't be
    sad;
Let us think of all the pleasures
    and the joys that we have had.
Let us keep a merry visage, and be
    happy till the last,
Let the future still be sweetened
    with the honey of the past.

"For I speak to you of summer
    nights upon the yellow sand,
When the Southern moon was
    sailing high and silvering all
    the land;
And if love tales were not sacred,
    there's a tale that I could
    tell
Of your many nightly wanderings
    with a dusk and lovely belle.

"And I speak to you of care-free
    songs when labour's hour was
    o'er,
And a woman waiting for your
    step outside the cabin door,
And of something roly-poly that
    you took upon your lap,
While you listened for the stum-
    bling, hesitating words, ' Pap,
    pap.'

"I could tell you of a 'possum
    hunt across the wooded
    grounds,
I could call to mind the sweetness
    of the baying of the hounds,
You could lift me up and smelling
    of the timber that's in me,
Build again a whole green forest
    with the mem'ry of a tree.

"So the future cannot hurt us
    while we keep the past in
    mind,
What care I for trembling fingers,
    — what care you that you are
    blind?

Time may leave us poor and
    stranded, circumstance may
    make us bend;
But they'll only find us mellower,
    won't they, comrade? — in
    the end."

THE STIRRUP CUP

COME, drink a stirrup cup with me,
    Before we close our rouse.
You're all aglow with wine, I
    know:
    The master of the house,
    Unmindful of our revelry,
    Has drowned the carking devil
    care,
    And slumbers in his chair.

Come, drink a cup before we start;
    We've far to ride to-night.
And Death may take the race we
    make,
    And check our gallant flight:
    But even he must play his part,
    And tho' the look he wears be
    grim,
We'll drink a toast to him!

For Death,— a swift old chap is
    he,
    And swift the steed He rides.
He needs no chart o'er main or
    mart,
    For no direction bides.
    So, come, a final cup with me,
    And let the soldiers' chorus
    swell,—
    To hell with care, to hell!

A CHOICE

THEY please me not — these
    solemn songs
That hint of sermons covered up.
'T is true the world should heed
    its wrongs,
    But in a poem let me sup,
Not simples brewed to cure or
    ease
Humanity's confessed disease,
But the spirit-wine of a singing
    line,
    Or a dew-drop in a honey cup!

Humor and Dialect

THEN AND NOW

THEN

HE loved her, and through many
   years,
Had paid his fair devoted court,
Until she wearied, and with sneers
Turned all his ardent love to sport.

That night within his chamber
   lone,
He long sat writing by his bed
A note in which his heart made
   moan
For love; the morning found him
   dead.

NOW

Like him, a man of later day
Was jilted by the maid he sought,
And from her presence turned
   away,
Consumed by burning, bitter
   thought.

He sought his room to write — a
   curse
Like him before and die, I ween.
Ah no, he put his woes in verse,
And sold them to a magazine.

AT CHESHIRE CHEESE

WHEN first of wise old Johnson
   taught,
My youthful mind its homage
   brought,

And made the pond'rous crusty
   sage
The object of a noble rage.

Nor did I think (How dense we
   are!)
That any day, however far,
Would find me holding, unre-
   pelled,
The place that Doctor Johnson
   held!

But change has come and time has
   moved,
And now, applauded, unreproved,
I hold, with pardonable pride,
The place that Johnson occupied.

Conceit! Presumption! What is
   this?
You surely read my words amiss;
Like Johnson I,— a man of mind‘
How could you ever be so blind?

No. At the ancient " Cheshire
   Cheese,"
Blown hither by some vagrant
   breeze,
To dignify my shallow wit,
In Doctor Johnson's seat I sit!

MY CORN-COB PIPE

Men may sing of their Havanas,
   elevating to the stars
The real or fancied virtues of their
   foreign-made cigars;

129

But I worship Nicotina at a dif-
ferent sort of shrine,
And she sits enthroned in glory in
this corn-cob pipe of mine.

It's as fragrant as the meadows
when the clover is in bloom;
It's as dainty as the essence of the
daintiest perfume;
It's as sweet as are the orchards
when the fruit is hanging ripe,
With the sun's warm kiss upon
them — is this corn-cob pipe.

Thro' the smoke about it clinging,
I delight its form to trace,
Like an oriental beauty with a veil
upon her face;
And my room is dim with vapour
as a church when censers
sway,
As I clasp it to my bosom — in a
figurative way.

It consoles me in misfortune and
it cheers me in distress,
And it proves a warm partaker of
my pleasures in success;
So I hail it as a symbol, friendship's
true and worthy type,
And I press my lips devoutly to
my corn-cob pipe.

IN AUGUST

WHEN August days are hot an'
dry,
When burning copper is the sky,
I'd rather fish than feast or fly
In airy realms serene and high.

I'd take a suit not made for looks,
Some easily digested books,
Some flies, some lines, some bait,
some hooks,
Then would I seek the bays and
brooks.

I would eschew mine every task,
In Nature's smiles my soul should
bask,
And I methinks no more could
ask,
Except — perhaps — one   little
flask.

In case of accident, you know,
Or should the wind come on to
blow,
Or I be chilled or capsized, so,
A flask would be the only go.

Then could I spend a happy
time,—
A bit of sport, a bit of rhyme
(A bit of lemon, or of lime,
To make my bottle's contents
prime).

When August days are hot an'
dry,
I won't sit by an' sigh or die,
I'll get my bottle (on the sly)
And go ahead, and fish, and lie!

THE DISTURBER

OH, what shall I do? I am wholly
    upset;
I am sure I 'll be jailed for a
    lunatic yet.
I 'll be out of a job — it 's the
    thing to expect
When I 'm letting my duty go by
    with neglect.
You may judge the extent and de-
    gree of my plight
When I 'm thinking all day and
    a-dreaming all night,
And a-trying my hand at a rhyme
    on the sly,
All on account of a sparkling eye.

There are those who say men
    should be strong, well-a-day!
But what constitutes strength in
    a man? Who shall say?
I am strong as the most when it
    comes to the arm.
I have aye held my own on the
    playground or farm.
And when I 've been tempted, I
    have n't been weak;
But now — why, I tremble to
    hear a maid speak.
I used to be bold, but now I 've
    grown shy,
And all on account of a sparkling
    eye.

There once was a time when my
    heart was devout,

But now my religion is open to
    doubt.
When parson is earnestly preach-
    ing of grace,
My fancy is busy with drawing
    a face,
Thro' the back of a bonnet most
    piously plain;
'I draw it, redraw it, and draw
    it again.'
While the songs and the sermon
    unheeded go by,—
All on account of a sparkling eye.

Oh, dear little conjurer, give o'er
    your wiles,
It is easy for you, you 're all
    blushes and smiles:
But, love of my heart, I am sorely
    perplexed;
I am smiling one minute and sigh-
    ing the next;
And if it goes on, I 'll drop hackle
    and flail,
And go to the parson and tell him
    my tale.
I warrant he 'll find me a cure
    for the sigh
That you 're aye bringing forth
    with the glance of your eye.

EXPECTATION

YOU 'LL be wonderin' whut 's de
    reason
    I 's a grinnin' all de time,
An' I guess you t'ink my sperits
    Mus' be feelin' mighty prime.

Well, I 'fess up, I is tickled
    As a puppy at his paws.
But you need n't think I 's crazy,
    I ain' laffin' 'dout a cause.

You 's a wonderin' too, I reckon,
    Why I does n't seem to eat,
An' I notice you a lookin'
    Lak you felt completely beat
When I 'fuse to tek de bacon,
    An' don' settle on de ham.
Don' you feel no feah erbout me,
    Jes' keep eatin', an' be ca'm.

Fu' I 's waitin' an' I 's watchin'
    'Bout a little t'ing I see —
D' othah night I 's out a walkin'
    An' I passed a 'simmon tree.
Now I 's whettin' up my hongry,
    An' I 's laffin' fit to kill,
Fu' de fros' done turned de 'sim-
        mons,
    An' de possum 's eat his fill.

He done go'ged hisse'f owdacious,
    An' he stayin' by de tree!
Don' you know, ol' Mistah Pos-
        sum
    Dat you gittin' fat fu' me?
'T ain't no use to try to 'spute it,
    'Case I knows you 's gittin'
        sweet
Wif dat 'simmon flavoh thoo you,
    So I 's waitin' fu' yo' meat.

An' some ebenin' me an' Towsah
    Gwine to come an' mek a call,

We jes' drap in onexpected
    Fu' to shek yo' han', dat 's all.
Oh, I knows dat you 'll be tickled,
    Seems lak I kin see you smile,
So pu'haps I mought pu'suade you
    Fu' to visit us a while.

LOVER'S LANE

SUMMAH night an' sighin' breeze,
    'Long de lovah's lane;
Frien'ly, shadder-mekin' trees,
    'Long de lovah's lane.
White folks' wo'k all done up
        gran'—
Me an' 'Mandy han'-in-han'
Struttin' lak we owned de lan',
    'Long de lovah's lane.

Owl a-settin' 'side de road,
    'Long de lovah's lane,
Lookin' at us lak he knowed
    Dis uz lovah's lane.
Go on, hoot yo' mou'nful tune,
You ain' nevah loved in June,
An' come hidin' f'om de moon
    Down in lovah's lane.

Bush it ben' an' nod an' sway,
    Down in lovah's lane,
Try'n' to hyeah me whut I say
    'Long de lovah's lane.
But I whispahs low lak dis,
An' my 'Mandy smile huh bliss —
Mistah Bush he shek his fis',
    Down in lovah's lane.

Whut I keer ef day is long,
  Down in lovah's lane.
I kin allus sing a song
  'Long de lovah's lane.
An' de wo'ds I hyeah an' say
Meks up fu' de weary day
W'en I 's strollin' by de way,
  Down in lovah's lane.

An' dis t'ought will allus rise
  Down in lovah's lane;
Wondah whethah in de skies
  Dey 's a lovah's lane.
Ef dey ain't, I tell you true,
'Ligion do look mighty blue,
'Cause I do' know whut I 'd do
  'Dout a lovah's lane.

PROTEST

WHO say my hea't ain't true to
    you?
  Dey bettah heish dey mouf.
I knows I loves you thoo an' thoo
  In watah time er drouf.
I wush dese people 'd stop dey
    talkin',
Don't mean no mo' dan chicken's
    squawkin':
I guess I knows which way I 's
    walkin',
  I knows de norf f'om souf.

I does not love Elizy Brown,
  I guess I knows my min'.
You allus try to tek me down
  Wid evaht'ing you fin'.

Ef dese hyeah folks will keep on
    fillin'
Yo' haid wid nonsense, an' you 's
    willin'
I bet some day dey 'll be a killin'
  Somewhaih along de line.

O' cose I buys de gal ice-cream,
  Whut else I gwine to do?
I knows jes' how de t'ing 'u'd
    seem
  Ef I 'd be sho't wid you.
On Sunday, you 's at chu'ch
    a-shoutin',
Den all de week you go 'roun'
    poutin'—
I 's mighty tiahed o' all dis
    doubtin',
  I tell you cause I 's true.

HYMN

O LI'L' lamb out in de col',
De Mastah call you to de fol',
    O li'l' lamb!
He hyeah you bleatin' on de hill;
Come hyeah an' keep yo' mou'nin'
    still,
    O li'l' lamb!

De Mastah sen' de Shepud fo'f;
He wandah souf, he wandah no'f,
    O li'l' lamb!
He wandah eas', he wandah
    wes';
De win' a-wrenchin' at his breas',
    O li'l' lamb!

Oh, tell de Shepud whaih you hide;
He want you walkin' by his side,
    O li'l' lamb!
He know you weak, he know you
    so';
But come, don' stay away no mo',
    O li'l' lamb!

An' af'ah while de lamb he hyeah
De Shepud's voice a-callin' cleah —
    Sweet li'l' lamb!
He answah f'om de brambles thick,
" O Shepud, I 's a-comin' quick "—
    O li'l' lamb!

LITTLE BROWN BABY

LITTLE brown baby wif spa'klin'
    eyes,
    Come to yo' pappy an' set on his
    knee.
What you been doin', suh — mak-
    in' san' pies?
    Look at dat bib — you 's ez
    du'ty ez me.
Look at dat mouf — dat 's mer-
    lasses, I bet;
    Come hyeah, Maria, an' wipe
    off his han's.
Bees gwine to ketch you an' eat
    you up yit,
    Bein' so sticky an sweet — good-
    ness lan's!

Little brown baby wif spa'klin'
    eyes,
    Who 's pappy's darlin' an'
    who 's pappy's chile?

Who is it all de day nevah once
    tries
    Fu' to be cross, er once loses dat
    smile?
Whah did you git dem teef? My,
    you 's a scamp!
    Whah did dat dimple come f'om
    in yo' chin?
Pappy do' know you — I b'lieves
    you 's a tramp;
    Mammy, dis hyeah 's some ol'
    straggler got in!

Let 's th'ow him outen de do' in
    de san',
    We do' want stragglers a-layin'
    'roun' hyeah;
Let's gin him 'way to de big
    buggah-man;
    I know he 's hidin' erroun'
    hyeah right neah.
Buggah-man, buggah-man, come
    in de do',
Hyeah 's a bad boy you kin have
    fu' to eat.
Mammy an' pappy do' want him
    no mo',
    Swaller him down f'om his haid
    to his feet!

Dah, now, I t'ought dat you 'd
    hug me up close.
    Go back, ol' buggah, you sha'n'
    have dis boy.
He ain't no tramp, ner no strag-
    gler, of co'se;
    He 's pappy's pa'dner an' play
    mate an' joy.

Come to you' pallet now — go to
    yo' res';
  Wisht you could allus know
    ease an' cleah skies;
  Wisht you could stay jes' a chile
    on my breas'—
    Little brown baby wif spa'klin'
    eyes!

TIME TO TINKER 'ROUN'!

SUMMAH 's nice, wif sun a-shinin',
  Spring is good wif greens and
    grass,
An' dey 's some t'ings nice 'bout
    wintah,
    Dough hit brings de freezin'
    blas;
But de time dat is de fines',
  Whethah fiel's is green er brown,
Is w'en de rain 's a-po'in'
  An' dey 's time to tinker 'roun.

Den you men's de mule's ol'
    ha'ness,
  An' you men's de broken chair.
Hummin' all de time you 's wo'kin'
  Some ol' common kind o' air.
Evah now an' then you looks out,
  Tryin' mighty ha'd to frown,
But you cain't, you 's glad hit 's
    rainin',
  An' dey 's time to tinker 'roun'.

Oh, you 'ten's lak you so anxious
  Evah time it so't o' stops.

W'en hit goes on, den you reckon
  Dat de wet 'll he'p de crops.
But hit ain't de crops you 's aftah;
  You knows w'en de rain comes
    down
Dat 's hit 's too wet out fu'
    wo'kin',
  An' dey 's time to tinker roun'.

Oh, dey 's fun inside de co'n-crib,
  An' dey 's laffin' at de ba'n;
An' dey 's allus some one jokin',
  Er some one to tell a ya'n.
Dah 's a quiet in yo' cabin,
  Only fu' de rain's sof' soun';
So you 's mighty blessed happy
  W'en dey 's time to tinker
    'roun'!

THE REAL QUESTION

FOLKS is talkin' 'bout de money,
  'bout de silvah an' de gold;
All de time de season 's changin'
    an' de days is gittin' cold.
An' dey 's wond'rin' 'bout de
    metals, whethah we'll have
    one er two.
While de price o' coal is risin' an'
    dey 's two months' rent
    dat 's due.

Some folks says dat gold 's de only
    money dat is wuff de name,
Den de othahs rise an' tell 'em
    dat dey ought to be ashame,

An' dat silvah is de only thing to
   save us f'om de powah
Of de gold-bug ragin' 'roun' an'
   seekin' who he may de-
   vowah.

Well, you folks kin keep on
   shoutin' wif yo' gold er
   silvah cry,
But I tell you people hams is
   sceerce an' fowls is roostin'
   high.
An' hit ain't de so't o' money dat
   is pesterin' my min',
But de question I want answehed 's
   how to get at any kin'!

JILTED

Lucy done gone back on me,
   Dat 's de way wif life.
Evaht'ing was movin' free,
   T'ought I had my wife.
Den some dahky comes along,
Sings my gal a little song,
Since den, evaht'ing 's gone wrong,
   Evah day dey 's strife.

Did n't answeh me to-day,
   W'en I called huh name,
Would you t'ink she 'd ac' dat way
   W'en I ain't to blame?
Dat 's de way dese women do,
W'en dey fin's a fellow true,
Den dey 'buse him thoo an' thoo;
   Well, hit 's all de same.

Somep'n's wrong erbout my lung,
   An' I 's glad hit 's so.
Doctah says 'at I 'll die young,
   Well, I wants to go!
Whut 's de use o' livin' hyeah,
W'en de gal you loves so deah,
Goes back on you clean an' cleah —
   I sh'd like to know?

THE NEWS

Whut dat you whisperin' keepin'
   f'om me?
Don't shut me out 'cause I 's ol'
   an' can't see.
Somep'n's gone wrong dat 's
   a-causin' you dread,—
Don't be afeared to tell — Whut!
   mastah dead?

Somebody brung de news early
   to-day,—
One of de sojers he led, do you
   say?
Did n't he foller whah ol' mastah
   lead?
How kin he live w'en his leadah
   is dead?

Let me lay down awhile, dah by
   his bed;
I wants to t'ink,— hit ain't cleah
   in my head: —
Killed while a-leadin' his men into
   fight,—
Dat 's whut you said, ain't it, did
   I hyeah right?

Mastah, my mastah, dead dah in
    de ficl'?
Lif' me up some,— dah, jes' so I
    kin kneel.
I was too weak to go wid him, dey
    said,
Well, now I 'll — fin' him — so —
    mastah is dead.

Yes, suh, I 's comin' ez fas' ez I
    kin,—
'T was kin' o' da'k, but hit 's
    lightah agin:
P'omised yo' pappy I 'd allus tek
    keer
Of you,— yes, mastah,— I 's fol-
    lerin',— hyeah!

CHRISMUS ON THE PLAN-
TATION

IT was Chrismus Eve, I mind hit
    fu' a mighty gloomy day —
Bofe de weathah an' de people —
    not a one of us was gay;
Cose you 'll t'ink dat 's mighty
    funny 'twell I try to mek hit
    cleah,
Fu' a da'ky 's allus happy when de
    holidays is neah.

But we was n't, fu' dat mo'nin'
    Mastah 'd tol' us we mus' go,
He 'd been payin' us sence free-
    dom, but he could n't pay no
    mo';

He wa'n't nevah used to plannin'
    'fo' he got so po' an' ol',
So he gwine to give up tryin', an'
    de homestead mus' be sol'.

I kin see him stan'in' now erpon
    de step ez cleah ez day,
Wid de win' a-kind o' fondlin'
    thoo his haih all thin an'
    gray;
An' I 'membah how he trimbled
    when he said, " It 's ha'd fu'
    me,
Not to mek yo' Chrismus brightah,
    but I 'low it wa'n't to be."

All de women was a-cryin', an' de
    men, too, on de sly,
An' I noticed somep'n shinin' even
    in ol' Mastah's eye.
But we all stood still to listen ez
    ol' Ben come f'om de crowd
An' spoke up, a-try'n' to steady
    down his voice and mek it
    loud: —

" Look hyeah, Mastah, I 's been
    servin' you' fu' lo! dese many
    yeahs,
An' now, sence we 's got freedom
    an' you 's kind o' po', hit
    'pears
Dat you want us all to leave you
    'cause you don't t'ink you can
    pay.
Ef my membry has n't fooled me,
    seem dat whut I hyead you
    say.

" Er in othah wo'ds, you wants us
  to fu'git dat you 's been kin',
An' ez soon ez you is he'pless, we 's
  to leave you hyeah behin'.
Well, ef dat 's de way dis freedom
  ac's on people, white er black,
You kin jes' tell Mistah Lincum
  fu' to tek his freedom back.

" We gwine wo'k dis ol' planta-
  tion fu' whatevah we kin git,
Fu' I know hit did suppo't us, an'
  de place kin do it yit.
Now de land is yo's, de hands is
  ouahs, an' I reckon we 'll be
  brave,
An' we 'll bah ez much ez you do
  w'en we has to scrape an'
  save."

Ol' Mastah stood dah trimblin',
  but a-smilin' thoo his teahs,
An' den hit seemed jes' nachul-
  like, de place fah rung wid
  cheahs,
An' soon ez dey was quiet, some
  one sta'ted sof' an' low:
" Praise God," an' den we all
  jined in, " from whom all
  blessin's flow! "

Well, dey was n't no use tryin',
  ouah min's was sot to stay,
An' po' ol' Mastah could n't plead
  ner baig, ner drive us 'way,
An' all at once, hit seemed to us,
  de day was bright agin,
So evahone was gay dat night, an'
  watched de Chrismus in.

ANGELINA

When de fiddle gits to singin' out
  a ol' Vahginny reel,
An' you 'mence to feel a ticklin' in
  yo' toe an' in yo' heel;
Ef you t'ink you got 'uligion an'
  you wants to keep it, too,
You jes' bettah tek a hint an' git
  yo'self clean out o' view.
Case de time is mighty temptin'
  when de chune is in de
  swing,
Fu' a darky, saint or sinner man,
  to cut de pigeon-wing.
An' you could n't he'p f'om danc-
  in' ef yo' feet was boun' wif
  twine,
When Angelina Johnson comes
  a-swingin' down de line.

Don't you know Miss Angelina?
  She 's de da'lin' of de place.
W'y, dey ain't no high-toned lady
  wif sich mannahs an' sich
  grace.
She kin move across de cabin, wif
  its planks all rough an' wo';
Jes' de same 's ef she was dancin'
  on ol' mistus' ball-room flo'.
Fact is, you do' see no cabin —
  evaht'ing you see look grand,
An' dat one ol' squeaky fiddle
  soun' to you jes' lak a ban';
Cotton britches look lak broadclof
  an' a linsey dress look fine,
When Angelina Johnson comes
  a-swingin' down de line.

Some folks say dat dancin's sin-
  ful, an' de blessed Lawd, dey
  say,
Gwine to punish us fu' steppin'
  w'en we hyeah de music play.
But I tell you I don' b'lieve it, fu'
  de Lawd is wise and good,
An' he made de banjo's metal an'
  he made de fiddle's wood,
An' he made de music in dem, so
  I don' quite t'ink he 'll keer
Ef our feet keeps time a little to
  de melodies we hyeah.
W'y, dey 's somep'n' downright
  holy in de way our faces
  shine,
When Angelina Johnson comes
  a-swingin' down de line.

Angelina steps so gentle, Angelina
  bows so low,
An' she lif' huh sku't so dainty dat
  huh shoetop skacely show:
An' dem teef o' huh'n a-shinin', ez
  she tek you by de han'—
Go 'way, people, d' ain't anothah
  sich a lady in de lan'!
When she 's movin' thoo de figgers
  er a-dancin' by huhse'f,
Folks jes' stan' stock-still a-sta'-
  in', an' dey mos' nigh hol's
  dey bref;
An' de young mens, dey 's a-sayin',
  " I 's gwine mek dat damsel
  mine,"
When Angelina Johnson comes
  a-swingin' down de line.

FOOLIN' WID DE SEASONS

SEEMS lak folks is mighty curus
  In de way dey t'inks an' ac's.
Dey jes' spen's dey days a-mixin'
  Up de t'ings in almanacs.
Now, I min' my nex' do' neigh-
  bour,—
  He 's a mighty likely man,
But he nevah t'inks o' nuffin
  'Ceptin' jes' to plot an' plan.

All de wintah he was plannin'
  How he 'd gethah sassafras
Jes' ez soon ez evah Springtime
  Put some greenness in de grass.
An' he 'lowed a little soonah
  He could stan' a coolah breeze
So 's to mek a little money
  F'om de sugah-watah trees.

In de summah, he 'd be waihin'
  Out de linin' of his soul,
Try 'n' ca'ci'late an' fashion
  How he 'd git his wintah coal;
An' I b'lieve he got his jedgement
  Jes' so tuckahed out an' thinned
Dat he t'ought a robin's whistle
  Was de whistle of de wind.

Why won't folks gin up dey plan-
  nin',
  An' jes' be content to know
Dat dey 's gittin' all dat 's fu' dem
  In de days dat come an' go?
Why won't folks quit movin' for-
  rard?
  Ain't hit bettah jes' to stan'

An' be satisfied wid livin'
  In de season dat's at han'?

Hit's enough fu' me to listen
  W'en de birds is singin' 'roun',
'Dout a-guessin' whut'll happen
  W'en de snow is on de groun'.
In de Springtime an' de summah,
  I lays sorrer on de she'f;
An' I knows ol' Mistah Wintah
  Gwine to hustle fu' hisse'f.

We been put hyeah fu' a pu'pose,
  But de questun dat has riz
An' made lots o' people diffah
  Is jes' whut dat pu'pose is.
Now, accordin' to my reas'nin',
  Hyeah's de p'int whaih I's
    arriv,
Scnce de Lawd put life into us,
  We was put hyeah fu' to live!

MY SORT O' MAN

I DON'T believe in 'ristercrats
  An' never did, you see;
The plain ol' homelike sorter folks
  Is good enough fur me.
O' course, I don't desire a man
  To be too tarnal rough,
But then, I think all folks should
    know
  When they air nice enough.

Now there is folks in this here
    world,
  From peasant up to king,

Who want to be so awful nice
  They overdo the thing.
That's jest the thing that makes
    me sick,
  An' quicker 'n a wink
I set it down that them same
    folks
  Ain't half so good 's you
    think.

I like to see a man dress nice,
  In clothes becomin' too;
I like to see a woman fix
  As women orter to do;
An' boys an' gals I like to see
  Look fresh an' young an'
    spry,—
We all must have our vanity
  An' pride before we die.

But I jedge no man by his
    clothes,—
  Nor gentleman nor tramp;
The man that wears the finest suit
  May be the biggest scamp,
An' he whose limbs air clad in rags
  That make a mournful sight,
In life's great battle may have
    proved
  A hero in the fight.

I don't believe in 'ristercrats;
  I like the honest tan
That lies upon the healthful cheek
  An' speaks the honest man;
I like to grasp the brawny hand
  That labor's lips have kissed,

For he who has not labored here
   Life's greatest pride has
      missed:

The pride to feel that yore own
   strength
   Has cleaved fur you the way
To heights to which you were not
   born,
   But struggled day by day.
What though the thousands sneer
   an' scoff,
   An' scorn yore humble birth?
Kings are but puppets; you are
   king
   By right o' royal worth.

The man who simply sits an' waits
   Fur good to come along,
Ain't worth the breath that one
   would take
   To tell him he is wrong.
Fur good ain't flowin' round this
   world
   Fur every fool to sup;
You 've got to put yore see-ers on,
   An' go an' hunt it up.

Good goes with honesty, I say,
   To honour an' to bless;
To rich an' poor alike it brings
   A wealth o' happiness.
The 'ristercrats ain't got it all,
   Fur much to their su'prise,
That 's one of earth's most blessed
   things
   They can't monopolize.

POSSUM

Ef dey 's anyt'ing dat riles me
   An' jes' gits me out o' hitch,
Twell I want to tek my coat off,
   So 's to r'ar an' t'ar an' pitch,
Hit 's to see some ign'ant white
   man
   'Mittin' dat owdacious sin —
W'en he want to cook a possum
   Tekin' off de possum's skin.

W'y dey ain't no use in talkin',
   Hit jes' hu'ts me to de hea't
Fu' to see dem foolish people
   Th'owin' 'way de fines' pa't.
W'y, dat skin is jes' ez tendah
An' ez juicy ez kin be;
I knows all erbout de critter —
   Hide an' haih — don't talk to
   me!

Possum skin is jes lak shoat skin;
   Jes' you swinge an' scrope it
   down,
Tek a good sha'p knife an' sco' it,
   Den you bake it good an' brown.
Huh-uh! honey, you 's so happy
Dat yo' thoughts is 'mos' a sin
When you 's settin' dah a-chawin'
   On dat possum's cracklin' skin.

White folks t'ink dey know 'bout
   eatin',
   An' I reckon dat dey do
Sometimes git a little idee
   Of a middlin' dish er two;

But dey ain't a t'ing dey knows of
  Dat I reckon cain't be beat
W'en we set down at de table
  To a unskun possum's meat!

ON THE ROAD

I 's boun' to see my gal to-night —
  Oh, lone de way, my dearie!
De moon ain't out, de stars ain't
    bright —
  Oh, lone de way, my dearie!
Dis hoss o' mine is pow'ful slow,
But when I does git to yo' do'
Yo' kiss 'll pay me back, an' mo',
  Dough lone de way, my dearie.

De night is skeery-lak an' still —
  Oh, lone de way, my dearie!
'Cept fu' dat mou'nful whippo'-
    will —
  Oh, lone de way, my dearie!
De way so long wif dis slow pace,
'T 'u'd seem to me lak savin' grace
Ef you was on a nearer place,
  Fu' lone de way, my dearie.

I hyeah de hootin' of de owl —
  Oh, lone de way, my dearie!
I wish dat watch-dog would n't
    howl —
  Oh, lone de way, my dearie!
An' evaht'ing, bofe right an' lef',
Seem p'int'ly lak hit put itse'f
In shape to skeer me half to def —
  Oh, lone de way, my dearie!

I whistles so 's I won't be feared —
  Oh lone de way, my dearie!
But anyhow I 's kin' o' skeered,
  Fu' lone de way, my dearie.
De sky been lookin' mighty glum,
But you kin mek hit lighten some,
Ef you 'll jes' say you 's glad I
    come,
  Dough lone de way, my dearie.

A DEATH SONG

LAY me down beneaf de willers in
    de grass,
Whah de branch 'll go a-singin' as
    it pass.
  An' w'en I 's a-layin' low,
  I kin hyeah it as it go
Singin', " Sleep, my honey, tek yo'
    res' at las'."

Lay me nigh to whah hit meks a
    little pool,
An' de watah stan's so quiet lak
    an' cool,
  Whah de little birds in spring,
  Ust to come an' drink an' sing,
An' de chillen waded on dey way
    to school.

Let me settle w'en my shouldahs
    draps dey load
Nigh enough to hyeah de noises in
    de road;
  Fu' I t'ink de las' long res'
  Gwine to soothe my sperrit bes'
Ef I 's layin' 'mong de t'ings I 's
    allus knowed.

A BACK-LOG SONG

DE axes has been ringin' in de
  woods de blessid day,
An' de chips has been a-fallin'
  fa' an' thick;
Dey has cut de bigges' hick'ry dat
  de mules kin tote away,
An' dey 's laid hit down and
  soaked it in de crik.
Den dey tuk hit to de big house an'
  dey piled de wood erroun'
In de fiah-place f'om ash-flo' to
  de flue,
While ol' Ezry sta'ts de hymn dat
  evah yeah has got to soun'
When de back-log fus' com-
  mence a-bu'nin' thoo.

Ol' Mastah is a-smilin' on de
  da'kies f'om de hall,
Ol' Mistus is a-stannin' in de do',
An' de young folks, males an'
  misses, is a-tryin', one an'
  all,
  Fu' to mek us feel hit 's Chris-
  mus time fu' sho'.
An' ouah hea'ts are full of pleasure,
  fu' we know de time is
  ouahs
  Fu' to dance er do jes' whut we
  wants to do.
An' dey ain't no ovahseer an' no
  othah kind o' powahs
  Dat kin stop us while dat log
  is bu'nin thoo.

Dey 's a-wokin' in de qua'tahs a-
  preparin' fu' de feas',
  So de little pigs is feelin' kind o'
  shy.
De chickens ain't so trus'ful ez
  dey was, to say de leas',
  An' de wise ol' hens is roostin'
  mighty high.
You could n't git a gobblah fu' to
  look you in de face —
  I ain't sayin' whut de tu'ky
  'spects is true;
But hit 's mighty dange'ous trav'-
  lin' fu' de critters on de
  place
F'om de time dat log commence a
  bu'nin' thoo.

Some one 's tunin' up his fiddle
  dah, I hyeah a banjo's ring,
  An', bless me, dat 's de tootin' of
  a ho'n!
Now dey 'll evah one be runnin'
  dat has got a foot to fling,
  An' dey 'll dance an' frolic on
  f'om now 'twell mo'n.
Plunk de banjo, scrap de fiddle,
  blow dat ho'n yo' level bes',
  Keep yo' min' erpon de chune
  an' step it true.
Oh, dey ain't no time fu' stoppin'
  an' dey ain't no time fu'
  res',
  Fu' hit 's Chrismus an' de back-
  log 's bu'nin' thoo!

LULLABY

BEDTIME 's come fu' little boys.
Po' little lamb.
Too tiahed out to make a noise,
Po' little lamb.
You gwine t' have to-morrer sho'?
Yes, you tole me dat befo',
Don't you fool me, chile, no mo',
Po' little lamb.

You been bad de livelong day,
Po' little lamb.
Th'owin' stones an' runnin' 'way,
Po' little lamb.
My, but you 's a-runnin' wil',
Look jes' lak some po' folks chile;
Mam' gwine whup you atter while,
Po' little lamb.

Come hyeah! you mos' tiahed to
def,
Po' little lamb.
Played yo'se'f clean out o' bref,
Po' little lamb.
See dem han's now — sich a sight!
Would you evah b'lieve dey's
white?
Stan' still twell I wash 'em right,
Po' little lamb.

Jes' cain't hol' yo' haid up straight,
Po' little lamb.
Had n't oughter played so late,
Po' little lamb.
Mammy do' know whut she 'd do,
Ef de chillun's all lak you;
You 's a caution now fu' true,
Po' little lamb.

Lay yo' haid down in my lap,
Po' little lamb.
Y' ought to have a right good slap,
Po' little lamb.
You been runnin' roun' a heap.
Shet dem eyes an' don't you peep,
Dah now, dah now, go to sleep,
Po' little lamb.

THE PHOTOGRAPH

SEE dis pictyah in my han'?
Dat 's my gal;
Ain't she purty? goodness lan'!
Huh name Sal.
Dat 's de very way she be —
Kin' o' tickles me to see
Huh a-smilin' back at me.

She sont me dis photygraph
Jes' las' week;
An' aldough hit made me laugh —
My black cheek
Felt somethin' a-runnin' queer;
Bless yo' soul, it was a tear
Jes' f'om wishin' she was here.

Often when I 's all alone
Layin' here,
I git t'inkin' 'bout my own
Sallie dear;
How she say dat I 's huh beau,
An' hit tickles me to know
Dat de gal do love me so.

Some bright day I 's goin' back,
Fo' de la!

An' ez sho' 's my face is black,
　　Ax huh pa
Fu' de blessed little miss
Who 's a-smilin' out o dis
Pictyah, lak she wan'ed a kiss!

JEALOUS

HYEAH come Cæsar Higgins,
Don't he think he 's fine?
Look at dem new riggin's
Ain't he tryin' to shine?
Got a standin' collar
An' a stove-pipe hat,
I 'll jes' bet a dollar
Some one gin him dat.

Don't one o' you mention,
Nothin' 'bout his cloes,
Don't pay no attention,
Er let on you knows
Dat he 's got 'em on him,
Why, 't 'll mek him sick,
Jes go on an' sco'n him,
My, ain't dis a trick!

Look hyeah, whut 's he doin'
Lookin' t' othah way?
Dat ere move 's a new one,
Some one call him, " Say! "
Can't you see no pusson —
Puttin' on you' airs,
Sakes alive, you 's wuss'n
Dese hyeah millionaires.

Need n't git so flighty,
Case you got dat suit.
Dem cloes ain't so mighty,—

Second hand to boct,
I 's a-tryin' to spite you!
Full of jealousy!
Look hyeah, man, I 'll fight
　　you,
Don't you fool wid me!

PARTED

DE breeze is blowin' 'cross de bay.
　　My lady, my lady;
De ship hit teks me far away,
　　My lady, my lady;
Ole Mas' done sol' me down de
　　　　stream;
Dey tell me 't ain't so bad 's hit
　　　　seem,
　　My lady, my lady.

O' co'se I knows dat you 'll be
　　　　true,
　　My lady, my lady;
But den I do' know whut to do,
　　My lady, my lady;
I knowed some day we 'd have to
　　　　pa't,
But den hit put' nigh breaks my
　　　　hea't,
　　My lady, my lady.

De day is long, de night is black,
　　My lady, my lady;
I know you 'll wait twell I come
　　　　back,
　　My lady, my lady;
I 'll stan' de ship, I 'll stan' de
　　　　chain,

But I 'll come back, my darlin'
    Jane,
    My lady, my lady.

Jes' wait, jes' b'lieve in whut I
    say,
    My lady, my lady;
D' ain't nothin' dat kin keep me
    'way,
    My lady, my lady;
A man 's a man, an' love is love;
God knows ouah hea'ts, my little
    dove;
He 'll he'p us f'om his th'one
    above,
    My lady, my lady.

TEMPTATION

I DONE got 'uligion, honey, an' I 's
    happy ez a king;
Evahthing I see erbout me 's jes'
    lak sunshine in de spring;
An' it seems lak I do' want to do
    anothah blessid thing
But jes' run an' tell de neighbours,
    an' to shout an' pray an'
    sing.

I done shuk my fis' at Satan, an'
    I 's gin de worl' my back;
I do' want no hendrin' causes now
    a-both'rin' in my track;
Fu' I 's on my way to glory, an' I
    feels too sho' to miss.
W'y, dey ain't no use in sinnin'
    when 'uligion 's sweet ez dis.

Talk erbout a man backslidin' w'en
    he 's on de gospel way;
No, suh, I done beat de debbil, an'
    Temptation 's los' de day.
Gwine to keep my eyes right
    straight up, gwine to shet my
    eahs, an' see
Whut ole projick Mistah Satan 's
    gwine to try to wuk on me.

Listen, whut dat soun' I hyeah
    dah? 'tain't no one commence
    to sing;
It 's a fiddle; git erway dah! don'
    you hyeah dat blessid
    thing?
W'y, dat 's sweet ez drippin' honey,
    'cause, you knows, I draws de
    bow,
An' when music 's sho' 'nough
    music, I 's de one dat 's sho'
    to know.

W'y, I 's done de double shuffle,
    twell a body could n't res',
Jes' a-hyeahin' Sam de fiddlah play
    dat chune his level bes';
I could cut a mighty caper, I could
    gin a mighty fling
Jes' right now, I 's mo' dan suttain
    I could cut de pigeon wing.

Look hyeah, whut 's dis I 's been
    sayin'? whut on urf 's tuk
    holt o' me?
Dat ole music come nigh runnin'
    my 'uligion up a tree!

Cleah out wif dat dah ole fiddle,
    don' you try dat trick agin;
Did n't think I could be tempted,
    but you lak to made me sin!

POSSUM TROT

I 'VE journeyed 'roun' consid'able,
    a-seein' men an' things,
An' I 've learned a little of the
    sense that meetin' people
    brings;
But in spite of all my travellin',
    an' of all I think I know,
I 've got one notion in my head,
    that I can't git to go;
An' it is that the folks I meet in
    any other spot
Ain't half so good as them I
    knowed back home in Possum
    Trot.

I know you 've never heerd the
    name, it ain't a famous
    place,
An' I reckon ef you 'd search the
    map you could n't find a trace
Of any sich locality as this I 've
    named to you;
But never mind, I know the place,
    an' I love it dearly too.
It don't make no pretensions to
    bein' great or fine,
The circuses don't come that way,
    they ain't no railroad line.
It ain't no great big city, where
    the schemers plan an' plot,

But jest a little settlement, this
    place called Possum Trot.

But don't you think the folks that
    lived in that outlandish place
Were ignorant of all the things
    that go for sense or grace.
Why, there was Hannah Dyer, you
    may search this teemin' earth
An' never find a sweeter girl, er
    one o' greater worth;
An' Uncle Abner Williams, a-
    leanin' on his staff,
It seems like I kin hear him talk,
    an' hear his hearty laugh.
His heart was big an' cheery as a
    sunny acre lot,
Why, that 's the kind o' folks we
    had down there at Possum
    Trot.

Good times? Well, now, to suit
    my taste,— an' I 'm some hard
    to suit,—
There ain't been no sich pleasure
    sence, an' won't be none to
    boot,
With huskin' bees in Harvest time,
    an' dances later on,
An' singin' school, an taffy pulls,
    an' fun from night till
    dawn.
Revivals come in winter time, bap-
    tizin's in the spring,
You 'd ought to seen those people
    shout, an' heerd 'em pray an'
    sing;

You 'd ought to 've heard ole Par-
    son Brown a-throwin' gospel
    shot
Among the saints an' sinners in
    the days of Possum Trot.

We live up in the city now, my
    wife was bound to come;
I hear aroun' me day by day the
    endless stir an' hum.
I reckon that it done me good, an'
    yet it done me harm,
That oil was found so plentiful
    down there on my ole farm.
We 've got a new-styled preacher,
    our church is new-styled too,
An' I 've come down from what I
    knowed to rent a cushioned
    pew.
But often when I 'm settin' there,
    it 's foolish, like as not,
To think of them ol' benches in
    the church at Possum Trot.

I know that I 'm ungrateful, an'
    sich thoughts must be a sin,
But I find myself a wishin' that
    the times was back agin.
With the huskin's an' the frolics,
    an' the joys I used to know,
When I lived at the settlement, a
    dozen years ago.
I don't feel this way often, I 'm
    scarcely ever glum,
For life has taught me how to take
    her chances as they come.
But now an' then my mind goes
    back to that ol' buryin' plot,

That holds the dust of some I
    loved, down there at Possum
    Trot.

DELY

Jes' lak toddy wahms you thoo'
    Sets yo' haid a reelin',
Meks you ovah good and new,
    Dat 's de way I 's feelin'.
Seems to me hit's summah time,
    Dough hit 's wintah reely,
I 's a feelin' jes' dat prime —
    An' huh name is Dely.

Dis hyeah love 's a cu'rus thing,
    Changes 'roun' de season,
Meks you sad or meks you sing,
    'Dout no urfly reason.
Sometimes I go mopin' 'roun',
    Den agin I 's leapin';
Sperits allus up an' down
    Even when I 's sleepin'.

Fu' de dreams comes to me den,
    An' dey keeps me pitchin',
Lak de apple dumplin's w'en
    Bilin' in de kitchen.
Some one sot to do me hahm,
    Tryin' to ovahcome me,
Ketchin' Dely by de ahm
    So 's to tek huh f'om me.

Mon, you bettah b'lieve I fights
    (Dough hit 's on'y seemin');
I 's a hittin' fu' my rights
    Even w'en I 's dreamin'.

But I 'd let you have 'em all,
   Give 'em to you freely,
Good an' bad ones, great an' small,
   So 's you leave me Dely.

Dely got dem meltin' eyes,
   Big an' black an' tendah.
Dely jes' a lady-size,
   Delikit an' slendah.
Dely brown ez brown kin be
   An' huh haih is curly;
Oh, she look so sweet to me,—
   Bless de precious girlie!

Dely brown ez brown kin be,
   She ain' no mullatter;
She pure cullud,— don' you see
   Dat 's jes' whut 's de mattah?
Dat 's de why I love huh so,
   D' ain't no mix about huh,
Soon 's you see huh face you know
   D' ain't no chanst to doubt huh.

Folks dey go to chu'ch an' pray
   So 's to git a blessin'.
Oomph, dey bettah come my way,
   Dey could lu'n a lesson.
Sabbaf day I don' go fu',
   Jes' to see my pigeon;
I jes' sets an' looks at huh,
   Dat 's enuff 'uligion.

BREAKING THE CHARM

Caught Susanner whistlin'; well,
It 's most nigh too good to tell.
'Twould 'a' b'en too good to see
Ef it had n't b'en fur me,
Comin' up so soft an' sly
That she didn' hear me nigh.
I was pokin' 'round that day,
An' ez I come down the way,
First her whistle strikes my ears,—
Then her gingham dress appears;
So with soft step up I slips.
Oh, them dewy, rosy lips!
Ripe ez cherries, red an' round,
Puckered up to make the sound.
She was lookin' in the spring,
Whistlin' to beat anything,—
"Kitty Dale" er "In the Sweet."
I was jest so mortal beat
That I can't quite ricoleck
What the toon was, but I 'speck
'T was some hymn er other, fur
Hymny things is jest like her.
Well she went on fur awhile
With her face all in a smile,
An' I never moved, but stood
Stiller 'n a piece o' wood —
Would n't wink ner would n't stir,
But a-gazin' right at her,
Tell she turns an' sees me — my!
Thought at first she 'd try to fly.
But she blushed an' stood her
   ground.
Then, a-slyly lookin' round,
She says: "Did you hear me,
   Ben?"
"Whistlin' woman, crowin' hen,"
Says I, lookin' awful stern.
Then the red commenced to burn
In them cheeks o' hern. Why, la!
Reddest red you ever saw —
Pineys wa'n't a circumstance.

You 'd 'a' noticed in a glance
She was pow'rful shamed an'
    skeart;
But she looked so sweet an' peart,
That a idee struck my head;
So I up an' slowly said:
" Woman whistlin' brings shore
    harm,
Jest one thing 'll break the charm."
" And what 's that?" " Oh,
    my!" says I,
" I don't like to tell you."
    " Why?"
Says Susanner. " Well, you see
It would kinder fall on me."
Course I knowed that she 'd in-
    sist,—
So I says: " You must be kissed
By the man that heard you whistle;
Everybody says that this 'll
Break the charm and set you free
From the threat'nin' penalty."
She was blushin' fit to kill,
But she answered, kinder still:
" I don't want to have no harm,
Please come, Ben, an' break the
    charm."
Did I break that charm? — oh,
    well,
There 's some things I must n't
    tell.
I remember, afterwhile,
Her a-sayin' with a smile:
" Oh, you quit,— you sassy dunce,
You jest caught me whistlin' *once.*"
Ev'ry sence that when I hear
Some one whistlin' kinder clear,

I most break my neck to see
Ef it 's Susy; but, dear me,
I jest find I 've b'en to chase
Some blamed boy about the place.
Dad 's b'en noticin' my way,
An' last night I heerd him say:
" We must send fur Dr. Glenn,
Mother; somethin 's wrong with
    Ben!"

HUNTING SONG

TEK a cool night, good an'
    cleah,
    Skiff o' snow upon de groun';
Jes' 'bout fall-time o' de yeah
    W'en de leaves is dry an
        brown;
Tek a dog an' tek a axe,
    Tek a lantu'n in yo' han',
Step light whah de switches
    cracks,
    Fu' dey 's huntin' in de lan'.
Down thoo de valleys an' ovah de
    hills,
    Into de woods whah de 'simmon-
        tree grows,
Wakin' an' skeerin' de po' whip-
    po'wills,
    Huntin' fu' coon an' fu' 'possum
        we goes.

Blow dat ho'n dah loud an'
    strong,
    Call de dogs an' da'kies neah;
Mek its music cleah an' long,
    So de folks at home kin hyeah.

Blow it twell de hills an' trees
   Sen's de echoes tumblin' back;
Blow it twell de back'ard breeze
   Tells de folks we's on de
     track.
Coons is a-ramblin' an' 'possums
   is out;
   Look at dat dog; you could set
   'on his tail!
Watch him now — steady,— min'
     — what you's about,
   Bless me, dat animal 's got on
   de trail!

Listen to him ba'kin now!
   Dat means bus'ness, sho 's you
   bo'n;
Ef he 's struck de scent I 'low
   Dat ere 'possum 's sholy gone.
Knowed dat dog fu' fo'teen
   yeahs,
   An' I nevah seed him fail
W'en he sot dem flappin' eahs
   An' went off upon a trail.
Run, Mistah 'Possum, an' run,
   Mistah Coon,
   No place is safe fu' yo' ramblin'
   to-night;
Mas' gin' de lantu'n an' God gin
   de moon,
   An' a long hunt gins a good ap-
   petite.

Look hyeah, folks, you hyeah
   dat change?
   Dat ba'k is sha'per dan de res'.
Dat ere soun' ain't nothin'
   strange,—

Dat dog 's talked his level
   bes'.
Somep'n' 's treed, I know de
   soun'.
   Dah now,— wha 'd I tell
   you? see!
Dat ere dog done run him
   down;
   Come hyeah, he'p cut down
   dis tree.
Ah, Mistah 'Possum, we got you
   at las'—
   Need n't play daid, laying dah
   on de groun';
Fros' an' de 'simmons has made
   you grow fas',—
   Won't he be fine when he 's
   roasted up brown!

A LETTER

DEAR MISS LUCY: I been t'inkin'
   dat I 'd write you long fo' dis,
But dis writin' 's mighty tejous, an'
   you know jes' how it is.
But I 's got a little lesure, so I teks
   my pen in han'
Fu' to let you know my feelin's
   since I retched dis furrin' lan'.
I 's right well, I 's glad to tell you
   (dough dis climate ain't to
   blame),
An' I hopes w'en dese lines reach
   you, dat dey 'll fin' yo' se'f de
   same.
Cose I 'se feelin kin' o' homesick
   — dat 's ez nachul ez kin be,

W'en a feller 's mo'n th'ee thou-
    sand miles across dat awful
    sea.
(Don't you let nobidy fool you
    'bout de ocean bein' gran';
If you want to see de billers, you
    jes' view dem f'om de lan'.)
'Bout de people? We been t'inkin'
    dat all white folks was alak;
But dese Englishmen is diffunt,
    an' dey 's curus fu' a fac'.
Fust, dey 's heavier an' redder in
    dey make-up an' dey looks,
An' dey don't put salt nor pepper
    in a blessed t'ing dey cooks!
W'en dey gin you good ol' tu'nips,
    ca'ots, pa'snips, beets, an'
    sich,
Ef dey ain't some one to tell you,
    you cain't 'stinguish which is
    which.
W'en I t'ought I 's eatin' chicken
    — you may b'lieve dis hyeah 's
    a lie —
But de waiter beat me down dat I
    was eatin' rabbit pie.
An' dey 'd t'ink dat you was crazy
    — jes' a reg'lar ravin' loon,
Ef you 'd speak erbout a 'possum
    or a piece o' good ol' coon.
O, hit 's mighty nice, dis trav'lin',
    an' I 's kin' o' glad I come.
But, I reckon, now I 's willin' fu'
    to tek my way back home.
I done see de Crystal Palace, an'
    I 's hyeahd dey string-band
    play,

But I has n't seen no banjos lay in'
    nowhahs roun' dis way.
Jes' gin ol' Jim Bowles a banjo,
    an' he 'd not go very fu',
'Fo' he 'd outplayed all dese fid-
    dlers, wif dey flourish and
    dey stir.
Evahbiddy dat I 's met wif has
    been monst'ous kin an' good;
But I t'ink I 'd lak it better to be
    down in Jones's wood,
Where we ust to have sich frolics,
    Lucy, you an' me an' Nelse,
Dough my appetite 'ud call me, ef
    dey was n't nuffin else.
I 'd jes' lak to have some sweet-
    pertaters roasted in de skin;
I 's a-longin' fu' my chittlin's an'
    my mustard greens ergin;
I 's a-wishin' fu' some buttermilk,
    an' co'n braid, good an'
    brown,
An' a drap o' good ol' bourbon fu'
    to wash my feelin's down!
An' I 's comin' back to see you jes'
    as ehly as I kin,
So you better not go spa'kin' wif
    dat wuffless scoun'el Quin!
Well, I reckon, I mus' close now;
    write ez soon 's dis reaches
    you;
Gi' my love to Sister Mandy an'
    to Uncle Isham, too.
Tell de folks I sen' 'em howdy;
    gin a kiss to pap an' mam;
Closin' I is, deah Miss Lucy,
    Still Yo' Own True-Lovin' SAM.

P. S. Ef you cain't mek out dis
 letter, lay it by erpon de she'f,
An' when I git home, I 'll read
 it, darlin', to you my own se'f.

CHRISMUS IS A-COMIN'

BONES a-gittin' achy,
Back a-feelin' col',
Han's a-growin' shaky,
Jes' lak I was ol'.
Fros' erpon de meddah
Lookin' mighty white;
Snowdraps lak a feddah
Slippin' down at night.
Jes' keep t'ings a-hummin'
Spite o' fros' an' showahs,
Chrismus is a-comin'
An' all de week is ouahs.

Little mas' a-axin',
"Who is Santy Claus?"
Meks it kin' o' taxin'
Not to brek de laws.
Chillun 's pow'ful tryin'
To a pusson's grace
W'en dey go a pryin'
Right on th'oo you' face
Down ermong yo' feelin's;
Jes' 'pears lak dat you
Got to change you' dealin's
So 's to tell 'em true.

An' my pickaninny —
Dreamin' in his sleep!
Come hyeah, Mammy Jinny,
Come an' tek a peep.

Ol' Mas' Bob an' Missis
In dey house up daih
Got no chile lak dis is,
D' ain't none anywhaih.
Sleep, my little lammy,
Sleep, you little limb,
He do' know whut mammy
Done saved up fu' him.

Dey 'll be banjo pickin',
Dancin' all night thoo.
Dey 'll be lots o' chicken,
Plenty tukky, too.
Drams to wet yo' whistles
So 's to drive out chills.
Whut I keer fu' drizzles
Fallin' on de hills?
Jes' keep t'ings a-hummin'
Spite o' col' an' showahs,
Chrismus day 's a-comin',
An' all de week is ouahs.

A CABIN TALE

THE YOUNG MASTER ASKS FOR A STORY

WHUT you say, dah? huh, uh! chile,
You 's enough to dribe me wile.
Want a sto'y; jes' hyeah dat!
Whah' 'll I git a sto'y at?
Di'n' I tell you th'ee las' night?
Go 'way, honey, you ain't right.
I got somep'n' else to do,
'Cides jes' tellin' tales to you.
Tell you jes' one? Lem me see
Whut dat one 's a-gwine to be.

When you 's ole, yo membry fails;
Seems lak I do' know no tales.
Well, set down dah in dat cheer,
Keep still ef you wants to hyeah.
Tek dat chin up off yo' han's,
Set up nice now. Goodness lan's!
Hol' yo'se'f up lak yo' pa.
Bet nobidy evah saw
Him scrunched down lak you was
   den —
High-tone boys meks high-tone
   men.

Once dey was a ole black bah,
Used to live 'roun' hyeah some-
   whah
In a cave. He was so big
He could ca'y off a pig
Lak you picks a chicken up,
Er yo' leetles' bit o' pup.
An' he had two gread big eyes,
Jes' erbout a saucer's size.
Why, dey looked lak balls o' fiah
Jumpin' 'roun' erpon a wiah
W'en dat bah was mad; an' laws!
But you ought to seen his paws!
Did I see 'em? How you 'spec
I 's a-gwine to ricollec'
Dis hyeah ya'n I 's try'n' to spin
Ef you keeps on puttin' in?
You keep still an' don't you cheep
Less I 'll sen' you off to sleep.
Dis hyeah bah 'd go trompin'
   'roun'
Eatin' evahthing he foun';
No one could n't have a fa'm
But dat bah 'u'd do' em ha'm;

And dey could n't ketch de scamp.
Anywhah he wan'ed to tramp.
Dah de scoun'el 'd mek his track,
Do his du't an' come on back.
He was sich a sly ole limb,
Traps was jes' lak fun to him.

   Now, down neah whah Mistah
     Bah
Lived, dey was a weasel dah;
But dey was n't fren's a-tall
Case de weasel was so small.
An' de bah 'u'd, jes' fu' sass,
Tu'n his nose up w'en he 'd pass.
Weasels 's small o' cose, but my!
Dem air animiles is sly.
So dis hyeah one says, says he,
" I 'll jes' fix dat bah, you see."
So he fixes up his plan
An' hunts up de fa'merman.
When de fa'mer see him come,
He 'mence lookin' mighty glum,
An' he ketches up a stick;
But de weasel speak up quick:
" Hol' on, Mistah Fa'mer man,
I wan' 'splain a little plan.
Ef you waits, I 'll tell you whah
An' jes' how to ketch ol' Bah.
But I tell yow now you mus'
Gin me one fat chicken fus'."
Den de man he scratch his haid,
Las' he say, " I'll mek de trade."
So de weasel et his hen,
Smacked his mouf and says,
    " Well, den,
Set yo' trap an' bait ternight,
An' I 'll ketch de bah all right."

Den he ups an' goes to see
Mistah Bah, an' says, says he:
"Well, fren' Bah, we *ain't* been
    fren's,
But ternight ha'd feelin' 'en's.
Ef you ain't too proud to steal,
We kin git a splendid meal.
Cose I would n't come to you,
But it mus' be done by two;
Hit 's a trap, but we kin beat
All dey tricks an' git de meat."
"Cose I 's wif you," says de bah,
"Come on, weasel, show me
    whah."
Well, dey trots erlong ontwell
Dat air meat beginned to smell
In de trap. Den weasel say:
"Now you put yo' paw dis way
While I hol' de spring back so,
Den you grab de meat an' go."
Well, de bah he had to grin
Ez he put his big paw in,
Den he juked up, but — kerbing!
Weasel done let go de spring.
"Dah now," says de weasel, "dah,
I done cotched you, Mistah Bah!"
O, dat bah did sno't and spout,
Try'n' his bestes' to git out,
But de weasel say, "Goo'-bye!
Weasel small, but weasel sly."
Den he tu'ned his back an' run
Tol' de fa'mer whut he done.
So de fa'mer come down dah,
Wif a axe and killed de bah.

Dah now, ain't dat sto'y fine?
Run erlong now, nevah min'.

Want some mo', you rascal, you?
No, suh! no, suh! dat 'll do.

AT CANDLE-LIGHTIN'
TIME

WHEN I come in f'om de co'n-fiel'
    aftah wo'kin' ha'd all day,
It 's amazin' nice to fin' my sup-
    pah all crpon de way;
An' it 's nice to smell de coffee
    bubblin' ovah in de pot,
An' it 's fine to see de meat a-
    sizzlin' teasin'-lak an' hot.

But when suppah-time is ovah, an'
    de t'ings is cleahed away;
Den de happy hours dat foller are
    de sweetes' of de day.
When my co'ncob pipe is sta'ted,
    an' de smoke is drawin'
    prime,
My ole 'ooman says, "I reckon,
    Ike, it 's candle-lightin' time."

Den de chillun snuggle up to me,
    an' all commence to call,
"Oh, say, daddy, now it 's time
    to mek de shadders on de
    wall."
So I puts my han's togethah —
    evah daddy knows de way,—
An' de chillun snuggle closer roun'
    ez I begin to say: —

"Fus' thing, hyeah come Mistah
    Rabbit; don' you see him wo'k
    his eahs?

Huh, uh! dis mus' be a donkey,—
    look, how innercent he 'pears!
Dah 's de ole black swan a-swim-
    min'— ain't she got a' awful
    neck?
Who 's dis feller dat 's a-comin'?
    Why, dat 's ole dog Tray, I
    'spec'! "

Dat 's de way I run on, tryin' fu'
    to please 'em all I can;
Den I hollahs, " Now be keerful
    — dis hyeah las' 's de buga-
    man! "
An' dey runs an' hides dey faces;
    dey ain't skeered — dey 's let-
    tin' on:
But de play ain't raaly ovah twell
    dat buga-man is gone.

So I jes' teks up my banjo, an' I
    plays a little chune,
An' you see dem haids come peepin'
    out to listen mighty soon.
Den my wife says, " Sich a pappy
    fu' to give you sich a fright!
Jes, you go to baid, an' leave him:
    say yo' prayers an' say good-
    night."

WHISTLING SAM

I HAS hyeahd o' people dancin' an'
    I 's hyeahd o' people singin'.
An' I 's been 'roun' lots of othahs
    dat could keep de banjo
    ringin';

But of all de whistlin' da'kies dat
    have lived an' died since Ham,
De whistlin'est I evah seed was
    ol' Ike Bates's Sam.
In de kitchen er de stable, in de
    fiel' er mowin' hay,
You could hyeah dat boy a-whis-
    tlin' pu'ty nigh a mile er-
    way,—
Puck'rin' up his ugly features
    'twell you could n't see his
    eyes,
Den you 'd hyeah a soun' lak dis
    un f'om dat awful puckah
    rise:

When dey had revival meetin' an'
    de Lawd's good grace was
    flowin'
On de groun' dat needed wat'rin'
    whaih de seeds of good was
    growin',
While de othahs was a-singin' an'
    a-shoutin' right an' lef',
You could hyeah dat boy a-whis-
    tlin' kin' o' sof' beneaf his
    bref:

At de call fu' colo'ed soldiers,
    Sam enlisted 'mong de res'
Wid de blue o' Gawd's great ahmy
    wropped about his swellin'
    breas',
An' he laffed an' whistled loudah
    in his youfful joy an' glee
Dat de govament would let him
    he'p to mek his people free.
Daih was lots o' ties to bin' him,
    pappy, mammy, an' his
    Dinah,—
Dinah, min' you, was his sweet-
    hea't, an' dey was n't nary
    finah;
But he lef' 'em all, I tell you, lak
    a king he ma'ched away,
Try'n' his level bes' to whistle,
    happy, solemn, choky, gay:

To de front he went an' bravely
    fought de foe an' kep' his
    sperrit,
An' his comerds said his whistle
    made 'em strong when dey
    could hyeah it.
When a saber er a bullet cut some
    frien' o' his'n down,
An' de time 'u'd come to trench
    him an' de boys 'u'd gethah
    'roun',

An' dey could n't sta't a hymn-
    tune, mebbe none o' dem
    'u'd keer,
Sam 'u'd whistle " Sleep in Jesus,"
    an' he knowed de Mastah'd
    hyeah.
In de camp, all sad discouraged,
    he would cheer de hea'ts of
    all,
When above de soun' of labour
    dey could hyeah his whistle
    call:

When de cruel wah was ovah an'
    de boys come ma'chin' back,
Dey was shouts an' cries an'
    blessin's all erlong dey happy
    track,
An' de da'kies all was happy; souls
    an' bodies bofe was freed.
Why, hit seemed lak de Redeemah
    mus' 'a' been on earf indeed.
Dey was gethahed all one evenin'
    jes' befo' de cabin do',
When dey hyeahd somebody
    whistlin' kin' o' sof' an' sweet
    an' low.
Dey could n't see de whistlah, but
    de hymn was cleah and
    ca'm,
An' dey all stood daih a-listenin'
    ontwell Dinah shouted,
    " Sam! "

An' dey seed a little da'ky way off
    yandah thoo de trees
Wid his face all in a puckah mekin'
    jes' sich soun's ez dese:

HOW LUCY BACKSLID

DE times is mighty stirrin' 'mong
    de people up ouah way,
Dey 'sputin' an' dey argyin' an'
    fussin' night an' day;
An' all dis monst'ous trouble dat
    hit meks me tiahed to tell
Is 'bout dat Lucy Jackson dat was
    sich a mighty belle.

She was de preachah's favoured,
    an' he tol' de chu'ch one
    night
Dat she travelled thoo de cloud o'
    sin a-bearin' of a light;
But, now, I 'low he t'inkin' dat she
    mus' 'a' los' huh lamp,
Case Lucy done backslided an' dey
    trouble in de camp.

Huh daddy wants to beat huh, but
    huh mammy daihs him to,
Fu' she lookin' at de question f'om
    a ooman's pint o' view;
An' she say dat now she would n't
    have it diff'ent ef she could;
Dat huh darter only acted jes' lak
    any othah would.

Cose you know w'en women argy,
    dey is mighty easy led
By dey hea'ts an' don't go foolin'
    'bout de reasons of de haid.
So huh mammy laid de law down
    (she ain' reckernizin' wrong),
But you got to mek erlowance fu'
    de cause dat go along.

Now de cause dat made Miss Lucy
    fu' to th'ow huh grace away
I 's afeard won't baih no 'spection
    w'en hit come to jedgement
    day;
Do' de same t'ing been a-wo'kin'
    evah sence de worl' began,—
De ooman disobeyin' fu' to 'tice
    along a man.

Ef you 'tended de revivals which
    we held de wintah pas',
You kin rickolec' dat convuts was
    a-comin' thick an' fas';
But dey ain't no use in talkin', dey
    was all lef' in de lu'ch
W'en ol' Mis' Jackson's dartah
    foun' huh peace an' tuk de
    chu'ch.

W'y, she shouted ovah evah inch
    of Ebenezah's flo';
Up into de preachah's pulpit an
    f'om dah down to de do';
Den she hugged an' squeezed huh
    mammy, an' she hugged an
    kissed huh dad,
An' she struck out at huh sistah
    people said, lak she was mad

I has 'tended some revivals dat
  was lively in my day,
An' I 's seed folks git 'uligion in
  mos' evah kin' o' way;
But I tell you, an' you b'lieve me
  dat I 's speakin' true indeed,
Dat gal tuk huh 'ligion ha'dah dan
  de ha'dest yit I 's seed.

Well, f'om dat, 't was " Sistah
  Jackson, won't you please do
  dis er dat? "
She mus' allus sta't de singin'
  w'en dey 'd pass erroun' de
  hat,
An' hit seemed dey was n't nuffin'
  in dat chu'ch dat could go by
'Dout sistah Lucy Jackson had a
  finger in de pie.

But de sayin' mighty trufeful dat
  hit easiah to sail
W'en de sea is ca'm an' gentle dan
  to weathah out a gale.
Dat 's whut made dis ooman's
  trouble; ef de sto'm had kep'
  away,
She 'd 'a' had enough 'uligion fu'
  to lasted out huh day.

Lucy went wid 'Lishy Davis, but
  w'en she jined chu'ch, you
  know
Dah was lots o' little places dat, of
  cose, she could n't go;
An' she had to gin up dancin' an'
  huh singin' an' huh play.—

Now hit 's nachul dat sich goin's-
  on 'u'd drive a man away.

So, w'en Lucy got so solemn, Ike
  he sta'ted fu' to go
Wid a gal who was a sinnah an'
  could mek a bettah show.
Lucy jes' went on to meetin' lak
  she did n't keer a rap,
But my 'sperunce kep' me t'inkin'
  dah was somep'n' gwine to
  drap.

Fu' a gal won't let 'uligion er no
  othah so't o' t'ing
Stop huh w'en she teks a notion
  dat she wants a weddin' ring.
You kin p'omise huh de blessin's
  of a happy aftah life
(An' hit 's nice to be a angel), but
  she 'd ravah be a wife.

So w'en Chrismus come an' mas-
  tah gin a frolic on de lawn,
Did n't 'sprise me not de littlest
  seein' Lucy lookin' on.
An' I seed a wa'nin' lightnin' go
  a-flashin' f'om huh eye
Jest ez 'Lishy an' his new gal went
  a-gallivantin' by.

An' dat Tildy, umph! she giggled,
  an' she gin huh dress a flirt
Lak de people she was passin' was
  ez common ez de dirt;
An' de minit she was dancin', w'y
  dat gal put on mo' aihs
Dan a cat a-tekin' kittens up a
  paih o' windin' staihs.

She could 'fo'd to show huh
    sma'tness, fu' she could n't
    he'p but know
Dat wid jes' de present dancahs
    she was ownah of de flo';
But I t'ink she'd kin' o' cooled
    down ef she happened on de
    sly
Fu' to noticed dat 'ere lightnin'
    dat I seed in Lucy's eye.

An' she would n't been so 'ston-
    ished w'en de people gin a
    shout,
An' Lucy th'owed huh mantle
    back an' come a-glidin' out.
Some ahms was dah to tek huh an'
    she fluttahed down de flo'
Lak a feddah f'om a bedtick w'en
    de win' commence to blow.

Soon ez Tildy see de trouble, she
    jes' tu'n an' toss huh haid,
But seem lak she los' huh sperrit,
    all huh darin'ness was daid.
Did n't cut anothah capah nary
    time de blessid night;
But de othah one, hit looked lak
    could n't git enough delight.

W'en you keeps a colt a-stan'nin'
    in de stable all along,
W'en he do git out hit's nachul
    he'll be pullin' mighty strong,
Ef you will tie up yo' feelin's,
    hyeah's de bes' advice to tek,
Look out fu' an awful loosin' w'en
    de string dat hol's 'em brek.

Lucy's mammy groaned to see huh,
    an' huh pappy sto'med an' to',
But she kep' right on a-hol'in' to
    de centah of de flo'.
So dey went an' ast de pastoh ef he
    could n't mek huh quit,
But de tellin' of de sto'y th'owed
    de preachah in a fit.

Tildy Taylor chewed huh hank'-
    cher twell she'd chewed it in
    a hole,—
All de sinnahs was rejoicin' 'cause
    a lamb had lef' de fol',
An' de las' I seed o' Lucy, she an'
    'Lish was side an' side:
I don't blame de gal fu' dancin',
    an' I could n't ef I tried.

Fu' de men dat wants to ma'y
    ain't a-growin' 'roun' on
    trees,
An' de gal dat wants to git one
    sholy has to try to please.
Hit's a ha'd t'ing fu' a ooman fu'
    to pray an' jes' set down,
An' to sacafice a husban' so's to
    try to gain a crown.

Now, I don' say she was justified
    in follerin' huh plan;
But aldough she los' huh 'ligion,
    yit she sholy got de man.
Latah on, w'en she is suttain dat
    de preachah's made 'em fas'
She kin jes' go back to chu'ch an'
    ax fu'giveness fu' de pas'!

Lyrics of
Love and Laughter

TWO LITTLE BOOTS

Two little boots all rough an' wo',
    Two little boots!
Law, I 's kissed 'em times befo',
    Dese little boots!
Seems de toes a-peepin' thoo
Dis hyeah hole an' sayin' " Boo! "
Evah time dey looks at you —
    Dese little boots.

Membah de time he put 'em on,
    Dese little boots;
Riz an' called fu' 'em by dawn,
    Dese little boots;
Den he tromped de livelong day,
Laffin' in his happy way,
Evaht'ing he had to say,
    " My little boots! "

Kickin' de san' de whole day long,
    Dem little boots;
Good de cobblah made 'em strong,
    Dem little boots!
Rocks was fu' dat baby's use,
I'on had to stan' abuse
W'en you tu'ned dese champeens
        loose,
    Dese little boots!

Ust to make de ol' cat cry,
    Dese little boots;
Den you walked it mighty high,
    Proud little boots!
Ahms akimbo, stan'in' wide,

Eyes a-sayin' " Dis is pride! "
Den de manny-baby stride!
    You little boots.

Somehow, you don' seem so gay,
    Po' little boots,
Sence yo' ownah went erway,
    Po' little boots!
Yo' bright tops don' look so red,
Dese brass tips is dull an' dead;
" Goo'-by," whut de baby said;
    Deah little boots!

Ain't you kin' o' sad yo'se'f,
    You little boots?
Dis is all his mammy 's lef',
    Two little boots.
Sence huh baby gone an' died.
Heav'n itse'f hit seem to hide
Des a little bit inside
    Two little boots.

TO THE ROAD

Cool is the wind, for the summer
        is waning,
    Who 's for the road?
Sun-flecked and soft, where the
        dead leaves are raining,
    Who 's for the road?
Knapsack and alpenstock press
        hand and shoulder,
Prick of the brier and roll of the
        boulder;

163

This be your lot till the season
  grow older;
   Who's for the road?

Up and away in the hush of the
  morning,
   Who's for the road?
Vagabond he, all conventions a-
  scorning,
   Who's for the road?
Music of warblers so merrily sing-
  ing,
Draughts from the rill from the
  roadside up-springing,
Nectar of grapes from the vines
  lowly swinging,
   These on the road.

Now every house is a hut or a
  hovel,
   Come to the road:
Mankind and moles in the dark
  love to grovel,
   But to the road.
Throw off the loads that are bend-
  ing you double;
Love is for life, only labor is
  trouble;
Truce to the town, whose best gift
  is a bubble:
   Come to the road!

A SPRING WOOING

Come on walkin' wid me, Lucy;
  't ain't no time to mope
  erroun'

W'en de sunshine's shoutin
  glory in de sky,
An' de little Johnny-Jump-Ups's
  jes' a-springin' f'om de
  groun',
  Den a-lookin' roun' to ax each
  othah w'y.
Don' you hyeah dem cows a-
  mooin'? Dat's dey howdy
  to de spring;
  Ain' dey lookin' most oncom-
  mon satisfied?
Hit's enough to mek a body want
  to spread dey mouf an'
  sing
  Jes' to see de critters all so
  spa'klin'-eyed.

W'y dat squir'l dat jes' run past
  us, ef I did n' know his
  tricks,
  I could swaih he 'd got 'uligion
  jes' to-day;
An' dem liza'ds slippin' back an'
  fofe ermong de stones an'
  sticks
  Is a-wigglin' 'cause dey feel so
  awful gay.
Oh, I see yo' eyes a-shinin' dough
  you try to mek me b'lieve
  Dat you ain' so monst'ous happy
  'cause you come;
But I tell you dis hyeah weathah
  meks it moughty ha'd to
  'ceive
  Ef a body's soul ain' blin' an
  deef an' dumb.

Robin whistlin' ovah yandah ez he
    buil' his little nes';
  Whut you reckon dat he sayin'
    to his mate?
He 's a-sayin' dat he love huh in de
    wo'ds she know de bes',
  An' she lookin' moughty pleased
    at whut he state.
Now, Miss Lucy, dat ah robin
    sholy got his sheer o' sense,
  An' de hen-bird got huh
    mothah-wit fu' true;
So I t'ink ef you 'll ixcuse me, fu'
    I do' mean no erfence,
  Dey 's a lesson in dem birds fu'
    me an' you.

I 's a-buil'in' o' my cabin, an' I 's
    vines erbove de do'
  Fu' to kin' o' gin it sheltah f'om
    de sun;
Gwine to have a little kitchen wid
    a reg'lar wooden flo',
  An' dey 'll be a back verandy
    w'en hit 's done.
I 's a-waitin' fu' you, Lucy, tek de'
    'zample o' de birds,
  Dat 's a-lovin' an' a-matin' evah-
    whaih.
I cain' tell you dat I loves you in
    de robin's music wo'ds,
  But my cabin 's talkin' fu' me
    ovah thaih!

JOGGIN' ERLONG

DE da'kest hour, dey allus say,
Is des' befo' de dawn,

But it 's moughty ha'd a-waitin'
W'ere de night goes frownin'
    on;
An' it 's moughty ha'd a-hopin'
W'en de clouds is big an' black,
An' all de t'ings you 's waited fu'
Has failed, er gone to wrack —
But des' keep on a-joggin' wid a
    little bit o' song,
De mo'n is allus brightah w'en de
    night 's been long.

Dey 's lots o' knocks you 's got to
    tek
Befo' yo' journey 's done,
An' dey 's times w'en you 'll be
    wishin'
Dat de weary race was run;
W'en you want to give up tryin'
An' des' float erpon de wave,
W'en you don't feel no mo' sorrer
Ez you t'ink erbout de grave —
Den, des' keep on a-joggin' wid a
    little bit o' song,
De mo'n is allus brightah w'en de
    night 's been long.

De whup-lash sting a good deal
    mo'
De back hit 's knowed befo',
An' de burden 's allus heavies'
Whaih hits weight has made a
    so';
Dey is times w'en tribulation
Seems to git de uppah han'
An' to whip de weary trav'lah
'Twell he ain't got stren'th to
    stan'—

But des' keep on a-joggin' wid a
  little bit o' song,
De mo'n is allus brightah w'en de
  night 's been long.

IN MAY

OH to have you in May,
  To talk with you under the
    trees,
Dreaming throughout the day,
  Drinking the wine-like breeze,

Oh it were sweet to think
  That May should be ours again,
Hoping it not, I shrink,
  Out of the sight of men.

May brings the flowers to bloom,
  It brings the green leaves to the
    tree,
And the fatally sweet perfume,
  Of what you once were to me.

DREAMS

WHAT dreams we have and how
  they fly
Like rosy clouds across the sky;
  Of wealth, of fame, of sure suc-
    cess,
    Of love that comes to cheer
      and bless;
  And how they wither, how they
    fade,
  The waning wealth, the jilting
    jade —

The fame that for a moment
  gleams,
Then flies forever,— dreams, ah
  — dreams!

O burning doubt and long regret.
O tears with which our eyes are
  wet,
  Heart-throbs, heart-aches, the
    glut of pain,
  The somber cloud, the bitter
    rain,
You were not of those dreams —
  ah! well,
Your full fruition who can tell?
  Wealth, fame, and love, ah!
    love that beams
    Upon our souls, all dreams —
      ah! dreams.

THE TRYST

DE night creep down erlong de
  lan',
  De shadders rise an' shake,
De frog is sta'tin' up his ban',
  De cricket is awake;
My wo'k is mos' nigh done, Celes',
  To-night I won't be late,
I 's hu'yin' thoo my level bes',
  Wait fu' me by de gate.

De mockin'-bird 'll sen' his glee
  A-thrillin' thoo and thoo,
I know dat ol' magnolia-tree
  Is smellin' des' fu' you;
De jessamine erside de road
  Is bloomin' rich an' white,

My hea't 's a-th'obbin' 'cause it
    knowed
    You 'd wait fu' me to-night.

Hit 's lonesome, ain't it, stan'in'
    thaih
    Wid no one nigh to talk?
But ain't dey whispahs in de aih
    Erlong de gyahden walk?
Don't somep'n kin' o' call my
    name,
    An' say " he love you bes' "?
Hit 's true, I wants to say de
    same,
    So wait fu' me, Celes'.

Sing somep'n fu' to pass de time,
    Outsing de mockin'-bird,
You got de music an' de rhyme,
    You beat him wid de word.
I 's comin' now, my wo'k is done,
    De hour has come fu' res',
I wants to fly, but only run —
    Wait fu' me, deah Celes'.

A PLEA

TREAT me nice, Miss Mandy
    Jane,
    Treat me nice.
Dough my love has tu'ned my
    brain,
    Treat me nice.
I ain't done a t'ing to shame,
Lovahs all ac's jes' de same:
Don't you know we ain't to blame?
    Treat me nice!

Cose I know I 's talkin' wild;
    Treat me nice;
I cain't talk no bettah, child,
    Treat me nice;
Whut a pusson gwine to do,
W'en he come a-cou'tin' you
All a-trimblin' thoo and thoo?
    Please be nice.

Reckon I mus' go de paf
    Othahs do:
Lovahs lingah, ladies laff;
    Mebbe you
Do' mean all the things you say,
An' pu'haps some latah day
W'en I baig you ha'd, you may
    Treat me nice!

THE DOVE

OUT of the sunshine and out of
    the heat,
Out of the dust of the grimy
    street,
A song fluttered down in the form
    of a dove,
And it bore me a message, the one
    word — Love!

Ah, I was toiling, and oh, I was
    sad:
I had forgotten the way to be glad.
Now, smiles for my sadness and
    for my toil, rest
Since the dove fluttered down to
    its home in my breast!

A WARM DAY IN WINTER

" Sunshine on de medders,
   Greenness on de way;
Dat's de blessed reason
   I sing all de day."
Look hyeah! Whut you axin'?
   Whut meks me so merry?
'Spect to see me sighin'
   W'en hit's wa'm in Febawary?

'Long de stake an' rider
   Seen a robin set;
W'y, hit 'mence a-thawin',
   Groun' is monst'ous wet.
Den you stan' dah wond'rin',
   Lookin' skeert an' stary;
I's a right to caper
   W'en hit's wa'm in Febawary.

Missis gone a-drivin',
   Mastah gone to shoot;
Ev'ry da'ky lazin'
   In de sun to boot.
Qua'tah's moughty pleasant,
   Hangin' 'roun' my Mary;
Cou'tin' boun' to prospah
   W'en hit's wa'm in Febawary.

Cidah look so pu'ty
   Po'in' f'om de jug —
Don' you see it's happy?
   Hyeah it laffin'— glug?
Now's de time fu' people
   Fu' to try an' bury
All dey grief an' sorrer,
   W'en hit's wa'm in Febawary.

SNOWIN'

Dey is snow upon de meddahs,
   dey is snow upon de hill,
An' de little branch's watahs is
   all glistenin' an' still;
De win' goes roun' de cabin lak a
   sperrit wan'erin' 'roun'.
An' de chillen shakes an' shivahs
   as dey listen to de soun'.
Dey is hick'ry in de fiahplace,
   whah de blaze is risin' high,
But de heat it meks ain't wa'min'
   up de gray clouds in de sky.
Now an' den I des peep outside,
   den I hurries to de do',
Lawd a mussy on my body, how I
   wish it would n't snow!

I kin stan' de hottes' summah, I
   kin stan' de wettes' fall,
I kin stan' de chilly springtime in
   de ploughland, but dat's
   all;
Fu' de ve'y hottes' fiah nevah tells
   my skin a t'ing,
W'en de snow commence a-flyin',
   an' de win' begin to sing.
Dey is plenty wood erroun' us, an'
   I chop an' tote it in,
But de t'oughts dat I's a t'inkin'
   while I's wo'kin' is a sin.
I kin keep f'om downright swahin'
   all de time I's on de go,
But my hea't is full o' cuss-wo'ds
   w'en I's trampin' thoo de
   snow.

What you say, you Lishy Davis,
  dat you see a possum's tracks?
Look hyeah, boy, you stop yo'
  foolin', bring ol' Spot, an'
  bring de ax.
Is I col'? Go way, now, Mandy,
  what you t'ink I 's made of?
  — sho,
W'y dis win' is des ez gentle, an'
  dis ain't no kin' o' snow.
Dis hyeah weathah 's des ez healthy
  ez de wa'mest summah days.
All you chillen step up lively, pile
  on wood an' keep a blaze.
What 's de use o' gittin' skeery
  case dey 's snow upon de
  groun'?
Huh-uh, I 's a reg'lar snowbird ef
  dey 's any possum 'roun'.

Go on, Spot, don' be so foolish;
  don' you see de signs o' feet.
What you howlin' fu'? Keep still,
  suh, cose de col' is putty
  sweet;
But we goin' out on bus'ness, an'
  hit 's bus'ness o' de kin'
Dat mus' put a dog an' dahky in
  a happy frame o' min'.
Yes, you 's col'; I know it, Spotty,
  but you des stay close to me,
An' I 'll mek you hot ez cotton
  w'en we strikes de happy tree.
No, I don' lak wintah weathah,
  an' I 'd wush 't uz allus
  June,
Ef it was n't fu' de trackin' o' de
  possum an' de coon.

KEEP A SONG UP ON DE WAY

OH, de clouds is mighty heavy
An' de rain is mighty thick;
  Keep a song up on de way.
An' de waters is a rumblin'
On de boulders in de crick,
  Keep a song up on de way.
Fu' a bird ercross de road
Is a-singin' lak he knowed
Dat we people did n't daih
Fu' to try de rainy aih
  Wid a song up on de way.

What 's de use o' gittin' mopy,
Case de weather ain' de bes'!
  Keep a song up on de way.
W'en de rain is fallin' ha'des',
Dey 's de longes' times to res'
  Keep a song up on de way.
Dough de plough 's a-stan'in' still
Dey 'll be watah fu' de mill,
Rain mus' come ez well ez sun
'Fo' de weathah's wo'k is done,
  Keep a song up on de way.

W'y hit 's nice to hyeah de showahs
Fallin' down ermong de trees:
  Keep a song up on de way.
Ef de birds don' bothah 'bout it,
But go singin' lak dey please,
  Keep a song up on de way.
You don' s'pose I 's gwine to see
Dem ah fowls do mo' dan me?
No, suh, I 'll des chase dis frown,
An' aldough de rain fall down,
  Keep a song up on de way.

THE TURNING OF THE BABIES IN THE BED

WOMAN 's sho' a cur'ous critter,
    an' dey ain't no doubtin' dat.
She 's a mess o' funny capahs f'om
    huh slippahs to huh hat.
Ef you tries to un'erstan' huh, an'
    you fails, des' up an' say:
" D' ain't a bit o' use to try to
    un'erstan' a woman's way."

I don' mean to be complainin', but
    I 's jes' a-settin' down
Some o' my own obserwations,
    w'en I cas' my eye eroun'.
Ef you ax me fu' to prove it, I
    ken do it mighty fine,
Fu' dey ain't no bettah 'zample
    den dis ve'y wife o' mine.

In de ve'y hea't o' midnight, w'en
    I 's sleepin' good an' soun',
I kin hyeah a so't o' rustlin' an'
    somebody movin' 'roun'.
An' I say, " Lize, whut you do-
    in'? " But she frown an' shek
    huh haid,
" Heish yo' mouf, I 's only tu'nin'
    of de chillun in de bed.

" Don' you know a chile gits rest-
    less, layin' all de night one
    way?
An' you' got to kind o' 'range him
    sev'al times befo' de day?
So de little necks won't worry, an'
    de little backs won't break;

Don' you t'ink case chillun 's chil-
    lun dey hain't got no pain an'
    ache."

So she shakes 'em, an' she twists
    'em, an' she tu'ns 'em 'roun'
    erbout,
'Twell I don' see how de chillun
    evah keeps f'om hollahin' out.
Den she lif's 'em up head down-
    'ards, so 's dey won't git livah-
    grown,
But dey snoozes des' ez peaceful
    ez a liza'd on a stone.

W'en hit 's mos' nigh time fu'
    wakin' on de dawn o' jedg-
    ment day,
Seems lak I kin hyeah ol' Gab'iel
    lay his trumpet down an' say,
" Who dat walkin' 'roun' so easy
    down on earf ermong de
    dead? "—
'T will be Lizy up a-tu'nin' of de
    chillun in de bed.

THE DANCE

HEEL and toe, heel and toe,
    That is the song we sing;
Turn to your partner and curtsey
    low,
    Balance and forward and swing
Corners are draughty and meadow
    are white,
This is the game for a winter's
    night.

Hands around, hands around,
  Trip it, and not too slow;
Clear is the fiddle and sweet its
    sound,
  Keep the girls' cheeks aglow.
Still let your movements be dainty
    and light,
This is the game for a winter's
    night.

Back to back, back to back,
  Turn to your place again;
Never let lightness nor nimble-
    ness lack,
  Either in maidens or men.
Time hasteth ever, beware of its
    flight,
Oh, what a game for a winter's
    night!

Slower now, slower now,
  Softer the music sighs;
Look, there are beads on your
    partner's brow
  Though there be light in her
    eyes.
Lead her away and her grace re-
  quite,
So goes the game on a winter's
    night.

SOLILOQUY OF A TURKEY

Dey 's a so't o' threatenin' feelin'
    in de blowin' of de breeze,
  An' I 's feelin' kin' o' squeamish
    in de night;

I 's a-walkin' 'roun' a-lookin' at
    de diffunt style o' trees,
  An' a-measurin' dey thickness
    an' dey height.
Fu' dey 's somep'n mighty 'spicious
    in de looks de da'kies give,
  Ez dey pass me an' my fambly
    on de groun',
So it 'curs to me dat lakly, ef I
    caihs to try an' live,
  It concehns me fu' to 'mence to
    look erroun'.

Dey 's a cu'ious kin' o' shivah
    runnin' up an' down my back,
  An' I feel my feddahs rufflin'
    all de day,
An' my laigs commence to trimble
    evah blessid step I mek;
  W'en I sees a ax, I tu'ns my
    head away.
Folks is go'gin' me wid goodies,
    an' dey 's treatin' me wid caih,
  An' I 's fat in spite of all dat I
    kin do.
I 's mistrus'ful of de kin'ness dat 's
    erroun' me evahwhaih,
  Fu' it 's jes' too good, an' fre-
    quent, to be true.

Snow 's a-fallin' on de medders, all
    erroun' me now is white,
  But I 's still kep' on a-roostin'
    on de fence;
Isham comes an' feels my breas'-
    bone, an' he hefted me las'
    night,

An' he 's gone erroun' a-grinnin'
   evah sence.
"T ain't de snow dat meks me
   shivah; 't ain't de col' dat
   meks me shake;
   'T ain't de wintah-time itse'f
   dat 's 'fectin' me;
But I t'ink de time is comin',
   an' I 'd bettah mek a break,
   Fu' to set wid Mistah Possum
   in his tree.

W'en you hyeah de da'kies singin',
   an' de quahtahs all is gay,
   'T ain't de time fu' birds lak me
   to be 'erroun';
W'en de hick'ry chips is flyin', an'
   de log 's been ca'ied erway,
   Den hit 's dang'ous to be roostin'
   nigh he groun'.

Grin on, Isham! Sing on, da'k-
   ies! But I flop my wings an'
   go
   Fu' de sheltah of de ve'y high-
   est tree,
Fu' dey 's too much close ertention
   — an' dey's too much fallin'
   snow —
   An' it 's too nigh Chris'mus
   mo'nin' now fu' me.

FISHING

W'EN I git up in de mo'nin' an'
   de clouds is big an' black,
Dey 's a kin' o' wa'nin' shivah goes
   a-scootin' down my back;

Den I says to my ol' ooman ez I
   watches down de lane,
"Don't you so't o' reckon, Lizy,
   dat we gwine to have some
   rain?"

"Go on, man," my Lizy answah,
   "you cain't fool me, not a
   bit,
I don't see no rain a-comin', ef
   you 's wishin' fu' it, quit;
Case de mo' you t'ink erbout it, an
   de mo' you pray an' wish,
W'y de rain stay 'way de longah,
   spechul ef you wants to fish."

But I see huh pat de skillet, an' I
   see huh cas' huh eye
Wid a kin' o' anxious motion to'ds
   de da'kness in de sky;
An' I knows whut she 's a-t'inkin',
   dough she tries so ha'd to
   hide.
She 's a-sayin', "Would n't catfish
   now tas'e monst'ous bully,
   fried?"

Den de clouds git black an' black-
   ah, an' de thundah 'mence to
   roll,
An' de rain, it 'mence a-fallin'.
   Oh, I 's happy, bless my
   soul!
Ez I look at dat ol' skillet, an' I
   'magine I kin see
Jes' a slew o' new-ketched catfish
   sizzlin' daih fu' huh an' me.

'T ain't no use to go a-ploughin',
    fu' de groun' 'll be too
    wet,
So I puts out fu' de big house at
    a moughty pace, you bet,
An' ol' mastah say, " Well, Lishy,
    ef you t'ink hit 's gwine to
    rain,
Go on fishin', hit's de weathah,
    an' I 'low we cain't com-
    plain."

Talk erbout a dahky walkin' wid
    his haid up in de aih!
Have to feel mine evah minute to
    be sho' I got it daih;
En' de win' is cuttin' capahs an'
    a-lashin' thoo de trees,
But de rain keeps on a-singin'
    blessed songs, lak " Tek yo'
    ease."

Wid my pole erpon my shouldah
    an' my wo'm can in my
    han',
I kin feel de fish a-waitin' w'en I
    strikes de rivah's san';
Nevah min', you ho'ny scoun'els,
    need n' swim erroun' an'
    grin,
I 'll be grinnin' in a minute w'en I
    'mence to haul you in.

W'en de fish begin to nibble, an'
    de co'k begin to jump,
I 's erfeahed dat dey 'll quit bitin',
    case dey hyeah my hea't go
    " thump,"

'Twell de co'k go way down
    undah, an' I raise a awful
    shout,
Ez a big ol' yallah belly comes a
    gallivantin' out.

Need n't wriggle, Mistah Catfish,
    case I got you jes' de same,
You been eatin', I 'll be eatin', an'
    we needah ain't to blame.
But you need n't feel so lonesome
    fu' I 's th'owin' out to see
Ef dey ain't some of yo' comrades
    fu' to keep you company.

Spo't, dis fishin'! now you talkin',
    w'y dey ain't no kin' to beat;
I don' keer ef I is soakin', laigs,
    an' back, an' naik, an' feet,
It 's de spo't I 's lookin' aftah.
    Hit 's de pleasure an' de fun,
Dough I knows dat Lizy 's waitin'
    wid de skillet w'en I 's done.

A PLANTATION PORTRAIT

HAIN'T you see my Mandy Lou,
    Is it true?
Whaih you been f'om day to day,
    Whaih, I say?
Dat you say you nevah seen
    Dis hyeah queen
Walkin' roun' f'om fiel' to street
    Smilin' sweet?

Slendah ez a saplin' tree;
    Seems to me

W'en de win' blow f'om de bay
    She jes' sway
Lak de reg'lar saplin' do
    Ef hit's grew
Straight an' graceful, 'dout a limb,
    Sweet an' slim.

Browner den de frush's wing,
    An' she sing
Lak he mek his wa'ble ring
    In de spring;
But she sholy beat de frush,
    Hyeah me, hush:
W'en she sing, huh teef kin show
    White ez snow.

Eyes ez big an' roun' an' bright
    Ez de light
Whut de moon gives in de prime
    Harvest time.
An' huh haih a woolly skein,
    Black an' plain.
Hol's you wid a natchul twis'
    Close to bliss.

Tendah han's dat mek yo' own
    Feel lak stone;
Easy steppin', blessid feet,
    Small an' sweet.
Hain't you seen my Mandy Lou,
    Is it true?
Look at huh befo' she's gone,
    Den pass on!

A LITTLE CHRISTMAS BASKET

De win' is hollahin' "Daih you"
    to de shuttahs an' de fiah,

De snow's a-sayin' "Got you" to
    de groun',
Fu' de wintah weathah's come
    widout a-askin' ouah de-
    siah,
    An' he's laughin' in his sleeve
        at whut he foun';
Fu' dey ain't nobody ready wid
    dey fuel er dey food,
    An' de money bag look timid
        lak, fu' sho',
So we want ouah Chrismus
    sermon, but we'd lak it ef
    you could
    Leave a little Chrismus basket
        at de do'.

Wha's de use o' tellin' chillen
    'bout a Santy er a Nick,
    An' de sto'ies dat a body allus
        tol'?
When de harf is gray wid ashes
    an' you hasn't got a stick
    Fu' to warm dem when dey
        little toes is col'?
Wha's de use o' preachin' 'ligion
    to a man dat's sta'ved to
    def,
    An' a-tellin' him de Mastah
        will pu'vide?
Ef you want to tech his feelin's,
    save yo' sermons an' yo'
    bref,
    Tek a little Chrismus basket by
        yo' side.

'T ain't de time to open Bibles an'
    to lock yo' cellah do',

'T ain't de time to talk o' bein'
    good to men;
Ef you want to preach a sermon
    ez you nevah preached
    befo',
    Preach dat sermon wid a shoat
      er wid er hen;
Bein' good is heap sight bettah den
    a-dallyin' wid sin,
    An' dey ain't nobody roun' dat
      knows it mo',
But I t'ink dat 'ligion 's sweeter
    w'en it kind o' mixes in
    Wid a little Chrismus basket at
      de do'.

THE VALSE

WHEN to sweet music my lady
    is dancing
    My heart to mild frenzy her
      beauty inspires.
Into my face are her brown eyes
    a-glancing,
    And swift my whole frame
      thrills with tremulous fires.
Dance, lady, dance, for the mo-
    ments are fleeting,
    Pause not to place yon refractory
      curl;
Life is for love and the night is
    for sweeting;
    Dreamily, joyously, circle and
      whirl.

Oh, how those viols are throbbing
    and pleading;

A prayer is scarce needed in
    sound of their strain.
Surely and lightly as round you
    are speeding,
    You turn to confusion my heart
      and my brain.
Dance, lady, dance to the viol's
    soft calling,
    Skip it and trip it as light as the
      air;
Dance, for the moments like rose
    leaves are falling,
    Strikes, now, the clock from its
      place on the stair.

Now sinks the melody lower and
    lower,
    The weary musicians scarce
      seeming to play.
Ah, love, your steps now are
    slower and slower,
    The smile on your face is more
      sad and less gay.
Dance, lady, dance to the brink of
    our parting,
    My heart and your step must not
      fail to be light.
Dance! Just a turn — tho' the
    tear-drop be starting.
    Ah — now it is done — so —
      my lady, good-night!

REPONSE

WHEN Phyllis sighs and from her
    eyes
The light dies out; my soul re-
    plies

With misery of deep-drawn breath,
E'en as it were at war with
    death.

When Phyllis smiles, her glance
    beguiles
My heart through love-lit wood-
    land aisles,
And through the silence high and
    clear,
A wooing warbler's song I hear.

But if she frown, despair comes
    down,
I put me on my sack-cloth gown;
So frown not, Phyllis, lest I die,
But look on me with smile or
    sigh.

MY SWEET BROWN GAL

W'EN de clouds is hangin' heavy
    in de sky,
An' de win's 's a-taihin' moughty
    vig'rous by,
I don' go a-sighin' all erlong de
    way;
I des' wo'k a-waitin' fu' de close
    o' day.

Case I knows w'en evenin' draps
    huh shadders down,
I won' care a smidgeon fu' de
    weathah's frown;
Let de rain go splashin', let de
    thundah raih,
Dey's a happy sheltah, an' I's
    goin' daih.

Down in my ol' cabin wa'm ez
    mammy's toas',
'Taters in de fiah layin' daih to
    roas';
No one daih to cross me, got no
    talkin' pal,
But I's got de comp'ny o' my
    sweet brown gal.

So I spen's my evenin' listenin' to
    huh sing,
Lak a blessid angel; how huh
    voice do ring!
Sweetah den a bluebird flutterin'
    erroun',
W'en he sees de steamin' o' de
    new ploughed groun'.

Den I hugs huh closah, closah to
    my breas'.
Need n't sing, my da'lin', tek you'
    hones' res'.
Does I mean Malindy, Mandy,
    Lize er Sal?
No, I means my fiddle — dat's
    my sweet brown gal!

SPRING FEVER

GRASS commence a-comin'
    Thoo de thawin' groun',
Evah bird dat whistles
    Keepin' noise erroun';
Cain't sleep in de mo'nin',
    Case befo' it's light
Bluebird an' de robin,
    Done begun to fight.

Bluebird sass de robin,
  Robin sass him back,
Den de bluebird scol' him
  'Twell his face is black.
Would n' min' de quoilin'
  All de mo'nin' long,
'Cept it wakes me early,
  Case hit 's done in song.

Anybody wo'kin'
  Wants to sleep ez late
Ez de folks 'll 'low him,
  An' I wish to state
(Co'se dis ain't to scattah,
  But 'twix' me an' you),
I could stan' de bedclothes,
  Kin' o' latah, too.

'T ain't my natchul feelin',
  Dis hyeah mopin' spell.
I stan's early risin'
  Mos'ly moughty well;
But de ve'y minute,
  I feel Ap'il's heat,
Bless yo' soul, de bedclothes
  Nevah seemed so sweet.

Mastah, he 's a-scol'in',
  Case de han's is slow,
All de hosses balkin',
  Jes' cain't mek 'em go.
Don' know whut 's de mattah,
  Hit 's a funny t'ing,
Less'n hit 's de fevah
  Dat you gits in spring.

THE VISITOR

LITTLE lady at de do',
  W'y you stan' dey knockin'?
Nevah seen you ac' befo'
  In er way so shockin'.
    Don' you know de sin it is
    Fu' to git my temper riz
    W'en I 's got de rheumatiz
  An' my jints is lockin'?

No, ol' Miss ain't sont you down,
  Don' you tell no story;
I been seed you hangin' 'roun'
  Dis hyeah te'itory.
    You des come fu' me to tell
    You a tale, an' I ain'—
      well —
    Look hyeah, what is dat I
      smell?
  Steamin' victuals? Glory!

Come in, Missy, how you do?
  Come up by de fiah,
I was jokin', chile, wid you;
  Bring dat basket nighah.
    Huh uh, ain't dat lak ol'
      Miss,
    Sen'in' me a feas' lak dis?
    Rheumatiz cain't stop my
      bliss,
  Case I 's feelin' spryah.

Chicken meat an' gravy, too,
  Hot an' still a-heatin';
Good ol' sweet pertater stew;
  Missy b'lieves in treatin'.
    Des set down, you blessed
      chile,

Daddy got to t'ink a while,
Den a story mek you smile
W'en he git thoo eatin'.

SONG

WINTAH, summah, snow er
    shine,
Hit 's all de same to me,
Ef only I kin call you mine,
    An' keep you by my knee.

Ha'dship, frolic, grief er caih,
    Content by night an' day,
Ef only I kin see you whaih
    You wait beside de way.

Livin', dyin', smiles er teahs,
    My soul will still be free,
Ef only thoo de comin' yeahs
    You walk de worl' wid me.

Bird-song, breeze-wail, chune er
    moan,
What puny t'ings dey 'll be,
Ef w'en I 's seemin' all erlone,
    I knows yo' hea't 's wid me.

THE COLORED BAND

W'EN de colo'ed ban' comes
    ma'chin' down de street,
Don't you people stan' daih
    starin'; lif' yo' feet!
    Ain't dey playin'? Hip, hoo-
    ray!

Stir yo' stumps an' cleah de
    way,
Fu' de music dat dey mekin' can't
    be beat.

Oh, de major man 's a-swingin'
    of his stick,
An' de pickaninnies crowdin'
    roun' him thick;
    In his go'geous uniform,
    He 's de lightnin' of de sto'm,
An' de little clouds erroun' look
    mighty slick.

You kin hyeah a fine perfo'mance
    w'en de white ban's sere-
    nade,
    An' dey play dey high-toned
    music mighty sweet,
But hit 's Sousa played in rag-
    time, an' hit 's Rastus on
    Parade,
    W'en de colo'ed ban' comes
    ma'chin' down de street.

W'en de colo'ed ban' comes ma'ch-
    in' down de street
You kin hyeah de ladies all erroun'
    repeat:
    "Ain't dey handsome? Ain't
    dey gran'?
    Ain't dey splendid? Goodness,
    lan'!
W'y dey 's pu'fect f'om dey fo'-
    heads to dey feet!"
An' sich steppin' to de music down
    de line,

'T ain't de music by itself dat meks
    it fine,
  Hit 's de walkin', step by step,
  An' de keepin' time wid " Hep,"
Dat it mek a common ditty soun'
    divine.

Oh, de white ban' play hits music,
    an' hit 's mighty good to
    hyeah,
An' it sometimes leaves a ticklin'
    in yo' feet;
But de hea't goes into bus'ness fu'
    to he'p erlong de eah,
  W'en de colo'ed ban' goes ma'ch-
    in' down de street.

TO A VIOLET FOUND ON
ALL SAINTS' DAY

BELATED wanderer of the ways of
    spring,
  Lost in the chill of grim No-
    vember rain,
Would I could read the message
    that you bring
  And find in it the antidote for
    pain.

Does some sad spirit out beyond
    the day,
  Far looking to the hours forever
    dead,
Send you a tender offering to lay
  Upon the grave of us, the liv-
    ing dead?

Or does some brighter spirit, un-
    forlorn,
  Send you, my little sister of the
    wood,
To say to some one on a cloudful
    morn,
  " Life lives through death, my
    brother, all is good? "

With meditative hearts the others
    go
  The memory of their dead to
    dress anew.
But, sister mine, bide here that I
    may know,
  Life grows, through death, as
    beautiful as you.

INSPIRATION

AT the golden gate of song
Stood I, knocking all day long,
But the Angel, calm and cold,
Still refused and bade me, " Hold."

Then a breath of soft perfume,
Then a light within the gloom;
Thou, Love, camest to my side,
And the gates flew open wide.

Long I dwelt in this domain,
Knew no sorrow, grief, or pain;
Now you bid me forth and free,
Will you shut these gates on me?

MY LADY OF CASTLE GRAND

GRAY is the palace where she
dwells,
Grimly the poplars stand
There by the window where she
sits,
My Lady of Castle Grand.

There does she bide the livelong
day,
Grim as the poplars are,
Ever her gaze goes reaching out,
Steady, but vague and far.

Bright burn the fires in the castle
hall,
Brightly the fire-dogs stand;
But cold is the body and cold the
heart
Of my Lady of Castle Grand.

Blue are the veins in her lily-white
hands,
Blue are the veins in her brow;
Thin is the line of her blue drawn
lips,
Who would be haughty now?

Pale is the face at the window-
pane,
Pale as the pearl on her breast,
" Roderick, love, wilt come again?
Fares he to east or west? "

The shepherd pipes to the shep-
herdess,
The bird to his mate in the
tree,
And ever she sighs as she hears
their song,
" Nobody sings for me."

The scullery maids have swains
enow
Who lead them the way of love,
But lonely and loveless their mis-
tress sits
At her window up above.

Loveless and lonely she waits and
waits,
The saddest in all the land;
Ah, cruel and lasting is love-blind
pride,
My Lady of Castle Grand.

DRIZZLE

HIT 's been drizzlin' an' been
sprinklin',
Kin' o' techy all day long.
I ain't wet enough fu' toddy,
I 's too damp to raise a song,
An' de case have set me t'inkin',
Dat dey 's folk des lak de rain,
Dat goes drizzlin' w'en dey 's
talkin',
An' won't speak out flat an'
plain.

Ain't you nevah set an' listened
At a body 'splain his min'?

W'en de t'oughts dey keep on
    drappin'
Was n't big enough to fin'?
Dem's whut I call drizzlin'
    people,
Othahs call 'em mealy mouf,
But de fust name hits me bettah,
    Case dey nevah tech a drouf.

Dey kin talk from hyeah to yandah,
    An' f'om yandah hyeah ergain,
An' dey don' mek no mo' 'pression,
    Den dis powd'ry kin' o' rain.
En yo' min' is dry ez cindahs,
    Er a piece o' kindlin' wood,
'T ain't no use a-talkin' to 'em,
    Fu' dey drizzle ain't no good.

Gimme folks dat speak out nachul,
    Whut 'll say des whut dey mean,
Whut don't set dey wo'ds so
    skimpy
Dat you got to guess between.
I want talk des' lak de showahs
    Whut kin wash de dust erway,
Not dat sprinklin' convusation,
    Dat des drizzle all de day.

DE CRITTERS' DANCE

AIN'T nobody nevah tol' you not a
    wo'd a-tall,
'Bout de time dat all de critters
    gin dey fancy ball?
Some folks tell it in a sto'y, some
    folks sing de rhyme,
'Peahs to me you ought to hyeahed
    it, case hit's ol' ez time.

Well, de critters all was p'osp'ous,
    now would be de chance
Fu' to tease ol' Pa'son Hedgehog,
    givin' of a dance;
Case, you know, de critters'
    preachah was de stric'est kin',
An' he nevah made no 'lowance fu'
    de frisky min'.

So dey sont dey inbitations, Rac-
    coon writ 'em all,
"Dis hyeah note is to inbite you
    to de Fancy Ball;
Come erlong an' bring yo' ladies,
    bring yo' chillun too,
Put on all yo' bibs an' tuckahs,
    show whut you kin do."

W'en de night come, dey all
    gathahed in a place dey
    knowed,
Fu' enough erway f'om people,
    nigh enough de road,
All de critters had ersponded, Hop-
    Toad up to Baih,
An' I's hyeah to tell you, Pa'son
    Hedgehog too, was daih.

Well, dey talked an' made dey
    'bejunce, des lak critters
    do,
An' dey walked an' p'omenaded
    'roun' an' thoo an' thoo;
Jealous ol' Mis' Fox, she whispah,
    "See Mis' Wildcat daih,
Ain't hit scan'lous, huh a-comin'
    wid huh shouldahs baih?"

Ol' man T'utle was n't honin' fu'
    no dancin' tricks,
So he stayed by ol' Mis' Tu'tle,
    talkin' politics;
Den de ban' hit 'mence a-playin'
    critters all to place,
Fou' ercross an' fou' stan' side-
    ways, smilin' face to face.

'Fessah Frog, he play de co'net,
    Cricket play de fife,
Slews o' Grasshoppahs a-fiddlin'
    lak to save dey life;
Mistah Crow, 'he call de figgers,
    settin' in a tree,
Huh, uh! how dose critters sas-
    shayed was a sight to see.

Mistah Possom swing Mis' Rab-
    bit up an' down de flo',
Ol' man Baih, he ain't so nimble,
    an' it mek him blow;
Raccoon dancin' wid Mis' Squ'il
    squeeze huh little han',
She say, " Oh, now ain't you aw-
    ful, quit it, goodness lan'! "

Pa'son Hedgehog groanin' awful at
    his converts' shines,
'Dough he peepin' thoo his fingahs
    at dem movin' lines,
'Twell he cain't set still no longah
    w'en de fiddles sing,
Up he jump, an' bless you, honey,
    cut de pigeon-wing.

Well, de critters lak to fainted jes'
    wid dey su'prise,

Sistah Fox, she vowed she was n't
    gwine to b'lieve huh eyes;
But dey could n't be no 'sputin'
    'bout it any mo':
Pa'son Hedgehog was a-cape'in' all
    erroun' de flo.'

Den dey all jes' capahed scan'lous
    case dey did n't doubt,
Dat dey still could go to meetin';
    who could tu'n 'em out?
So wid dancin' an' uligion, dey
    was in de fol',
Fu' a-dancin' wid de Pa'son could-
    n't hu't de soul.

WHEN DEY 'LISTED COL
ORED SOLDIERS

DEY was talkin' in de cabin, dey
    was talkin' in de hall;
But I listened kin' o' keerless, no
    a-t'inkin' 'bout it all;
An' on Sunday, too, I noticed, dey
    was whisp'rin' mighty much
Stan'in' all erroun' de roadsid
    w'en dey let us out o
    chu'ch.
But I did n't t'ink erbout it 'twel
    de middle of de week,
An' my 'Lias come to see me, an
    somehow he could n't speak
Den I seed all in a minute wh
    he 'd come to see m
    for;—
Dey had 'listed colo'ed sojers an
    my 'Lias gwine to wah.

Oh, I hugged him, an' I kissed
him, an' I baiged him not to
go;
But he tol' me dat his conscience,
hit was callin' to him so,
An' he could n't baih to lingah
w'en he had a chanst to
fight
For de freedom dey had gin him
an' de glory of de right.
So he kissed me, an' he lef' me,
w'en I 'd p'omised to be true;
An' dey put a knapsack on him,
an' a coat all colo'ed blue.
So I gin him pap's ol' Bible f'om
de bottom of de draw',—
W'en dey 'listed colo'ed sojers an'
my 'Lias went to wah.

But I t'ought of all de weary miles
dat he would have to tramp,
An' I could n't be contented w'en
dey tuk him to de camp.
W'y my hea't nigh broke wid
grievin' 'twell I seed him on
de street;
Den I felt lak I could go an' th'ow
my body at his feet.
For his buttons was a-shinin', an'
his face was shinin', too,
An' he looked so strong an' mighty
in his coat o' sojer blue,
Dat I hollahed, "Step up, man-
ny," dough my th'oat was so'
an' raw,—
W'en dey 'listed colo'ed sojers an'
my 'Lias went to wah.

Ol' Mis' cried w'en mastah lef'
huh, young Miss mou'ned huh
brothah Ned,
An' I did n't know dey feelin's is
de ve'y wo'ds dey said
W'en I tol' 'em I was so'y. Dey
had done gin up dey all;
But dey only seemed mo' proudah
dat dey men had hyeahed de
call.
Bofe my mastahs went in gray
suits, an' I loved de Yankee
blue,
But I t'ought dat I could sorrer
for de losin' of 'em too;
But I could n't, for I did n't know
de ha'f o' whut I saw,
'Twell dey 'listed colo'ed sojers an'
my 'Lias went to wah.

Mastah Jack come home all sickly;
he was broke for life, dey
said;
An' dey lef' my po' young mastah
some'r's on de roadside,—
dead.
W'en de women cried an' mou'ned
'em, I could feel it thoo an'
thoo,
For I had a loved un fightin' in de
way o' dangah, too.
Den dey tol' me dey had laid him
some'r's way down souf to
res',
Wid de flag dat he had fit for
shinin' daih acrost his
breas'.

Well, I cried, but den I reckon
    dat's whut Gawd had called
    him for,
W'en dey 'listed colo'ed sojers an'
    my 'Lias went to wah.

LINCOLN

Hurt was the nation with a
    mighty wound,
And all her ways were filled with
    clam'rous sound.
Wailed loud the South with unre-
    mitting grief,
And wept the North that could
    not find relief.
Then madness joined its harshest
    tone to strife:
A minor note swelled in the song
    of life.
'Till, stirring with the love that
    filled his breast,
But still, unflinching at the right's
    behest,
Grave Lincoln came, strong
    handed, from afar,
The mighty Homer of the lyre of
    war.
'T was he who bade the raging
    tempest cease,
Wrenched from his harp the har-
    mony of peace,
Muted the strings, that made the
    discord,— Wrong,
And gave his spirit up in thun-
    d'rous song.

Oh mighty Master of the mighty
    lyre,
Earth heard and trembled at thy
    strains of fire:
Earth learned of thee what Heav'n
    already knew,
And wrote thee down among her
    treasured few.

ENCOURAGEMENT

Who dat knockin' at de do'?
Why, Ike Johnson,— yes, fu' sho!
Come in, Ike. I's mighty glad
You come down. I t'ought you's
    mad
At me 'bout de othah night,
An' was stayin' 'way fu' spite.
Say, now, was you mad fu' true
W'en I kin' o' laughed at you?
    Speak up, Ike, an' 'spress yo'se'f.

'T ain't no use a-lookin' sad,
An' a-mekin' out you's mad;
Ef you's gwine to be so glum,
Wondah why you evah come.
I don't lak nobidy 'roun'
Dat jes' shet dey mouf an'
    frown,—
Oh, now, man, don't act a dunce!
Cain't you talk? I tol' you once,
    Speak up, Ike, an' 'spress yo'se'f.

Wha'd you come hyeah fu' to-
    night?
Body'd t'ink yo' haid ain't right.
I's done all dat I kin do,—

Dressed perticler, jes' fu' you;
Reckon I 'd 'a' bettah wo'
My ol' ragged calico.
Aftah all de pains I 's took,
Cain't you tell me how I look?
    Speak up, Ike, an' 'spress yo'se'f.

Bless my soul! I 'mos' fu'got
Tellin' you 'bout Tildy Scott.
Don't you know, come Thu'sday
    night,
She gwine ma'y Lucius White?
Miss Lize say I allus wuh
Heap sight laklier 'n huh;
An' she 'll git me somep'n new,
Ef I wants to ma'y too.
    Speak up, Ike, an' 'spress yo'se'f.

I could ma'y in a week,
Ef de man I wants 'ud speak.
Tildy's presents 'll be fine,
But dey would n't ekal mine.
Him whut gits me fu' a wife
'Ll be proud, you bet yo' life.
I 's had offers; some ain't quit;
But I has n't ma'ied yit!
    Speak up, Ike, an' 'spress yo'se'f.

Ike, I loves you,— yes, I does;
You 's my choice, and allus was.
Laffin' at you ain't no harm.—
Go 'way, dahky, whah 's yo' arm?
Hug me closer — dah, dat 's
    right!
Was n't you a awful sight,
Havin' me to baig you so?
Now ax whut you want to
    know,—
    Speak up, Ike, an' 'spress yo'se'f!

THE BOOGAH MAN

W'en de evenin' shadders
    Come a-glidin' down,
Fallin' black an' heavy
    Ovah hill an' town,
Ef you listen keerful,
    Keerful ez you kin,
So 's you boun' to notice
    Des a drappin' pin;
Den you 'll hyeah a funny
    Soun' ercross de lan';
Lay low; dat 's de callin'
    Of de Boogah Man!

Woo-oo, woo-oo!
    Hyeah him ez he go erlong de
        way;
Woo-oo, woo-oo!
    Don' you wish de night 'ud tu'n
        to day?
Woo-oo, woo-oo!
    Hide yo' little peepers 'hind yo'
        han';
Woo-oo, woo-oo!
    Callin' of de Boogah Man.

W'en de win 's a-shiverin'
    Thoo de gloomy lane,
An' dey comes de patterin'
    Of de evenin' rain,
W'en de owl 's a-hootin',
    Out daih in de wood,
Don' you wish, my honey,
    Dat you had been good?
'T ain't no use to try to
    Snuggle up to Dan;
Bless you, dat 's de callin'
    Of de Boogah Man!

Ef you loves yo' mammy,
　An' you min's yo' pap,
Ef you nevah wriggles
　Outen Sukey's lap;
Ef you says yo' " Lay me "
　Evah single night
'Fo' dey tucks de kivers
　An' puts out de light,
Den de rain kin pattah
　Win' blow lak a fan,
But you need n' bothah
　'Bout de Boogah Man!

THE WRAITH

Ah me, it is cold and chill
　And the fire sobs low in the
　　grate,
While the wind rides by on the
　　hill,
　And the logs crack sharp with
　　hate.

And she, she is cold and sad
　As ever the sinful are,
But deep in my heart I am glad
　For my wound and the coming
　　scar.

Oh, ever the wind rides by
　And ever the raindrops grieve;
But a voice like a woman's sigh
　Says, " Do you believe, be-
　　lieve? "

Ah, you were warm and sweet,
Sweet as the May days be;

Down did I fall at your feet,
　Why did you hearken to me?

Oh, the logs they crack and whine,
　And the water drops from the
　　eaves;
But it is not rain but brine
　Where my dead darling grieves.

And a wraith sits by my side,
　A spectre grim and dark;
Are you gazing here open-eyed
　Out to the lifeless dark?

But ever the wind rides on,
　And we sit close within;
Out of the face of the dawn,
　I and my darling,— sin.

SILENCE

'T is better to sit here beside the
　　sea,
　Here on the spray-kissed beach,
In silence, that between such
　　friends as we
　Is full of deepest speech.

WHIP-POOR-WILL AND
KATY-DID

Slow de night 's a-fallin',
An' I hyeah de callin,
　Out erpon de lonesome hill;
Soun' is moughty dreary,
Solemn-lak an' skeery,
　Sayin' fu' to " whip po' Will."

Now hit 's moughty tryin',
Fu' to hycah dis cryin',
  'Deed hit 's mo' den I kin stan';
Sho' wid all our slippin',
Dey 's enough of whippin'
  'Dout a bird a'visin' any man.

In de noons o' summah
Dey 's anothah hummah
  Sings anothah song instid;
An' his th'oat 's a-swellin'
Wid de joy o' tellin',
  But he says dat " Katy did."

Now I feels onsuhtain;
Won't you raise de cu'tain
  Ovah all de ti'ngs dat 's hid?
W'y dat feathahed p'isen
Goes erbout a-visin'
  Whippin' Will w'en Katy
    did?

'LONG TO'DS NIGHT

Daih 's a moughty soothin'
    feelin'
  Hits a dahky man,
    'Long to'ds night.
W'en de row is mos' nigh ended,
  Den he stops to fan,
    'Long to'ds night.
De blue smoke f'om his cabin
    is a-callin' to him
    " Come; "
He smell de bacon cookin', an' he
    hyeah de fiah hum;

An' he 'mence to sing, 'dough
    wo'kin' putty nigh
    done made him dumb,
    'Long to'ds night.

Wid his hoe erpon his shouldah
  Den he goes erlong,
    'Long to'ds night.
An' he keepin' time a-steppin'
  Wid a little song,
    'Long to'ds night.
De restin'-time 's a-comin', an' de
    time to drink an' eat;
A baby's toddlin' to'ds him on hits
    little dusty feet,
An' a-goin' to'ds his cabin, an'
    his suppah 's moughty
    sweet,
    'Long to'ds night.

Daih his Ca'line min' de kettle,
  Rufus min' de chile,
    'Long to'ds night;
An' de sweat roll down his
    forred,
  Mixin' wid his smile,
    'Long to'ds night.
He toss his piccaninny, an' he hum
    a little chune;
De wokin' all is ovah, an' de sup-
    pah comin' soon;
De wo'kin' time 's Decembah, but
    de restin' time is
    June,
    'Long to'ds night.

Dey 's a kin' o' doleful feelin',
  Hits a tendah place,
    'Long to'ds night;

Dey 's a moughty glory in him
　Shinin' thoo his face,
　　Long to'ds night.
De cabin 's lak de big house, an'
　　　de fiah's lak de sun;
His wife look moughty lakly, an'
　　　de chile de puttiest
　　　one;
W'y, hit 's blessid, jes' a-livin'
　　　w'en a body's wo'k is
　　　done.
　　　'Long to'ds night.

A GRIEVANCE

W'EN de snow 's a-fallin'
　An' de win' is col'.
Mammy 'mence a-callin',
　Den she 'mence to scol',
"Lucius Lishy Brackett,
　Don't you go out do's,
Button up yo' jacket,
　Les'n you 'll git froze."

I sit at de windah
　Lookin' at de groun',
Nuffin nigh to hindah,
　Mammy ain' erroun';
Wish 't she would n' mek me
　Set down in dis chaih;
Pshaw, it would n't tek me
　Long to git some aih.

So I jump down nimble
　Ez a boy kin be,
Dough I 's all a-trimble
　Feahed some one 'll see;
Bet in a half a minute
　I fly out de do'

An' I 's knee-deep in it,
　Dat dah blessed snow.

Den I hyeah a pattah
　Come acrost de flo'.
Den dey comes a clattah
　At de cabin do';
An' my mammy holler
　Spoilin' all my joy,
"Come in f'om dat wallah,
　Don't I see you, boy?"

W'en de snow 's a-sievin'
　Down ez sof' ez meal,
Whut 's de use o' livin'
　'Cept you got de feel
Of de stuff dat 's fallin'
　'Roun' an' white an' damp,
'Dout some one a-callin',
　"Come in hyeah, you scamp!

DINAH KNEADING
DOUGH

I HAVE seen full many a sight
Born of day or drawn by night:
Sunlight on a silver stream,
Golden lilies all a-dream,
Lofty mountains, bold and proud,
Veiled beneath the lacelike cloud;
But no lovely sight I know
Equals Dinah kneading dough.

Brown arms buried elbow-deep
Their domestic rhythm keep,
As with steady sweep they go
Through the gently yielding
　　dough.

Maids may vaunt their finer
    charms—
Naught to me like Dinah's arms;
Girls may draw, or paint, or
    sew —
I love Dinah kneading dough.

Eyes of jet and teeth of pearl,
Hair, some say, too tight a-curl;
But the dainty maid I deem
Very near perfection's dream.
Swift she works, and only flings
Me a glance — the least of things.
And I wonder, does she know
That my heart is in the dough?

TO A CAPTIOUS CRITIC

DEAR critic, who my lightness so
    deplores,
Would I might study to be prince
    of bores,
Right wisely would I rule that
    dull estate —
But, sir, I may not, till you
    abdicate.

DAT OL' MARE O' MINE

WANT to trade me, do you, mis-
    tah? Oh, well, now, I
    reckon not,
W'y you could n't buy my Sukey
    fu' a thousan' on de spot.
    Dat ol' mare o' mine?

Yes, huh coat ah long an' shaggy,
    an' she ain't no shakes to
    see;
Dat's a ring-bone, yes, you right,
    suh, an' she got a on'ry
    knee,
But dey ain't no use in talkin',
    she de only hoss fu' me,
    Dat ol' mare o' mine.

Co'se, I knows dat Suke's con-
    tra'y, an' she moughty ap'
    to vex;
But you got to mek erlowance fu'
    de nature of huh sex;
    Dat ol' mare o' mine.
Ef you pull her on de lef' han';
    she plum 'termined to go
    right,
A cannon could n't skeer huh, but
    she boun' to tek a fright
At a piece o' common paper, or
    anyt'ing whut's white,
    Dat ol' mare o' mine.

W'en my eyes commence to fail
    me, dough, I trus'es to
    huh sight,
An' she 'll tote me safe an' hones'
    on de ve'y da'kes' night,
    Dat ol' mare o' mine.
Ef I whup huh, she jes' switch
    huh tail, an' settle to a
    walk,
Ef I whup huh mo', she shek huh
    haid, an' lak ez not, she
    balk.

But huh sense ain't no ways
    lackin',, she do evah t'ing
    but talk,
    Dat ol' mare o' mine.

But she gentle ez a lady w'en she
    know huh beau kin see.
An' she sholy got mo' gumption
    any day den you or me,
    Dat ol' mare o' mine.
She 's a leetle slow a-goin,' an' she
    moughty ha'd to sta't,
But we 's gittin' ol' togathah, an'
    she 's closah to my hea't,
An' I does n't reckon, mistah, dat
    she 'd sca'cely keer to pa't;
    Dat ol' mare o' mine.

W'y I knows de time dat cidah 's
    kin' o' muddled up my haid,
Ef it had n't been fu' Sukey
    hyeah, I reckon I 'd been
    daid;
    Dat ol' mare o' mine.
But she got me in de middle o'
    de road an' tuk me
    home,
An' she would n't let me wandah,
    ner she would n't let me
    roam,
Dat 's de kin' o' hoss to tie to
    w'en you 's seed de cidah's
    foam,
    Dat ol' mare o' mine.

You kin talk erbout yo' heaven,
    you kin talk erbout yo' hell,

Dey is people, dey is hosses, den
    dey 's cattle, den dey 's—
    well —
    Dat ol' mare o' mine;
She de beatenes' t'ing dat evah
    struck de medders o' de
    town,
An' aldough huh haid ain't fittin'
    fu' to waih no golden
    crown.
D' ain't a blessed way fu' Petah
    fu' to tu'n my Sukey down,
    Dat ol' mare o' mine.

IN THE MORNING

'Lias! 'Lias! Bless de Lawd!
Don' you know de day 's
    erbroad?
Ef you don' git up, you scamp,
Dey 'll be trouble in dis camp.
T'ink I gwine to let you sleep
W'ile I meks yo' boa'd an' keep?
Dat 's a putty howdy-do —
Don' you hyeah me, 'Lias — you?

Bet ef I come crost dis flo'
You won' fin' no time to sno'.
Daylight all a-shinin' in
W'ile you sleep — w'y hit 's a sin!
Ain't de can'le-light enough
To bu'n out widout a snuff,
But you go de mo'nin' thoo
Bu'nin' up de daylight too?

'Lias, don' you hyeah me call?
No use tu'nin' to'ds de wall;

I kin hyeah dat mattuss squeak;
Don' you hyeah me w'en I speak?
Dis hyeah clock done struck off
    six —
Ca'line, bring me dem ah sticks!
Oh, you down, suh; huh, you
    down —
Look hyeah, don' you daih to
    frown.

Ma'ch yo'se'f an' wash yo' face,
Don' you splattah all de place;
I got somep'n else to do,
'Sides jes' cleanin' aftah you.
Tek dat comb an' fix yo' haid —
Looks jes' lak a feddah baid.
Look hyeah, boy, I let you see
You sha' n't roll yo' eyes at me.

Come hyeah; bring me dat ah
    strap!
Boy, I 'll whup you 'twell you
    drap;
You done felt yo'se'f too strong,
An' you sholy got me wrong.
Set down at dat table thaih;
Jes' you whimpah ef you daih!
Evah mo'nin' on dis place,
Seem lak I mus' lose my grace.

Fol' yo' han's an' bow yo' haid —
Wait ontwell de blessin' 's said;
" Lawd, have mussy on ouah
    souls —"
(Don' you daih to tech dem
    rolls —)
" Bless de food we gwine to
    eat —"

(You set still — I *see* yo' feet;
You jes' try dat trick agin!)
" Gin us peace an' joy. Amen!"

THE POET

HE sang of life, serenely sweet,
    With, now and then, a deeper
    note.
    From some high peak, nigh yet
    remote,
He voiced the world's absorbing
    beat.

He sang of love when earth was
    young,
    And Love, itself, was in his
    lays.
    But ah, the world, it turned to
    praise
A jingle in a broken tongue.

A FLORIDA NIGHT

WIN' a-blowin' gentle so de san'
    lay low,
    San' a little heavy f'om de rain,
All de pa'ms a-wavin' an' a-weav-
    in' slow,
    Sighin' lak a sinnah-soul in
    pain.
Alligator grinnin' by de ol'
    lagoon,
Mockin'-bird a-singin' to be big
    full moon,

'Skeeter go a-skimmin' to his
    fightin' chune
    (Lizy Ann's a-waitin' in de
    lane!).

Moccasin a-sleepin' in de cyprus
    swamp;
    Need n't wake de gent'man, not
    fu' me.
Mule, you need n't wake him
    w'en you switch an' stomp,
    Fightin' off a 'skeeter er a flea.
Florida is lovely, she's de fines'
    lan'
Evah seed de sunlight f'om de
    Mastah's han',
'Ceptin' fu' de varmints an' huh
    fleas an' san'
    An' de nights w'en Lizy Ann
    ain' free.

Moon's a-kinder shaddered on de
    melon patch;
    No one ain't a-watchin' ez I
    go.
Climbin' of de fence so's not to
    click de latch
    Meks my gittin' in a little
    slow.
Watermelon smilin' as it say,
    "I's free;"
Alligator boomin', but I let him
    be,
Florida, oh, Florida's de lan' fu'
    me —
    (Lizy Ann a-singin' sweet an'
    low).

DIFFERENCES

My neighbor lives on the hill,
    And I in the valley dwell,
My neighbor must look down on
    me,
    Must I look up? — ah, well,
My neighbor lives on the hill,
    And I in the valley dwell.

My neighbor reads, and prays,
    And I — I laugh, God wot,
And sing like a bird when the
    grass is green
    In my small garden plot;
But ah, he reads and prays,
    And I — I laugh, God wot.

His face is a book of woe,
    And mine is a song of glee;
A slave he is to the great "They
    say,"
    But I — I am bold and free;
No wonder he smacks of woe,
    And I have the tang of glee.

My neighbor thinks me a fool,
    "The same to yourself," say I;
"Why take your books and take
    your prayers,
    Give me the open sky;"
My neighbor thinks me a fool,
    "The same to yourself," say I

LONG AGO

De ol' time's gone, de new
    time's hyeah
    Wid all hits fuss an' feddahs;

I done fu'got de joy an' cheah
  We knowed all kin's o' wed-
      dahs,
I done fu'got each ol'-time hymn
  We ust to sing in meetin';
I's leahned de prah's, so neat an'
      trim,
  De preachah keeps us 'peatin'.

Hang a vine by de chimney side,
  An' one by de cabin do';
An' sing a song fu' de day dat
      died,
  De day of long ergo.

My youf, hit's gone, yes, long
      ergo,
  An' yit I ain't a-moanin';
Hit's fu' somet'ings I ust to
      know
  I set to-night a-honin'.
De pallet on de ol' plank flo',
  De rain bar'l und' de eaves,
De live oak 'fo' de cabin do',
  Whaih de night dove comes an'
      grieves.

Hang a vine by de chimney side,
  An' one by de cabin do';
An' sing a song fu' de day dat
      died,
  De day of long ergo.

I'd lak a few ol' frien's to-night
  To come an' set wid me;
An' let me feel dat ol' delight
  I ust to in dey glee.
But hyeah we is, my pipe an' me,
  Wid no one else erbout;

We bofe is choked ez choked kin
      be,
  An' bofe 'll soon go out.

Hang a vine by de chimney side,
  An' one by de cabin do';
An' sing a song fu' de day dat
      died,
  De day of long ergo.

A PLANTATION MELODY

DE trees is bendin' in de sto'm,
De rain done hid de mountain's
      fo'm,
  I's 'lone an' in distress.
But listen, dah's a voice I hyeah,
A-sayin' to me, loud an' cleah,
  "Lay low in de wildaness."

De lightnin' flash, de bough sway
      low,
My po' sick hea't is trimblin' so,
  It hu'ts my very breas'.
But him dat give de lightnin'
      powah
Jes' bids me in de tryin' howah
  "Lay low in de wildaness."

O brothah, w'en de tempes' beat,
An' w'en yo' weary head an' feet
  Can't fin' no place to res',
Jes' 'membah dat de Mastah's
      nigh,
An' putty soon you'll hyeah de
      cry,
  "Lay low in de wildaness."

O sistah, w'en de rain come down,
An' all yo' hopes is 'bout to
    drown,
    Don't trus' de Mastah less.
He smilin' w'en you t'ink he
    frown,
He ain' gwine let yo' soul sink
    down —
    Lay low in de wildaness.

A SPIRITUAL

DE 'cession 's stahted on de gospel
    way,
    De Capting is a-drawin' nigh:
Bettah stop a-foolin' an' a-try to
    pray;
    Lif' up yo' haid w'en de King
    go by!

Oh, sinnah mou'nin' in de dusty
    road,
    Hyeah 's de minute fu' to dry
    yo' eye:
Dey 's a moughty One a-comin'
    fu' to baih yo' load;
    Lif' up yo' haid w'en de King
    go by!

Oh, widder weepin' by yo' hus-
    ban's grave,
    Hit 's bettah fu' to sing den
    sigh:
Hyeah come de Mastah wid de
    powah to save;
    Lif' up yo' haid w'en de King
    go by!

Oh, orphans a-weepin' lak de wid-
    der do,
    An' I wish you 'd tell me why:
De Mastah is a mammy an' a
    pappy too;
    Lif' up yo' haid w'en de King
    go by!

Oh, Moses sot de sarpint in de
    wildahness
    W'en de chillun had com-
    menced to die:
Some 'efused to look, but hit
    cuohed de res';
    Lif' up yo' haid w'en de King
    go by!

Bow down, bow 'way down,
        Bow down,
But lif' up yo' haid w'en de King
    go by!

THE MEMORY OF MARTHA

OUT in de night a sad bird moans
    An', oh, but hit 's mought
    lonely;
Times I kin sing, but mos'
    groans,
    Fu' oh, but hit 's mought
    lonely!
Is you sleepin' well dis evenin
    Marfy, deah?
W'en I calls you f'om de cabin
    kin you hyeah?
    'T ain't de same ol' place to me
    Nuffin' 's lak hit used to be,

W'en I knowed dat you was allus
  some'ers near.

Down by de road de shadders
  grows,
  An', oh, but hit's moughty
    lonely;
Seem lak de ve'y moonlight
  knows,
  An', oh, but hit's moughty
    lonely!
Does you know, I's cryin' fu' you,
  oh, my wife?
Does you know dey ain't no joy
  no mo' in life?
  An' my only t'ought is dis,
  Dat I's honin' fu' de bliss
Fu' to quit dis groun' o' worri-
  ment an' strife.

Dah on de baid my banjo lays,
  An', oh, but hit's moughty
    lonely;
Can't even sta't a chune o' praise,
  An', oh, but hit's moughty
    lonely!
Oh, hit's moughty slow a-waitin'
  hyeah below.
Is you watchin' fu' me, Marfy,
  at de do'?
  Ef you is, in spite o' sin,
  Dey'll be sho' to let me in,
W'en dey sees yo' face a-shinin',
  den dey'll know.

W'EN I GITS HOME

IT's moughty tiahsome layin'
  'roun'
Dis sorrer-laden earfly groun',
An' oftentimes I thinks, thinks
  I,
'T would be a sweet t'ing des to
  die,
  An' go 'long home.

Home whaih de frien's I loved 'll
  say,
"We've waited fu' you many a
  day,
Come hyeah an' res' yo'se'f, an'
  know
You's done wid sorrer an' wid
  woe,
  Now you's at home."

W'en I gits home some blessid
  day,
I 'lows to th'ow my caihs erway,
An' up an' down de shinin' street,
Go singin' sof' an' low an' sweet,
  W'en I gits home.

I wish de day was neah at han',
I's tiahed of dis grievin' lan',
I's tiahed of de lonely yeahs.
I want to des dry up my teahs,
  An' go 'long home.

Oh, Mastah, won't you sen' de
  call?
My frien's is daih, my hope, my
  all.

I 's waitin' whaih de road is rough,
I want to hyeah you say,
    " Enough,
    Ol' man, come home! "

" HOWDY, HONEY, HOWDY! "

Do' a-stan'in' on a jar, fiah
    a-shinin' thoo,
Ol' folks drowsin' 'roun' de place,
    wide awake is Lou,
W'en I tap, she answeh, an' I see
    huh 'mence to grin,
" Howdy, honey, howdy, won't
    you step right in? "

Den I step erpon de log layin' at
    de do',
Bless de Lawd, huh mammy an'
    huh pap 's done 'menced to
    sno',
Now 's de time, ef evah, ef I 's
    gwine to try an' win,
" Howdy, honey, howdy, won't
    you step right in? "

No use playin' on de aidge,
    trimblin' on de brink,
W'en a body love a gal, tell huh
    whut he t'ink;
W'en huh hea't is open fu' de love
    you gwine to gin,
Pull yo'se'f togethah, suh, an' step
    right in.

Sweetes' imbitation dat a body
    evah hyeahed,

Sweetah den de music of a love-
    sick mockin'-bird,
Comin' f'om de gal you loves bet-
    tah den yo' kin,
" Howdy, honey, howdy, won't
    you step right in? "

At de gate o' heaven w'en de
    storm o' life is pas',
'Spec' I 'll be a-stan'in', 'twell de
    Mastah say at las',
" Hyeah he stan' all weary, but
    he winned his fight wid sin.
Howdy, honey, howdy, won't you
    step right in? "

THE UNSUNG HEROES

A song for the unsung heroes
    who rose in the country's
    need,
When the life of the land was
    threatened by the slaver's
    cruel greed,
For the men who came from the
    cornfield, who came from the
    plough and the flail,
Who rallied round when they
    heard the sound of the
    mighty man of the rail.

They laid them down in the val-
    leys, they laid them down in
    the wood,
And the world looked on at the
    work they did, and whis-
    pered, " It is good."

They fought their way on the hillside, they fought their way in the glen,
And God looked down on their sinews brown, and said, " I have made them men."

They went to the blue lines gladly, and the blue lines took them in,
And the men who saw their muskets' fire thought not of their dusky skin.
The gray lines rose and melted beneath their scathing showers,
And they said, " 'T is true, they have force to do, these old slave boys of ours."

Ah, Wagner saw their glory, and Pillow knew their blood,
That poured on a nation's altar, a sacrificial flood.
Port Hudson heard their war-cry that smote its smoke-filled air,
And the old free fires of their savage sires again were kindled there.

They laid them down where the rivers the greening valleys gem.
And the song of the thund'rous cannon was their sole requiem,

And the great smoke wreath that mingled its hue with the dusky cloud,
Was the flag that furled o'er a saddened world, and the sheet that made their shroud.

Oh, Mighty God of the Battles Who held them in Thy hand,
Who gave them strength through the whole day's length, to fight for their native land,
They are lying dead on the hillsides, they are lying dead on the plain,
And we have not fire to smite the lyre and sing them one brief strain.

Give, Thou, some seer the power to sing them in their might,
The men who feared the master's whip, but did not fear the fight;
That he may tell of their virtues as minstrels did of old,
Till the pride of face and the hate of race grow obsolete and cold.

A song for the unsung heroes who stood the awful test,
When the humblest host that the land could boast went forth to meet the best;
A song for the unsung heroes who fell on the bloody sod,

Who fought their way from night
    to day and struggled up to
    God.

THE POOL

By the pool that I see in my
    dreams, dear love,
    I have sat with you time and
        again;
And listened beneath the dank
    leaves, dear love,
    To the sibilant sound of the
        rain.

And the pool, it is silvery bright,
    dear love,
    And as pure as the heart of a
        maid,
As sparkling and dimpling, it
    darkles and shines
    In the depths of the heart of
    the glade.

But, oh, I 've a wish in my soul,
    dear love,
    (The wish of a dreamer, it
        seems,)
That I might wash free of my
    sins, dear love,
    In the pool that I see in my
    dreams.

POSSESSION

Whose little lady is you, chile,
    Whose little gal is you?

What 's de use o' kiver'n up yo'
    face?
    Chile, dat ain't de way to do
Lemme see yo' little eyes,
    Tek yo' little han's down nice,
Lawd, you wuff a million bills,
    Huh uh, chile, dat ain't yo'
    price.

Honey, de money ain't been made
    Dat dey could pay fu' you;
'T ain't no use a-biddin'; you too
    high
    Fu' de riches' Jap er Jew.
Lemme see you smilin' now,
    How dem teef o' yo'n do
    shine,
An' de t'ing dat meks me laff
    Is dat all o' you is mine.

How 's I gwine to tell you how I
    feel,
    How 's I gwine to weigh yo'
    wuff?
Oh, you sholy is de sweetes' t'ing
    Walkin' on dis blessed earf.
Possum is de sweetes' meat,
    Cidah is the nices' drink,
But my little lady-bird
    Is de bes' of all, I t'ink.

Talk erbout 'uligion he'pin' folks
    All thoo de way o' life,
Gin de res' 'uligion, des' gin me
    You, my little lady-wife.
Den de days kin come all ha'd,
    Den de nights kin come all
    black,

Des' you tek me by de han',
　An' I 'll stumble on de track.

Stumble on de way to Gawd, my
　　chile,
　Stumble on, an' mebbe fall;
But I 'll keep a-trottin', while you
　　lead on,
　Pickin' an' a-trottin', dat 's all.
Hol' me mighty tight, dough,
　　chile,
　Fu' hit 's rough an' rocky lan',
Heaben 's at de en', I know,
　So I 's leanin' on yo' han'.

THE OLD FRONT GATE

W'EN daih 's chillun in de house,
　Dey keep on a-gittin' tall;
But de folks don' seem to see
　Dat dey 's growin' up at all,
'Twell dey fin' out some fine day
　Dat de gals has 'menced to
　　grow,
W'en dey notice as dey pass
　Dat de front gate 's saggin' low.

W'en de hinges creak an' cry,
　An' de bahs go slantin' down,
You kin reckon dat hit 's time
　Fu' to cas' yo' eye erroun',
'Cause daih ain't no 'sputin' dis,
　Hit 's de trues' sign to show
Dat daih 's cou'tin' goin' on
　W'en de ol' frcnt gate sags low.

Oh, you grumble an' complain,
　An' you prop dat gate up right;
But you notice right nex' day
　Dat hit 's in de same ol' plight.
So you fin' dat hit 's a rule,
　An' daih ain' no use to blow,
W'en de gals is growin' up,
　Dat de front gate will sag low.

Den you t'ink o' yo' young days,
　W'en you cou'ted Sally Jane,
An' you so't o' feel ashamed
　Fu' to grumble an' complain,
'Cause yo' ricerlection says,
　An' you know hits wo'ds is so,
Dat huh pappy had a time
　Wid his front gate saggin' low.

So you jes' looks on an' smiles
　At 'em leanin' on de gate,
Tryin' to t'ink whut he kin say
　Fu' to keep him daih so late,
But you lets dat gate erlone,
　Fu' yo' 'sperunce goes to show,
'Twell de gals is ma'ied off,
　It gwine keep on saggin' low.

DIRGE FOR A SOLDIER

IN the east the morning comes,
Hear the rollin' of the drums
　　On the hill.
But the heart that beat as they
　　beat
In the battle's raging day heat
　　Lieth still.
Unto him the night has come,
Though they roll the morning
　　drum.

What is in the bugle's blast?
It is: "Victory at last!
   Now for rest."
But, my comrades, come behold
   him,
Where our colors now enfold him,
   And his breast
Bares no more to meet the blade,
But lies covered in the shade.

What a stir there is to-day!
They are laying him away
   Where he fell.
There the flag goes draped before
   him;
Now they pile the grave sod o'er
   him
   With a knell.
And he answers to his name
In the higher ranks of fame.

There's a woman left to mourn
For the child that she has borne
   In travail.
But her heart beats high and
   higher,
With the patriot mother's fire,
   At the tale.
She has borne and lost a son,
But her work and his are done.

Fling the flag out, let it wave;
They're returning from the
   grave —
   "Double quick!"
And the cymbals now are crash-
   ing,

Bright his comrades' eyes are flash-
   ing
   From the thick
Battle-ranks which knew him
   brave,
No tears for a hero's grave.

In the east the morning comes,
Hear the rattle of the drums
   Far away.
Now no time for grief's pursuing,
Other work is for the doing,
   Here to-day.
He is sleeping, let him rest
With the flag across his breast.

A FROLIC

Swing yo' lady roun' an' roun',
   Do de bes' you know;
Mek yo' bow an' p'omenade
   Up an' down de flo';
Mek dat banjo hump huhse'f,
   Listen at huh talk:
Mastah gone to town to-night;
   'T ain't no time to walk.

Lif' yo' feet an' flutter thoo,
   Run, Miss Lucy, run;
Reckon you'll be cotched an'
   kissed
   'Fo' de night is done.
You don't need to be so proud —
   I's a-watchin' you,
An' I's layin' lots o' plans
   Fu' to git you, too.

Moonlight on de cotton-fiel'
   Shinin' sof' an' white,
Whippo'will a-tellin' tales
   Out thaih ir de night;
An' yo' cabin 's 'crost de lot:
   Run, Miss Lucy, run;
Reckon you 'll be cotched an'
     kissed
   'Fo' de night is done.

NODDIN' BY DE FIRE

SOME folks t'inks hit 's right an'
    p'opah,
   Soon ez bedtime come erroun',
Fu' to scramble to de kiver,
   Lak dey 'd hyeahed de trumpet
     soun'.
But dese people dey all misses
   Whut I mos'ly does desiah;
Dat 's de settin' roun' an' dozin',
   An' a-noddin' by de fiah.

When you 's tiahed out a-hoein',
   Er a-followin' de plough,
Whut 's de use of des a-fallin'
   On yo' pallet lak a cow?
W'y, de fun is all in waitin'
   In de face of all de tiah,
An' a-dozin' and a-drowsin'
   By a good ol' hick'ry fiah.

Oh, you grunts an' groans an'
    mumbles
   Case yo' bones is full o' col',

Dough you feels de joy a-tricklin'
   Roun' de co'nahs of yo' soul.
An' you 'low anothah minute
   'S sho to git you wa'm an'
    dryah,
W'en you set up pas' yo' bedtime,
   Case you hates to leave de fiah.

Whut 's de use o' downright
    sleepin'?
   You can't feel it while it las',
An' you git up feelin' sorry
   W'en de time fu' it is pas'.
Seem to me dat time too precious,
   An' de houahs too short entiah,
Fu' to sleep, w'en you could spen'
    'em
    Des a-noddin' by de fiah.

LOVE'S CASTLE

KEY and bar, key and bar,
   Iron bolt and chain!
And what will you do when the
    King comes
   To enter his domain?

Turn key and lift bar,
   Loose, oh, bolt and chain!
Open the door and let him in,
   And then lock up again.

But, oh, heart, and woe, heart,
   Why do you ache so sore?
Never a moment's peace have you
   Since Love hath passed the door.

Turn key and lift bar,
And loose bolt and chain;
But Love took in his esquire, Grief,
And there they both remain.

MORNING SONG OF LOVE

DARLING, my darling, my heart is
on the wing,
It flies to thee this morning like
a bird,
Like happy birds in springtime my
spirits soar and sing,
The same sweet song thine ears
have often heard.

The sun is in my window, the
shadow on the lea,
The wind is moving in the
branches green,
And all my life, my darling, is
turning unto thee,
And kneeling at thy feet, my
own, my queen.

The golden bells are ringing across
the distant hill,
Their merry peals come to me
soft and clear,
But in my heart's deep chapel all
incense-filled and still
A sweeter bell is sounding for
thee, dear.

The bell of love invites thee to
come and seek the shrine

Whose altar is erected unto
thee,
The offerings, the sacrifice, the
prayers, the chants are
thine,
And I, my love, thy humble
priest will be.

ON A CLEAN BOOK

TO F. N.

LIKE sea-washed sand upon the
shore,
So fine and clean the tale,
So clear and bright I almost see,
The flashing of a sail.

The tang of salt is in its veins,
The freshness of the spray
God give you love and lore and
strength,
To give us such alway.

TO THE EASTERN SHORE

I 's feelin' kin' o' lonesome in my
little room to-night,
An' my min 's done los' de min-
utes an' de miles,
W'ile it teks me back a-flyin' to
de country of delight,
Whaih de Chesapeake goes
grumblin' er wid smiles.
Oh, de ol' plantation 's callin'
to me, Come, come back,

Hyeah 's de place fu' you to la-
   bouh an' to res',
   'Fu my sandy roads is gleam-
   in' w'ile de city ways is
   black;
Come back, honey, case yo'
   country home is bes'.

I know de moon is shinin' down
   erpon de Eastern sho',
An' de bay 's a-sayin' " How-
   dy " to de lan';
An' de folks is all a-settin' out
   erroun' de cabin do',
   Wid dey feet a-restin' in de sil-
   vah san';
   An' de ol' plantation 's callin'
   to me, Come, oh, come,
F'om de life dat 's des' a-waih-
   in' you erway,
   F'om de trouble an' de bustle,
   an' de agernizin' hum
Dat de city keeps ergoin' all de
   day.

I 's tiahed of de city, tek me back
   to Sandy Side,
   Whaih de po'est ones kin live
   an' play an' eat;
Whaih we draws a simple livin'
   f'om de fo'est an' de tide,
   An' de days ah faih, an' evah
   night is sweet.
      Fu' de ol' plantation 's callin'
      to me, Come, oh, come.
   An' de Chesapeake 's a-sayin'
   " Dat 's de t'ing,"

W'ile my little cabin beckons,
   dough his mouf is closed
   an' dumb,
I 's a-comin, an' my hea't be-
   gins to sing.

RELUCTANCE

WILL I have some mo' dat pie?
No, ma'am, thank-ee, dat is —
      I —
   Bettah quit daihin' me.
Dat ah pie look sutny good:
How 'd you feel now ef I would?
I don' reckon dat I should;
   Bettah quit daihin' me.

Look hyeah, I gwine tell de truf,
Mine is sholy one sweet toof:
   Bettah quit daihin' me.
Yass'm, yass'm, dat 's all right,
I 's done tried to be perlite:
But dat pie 's a lakly sight,
   Wha 's de use o' daihin' me?

My, yo' lips is full an' red,
Don't I wish you 'd tu'n yo' haid?
   Bettah quit daihin' me.
Dat ain't faih, now, honey chile,
I 's gwine lose my sense erwhile
Ef you des set daih an' smile,
   Bettah quit daihin' me.

Nuffin' don' look ha'f so fine
Ez dem teef, deah, w'en dey shine:
   Bettah quit daihin' me.
Now look hyeah, I tells you dis;

I 'll give up all othah bliss
Des to have one little kiss,
　Bettah quit daihin' me.

Laws, I teks yo' little han',
Ain't it tendah? bless de lan'—
　Bettah quit daihin' me.
I 's so lonesome by myse'f,
'D ain't no fun in livin' lef';
Dis hyeah life 's ez dull ez def:
　Bettah quit daihin' me.

Why n't you tek yo' han' erway?
Yass, I 'll hol' it: but I say
　Bettah quit daihin' me.
Holin' han's is sholy fine.
Seems lak dat 's de weddin' sign.
Wish you 'd say dat you 'd be
　mine; —
　　Dah you been daihin' me.

BALLADE

By Mystic's banks I held my
　dream.
　(I held my fishing rod as well,)
The vision was of dace and bream,
　A fruitless vision, sooth to tell.
　But round about the sylvan dell
Were other sweet Arcadian
　shrines,
　Gone now, is all the rural spell,
Arcadia has trolley lines.

Oh, once loved, sluggish, darkling
　stream,

For me no more, thy waters
　swell,
Thy music now the engines'
　scream,
　Thy fragrance now the factory's
　　smell;
　Too near for me the clanging
　　bell;
A false light in the water shines
　While Solitude lists to her
　　knell,—
Arcadia has trolley lines.

Thy wooded lanes with shade and
　gleam
　Where bloomed the fragrant as-
　　phodel,
Now bleak commercially teem
　With signs "To Let," "To
　　Buy," "To Sell."
　And Commerce holds them
　　fierce and fell;
With vulgar sport she now com-
　bines
　Sweet Nature's piping voice to
　　quell.
Arcadia has trolley lines.

L'ENVOI.

Oh, awful Power whose works
　repel
　The marvel of the earth's de-
　　signs,—
I 'll hie me otherwhere to dwell,
Arcadia has trolley lines.

SPEAKIN' AT DE COU'T-HOUSE

DEY been speakin' at de cou't-
house,
  An' laws-a-massy me,
'T was de beatness kin' o' doin's
  Dat evah I did see.
Of cose I had to be dah
  In de middle o' de crowd,
An' I hallohed wid de othahs,
  W'en de speakah riz and bowed.

I was kind o' disapp'inted
  At de smallness of de man,
Case I 'd allus pictered great folks
  On a mo' expansive plan;
But I t'ought I could respect him
  An' tek in de wo'ds he said,
Fu' dey sho was somp'n knowin'
  In de bald spot on his haid.

But hit did seem so't o' funny
  Aftah waitin' fu' a week
Dat de people kep' on shoutin'
  So de man des could n't speak;
De ho'ns dey blared a little,
  Den dey let loose on de
    drums,—
Some one tol' me dey was playin'
  "See de conkerin' hero comes."

"Well," says I, "you all is white
  folks,
But you 's sutny actin' queer,
What 's de use of heroes comin'
  Ef dey cain't talk w'en dey 's
    here?"

Aftah while dey let him open,
  An' dat man he waded in,
An' he fit de wahs all ovah
  Winnin' victeries lak sin.

W'en he come down to de present,
  Den he made de feathahs fly.
He des waded in on money,
  An' he played de ta'iff high.
An' he said de colah question,
  Hit was ovah, solved, an' done,
Dat de dahky was his brothah,
  Evah blessed mothah's son.

Well he settled all de trouble
  Dat 's been pesterin' de lan',
Den he set down mid de cheerin'
  An' de playin' of de ban'.
I was feelin' moughty happy
  'Twell I hyeahed somebody
    speak,
"Well, dat 's his side of de bus'-
  ness,
  But you wait for Jones nex'
    week."

BLACK SAMSON OF BRANDYWINE

"In the fight at Brandywine, Black
Samson, a giant negro armed with a
scythe, sweeps his way through the
red ranks. . . ." C. M. SKINNER'S
"*Myths and Legends of Our Own
Land.*"

GRAY are the pages of record,
  Dim are the volumes of eld;
Else had old Delaware told us
  More that her history held.

Told us with pride in the story,
  Honest and noble and fine,
More of the tale of my hero,
  Black Samson of Brandywine.

Sing of your chiefs and your no-
    bles,
  Saxon and Celt and Gaul,
Breath of mine ever shall join you,
  Highly I honor them all.
Give to them all of their glory,
  But for this noble of mine,
Lend him a tithe of your tribute,
  Black Samson of Brandywine.

There in the heat of the battle,
  There in the stir of the fight,
Loomed he, an ebony giant,
  Black as the pinions of night.
Swinging his scythe like a mower
  Over a field of grain,
Needless the care of the gleaners,
  Where he had passed amain.

Straight through the human har-
    vest,
  Cutting a bloody swath,
Woe to you, soldier of Briton!
  Death is abroad in his path.
Flee from the scythe of the reaper,
  Flee while the moment is thine,
None may with safety withstand
    him,
  Black Samson of Brandywine.

Was he a freeman or bondman?
  Was he a man or a thing?

What does it matter? His brav
    'ry
  Renders him royal — a king.
If he was only a chattel,
  Honor the ransom may pay
Of the royal, the loyal black giant
  Who fought for his country
    that day.

Noble and bright is the story,
  Worthy the touch of the lyre,
Sculptor or poet should find it
  Full of the stuff to inspire.
Beat it in brass and in copper,
  Tell it in storied line,
So that the world may remember
  Black Samson of Brandywine.

THE LOOKING-GLASS

DINAH stan' befo' de glass,
  Lookin' moughty neat,
An' huh purty shadder sass
  At huh haid an' feet.
While she sasshay 'roun' an' bow
Smilin' den an' poutin' now,
An' de lookin'-glass, I 'low
  Say: " Now, ain't she sweet? "

All she do, de glass it see,
  Hit des see, no mo',
Seems to me, hit ought to be
  Drappin' on de flo'.
She go w'en huh time git slack
Kissin' han's an' smilin' back,
Lawsy, how my lips go smack,
  Watchin' at de do'

Wisht I was huh lookin'-glass,
  W'en she kissed huh han';
Does you t'ink I 'd let it pass,
  Settin' on de stan'?
No; I'd des' fall down an' break,
  Kin' o' glad 't uz fu' huh sake;
But de diffunce, dat whut make
  Lookin'-glass an' man.

A MISTY DAY

Heart of my heart, the day is
  chill,
The mist hangs low o'er the
  wooded hill,
The soft white mist and the heavy
  cloud
The sun and the face of heaven
  shroud.
The birds are thick in the dripping
  trees,
That drop their pearls to the beg-
  gar breeze;
No songs are rife where songs are
  wont,
Each singer crouches in his haunt.

Heart of my heart, the day is chill,
Whene'er thy loving voice is still,
The cloud and mist hide the sky
  from me,
Whene'er thy face I cannot see.
My thoughts fly back from the
  chill without,
My mind in the storm drops
  doubt on doubt,

No songs arise. Without thee,
  love,
My soul sinks down like a fright-
  ened dove.

LI'L' GAL

Oh, de weathah it is balmy an' de
  breeze is sighin' low.
      Li'l' gal,
An' de mockin' bird is singin' in
  de locus' by de do',
      Li'l' gal;
Dere 's a hummin' an' a bummin'
  in de lan' f'om eas' to wes',
I 's a-sighin' fu' you, honey, an' I
  nevah know no res'.
Fu' dey 's lots o' trouble brewin'
  an' a-stewin' in my breas',
      Li'l' gal.

Whut 's de mattah wid de weathah,
  whut 's de mattah wid de
  breeze,
      Li'l' gal?
Whut 's de mattah wid de locus'
  dat 's a-singin' in de trees,
      Li'l' gal?
W'y dey knows dey ladies love 'em,
  an' dey knows dey love 'em
  true,
An' dey love 'em back, I reckon,
  des' lak I 's a-lovin' you;
Dat 's de reason dey 's a-weavin'
  an' a-sighin', thoo an' thoo,
      Li'l' gal.

Don't you let no da'ky fool you
 'cause de clo'es he waihs is
 fine,
  Li'l' gal.
Dey's a hones' hea't a-beatin' un-
 nerneaf dese rags o' mine,
  Li'l' gal.
C'ose dey ain' no use in mockin'
 whut de birds an' weathah do,
But I's so'y I cain't 'spress it w'en
 I knows I loves you true,
Dat's de reason I's a-sighin' an'
 a-singin now fu' you,
  Li'l' gal.

DOUGLASS

Ah, Douglass, we have fall'n on
 evil days,
 Such days as thou, not even thou
  didst know,
 When thee, the eyes of that
  harsh long ago
Saw, salient, at the cross of devious
 ways,
And all the country heard thee
 with amaze.
 Not ended then, the passionate
  ebb and flow,
 The awful tide that battled to
  and fro;
We ride amid a tempest of dis-
 praise.

Now, when the waves of swift dis-
 sension swarm,

And Honor, the strong pilot,
 lieth stark,
Oh, for thy voice high-sounding
 o'er the storm,
 For thy strong arm to guide the
  shivering bark,
The blast-defying power of thy
 form,
 To give us comfort through the
  lonely dark.

WHEN SAM'L SINGS

Hyeah dat singin' in de medders
 Whaih de folks is mekin' hay?
Wo'k is pretty middlin' heavy
 Fu' a man to be so gay.
You kin tell dey's somep'n special
 F'om de canter o' de song;
Somep'n sholy pleasin' Sam'l,
 W'en he singin' all day long.

Hyeahd him wa'blin' 'way dis
 mo'nin'
 'Fo' 't was light enough to see.
Seem lak music in de evenin'
 Allus good enough fu' me.
But dat man commenced to hollah
 'Fo' he'd even washed his face;
Would you b'lieve, de scan'lous
 rascal
 Woke de birds erroun' de place?

Sam'l took a trip a-Sad'day;
 Dressed hisse'f in all he had,
Tuk a cane an' went a-strollin',
 Lookin' mighty pleased an' glad.

Some folks don' know whut de
    mattah,
  But I do, you bet yo' life;
Sam'l smilin' an' a-singin'
    'Case he been to see his wife.

She live on de fu' plantation,
    Twenty miles erway er so;
But huh man is mighty happy
    W'en he git de chanst to go.
Walkin' allus ain' de nices'—
    Mo'nin' fin's him on de way—
But he allus comes back smilin',
    Lak his pleasure was his pay.

Den he do a heap o' talkin',
    Do' he mos'ly kin' o' still,
But de wo'ds, dey gits to runnin'
    Lak de watah fu' a mill.
"Whut 's de use o' havin' trouble,
    Whut 's de use o' havin' strife?"
Dat 's de way dis Sam'l preaches
    W'en he been to see his wife.

An' I reckon I git jealous,
    Fu' I laff an' joke an' sco'n,
An' I say, "Oh, go on, Sam'l,
    Des go on, an' blow yo' ho'n."
But I know dis comin' Sad'day,
    Dey 'll be brighter days in life;
An' I 'll be ez glad ez Sam'l
    W'en I go to see my wife.

BOOKER T. WASHINGTON

THE word is writ that he who
    runs may read.
What is the passing breath of
    earthly fame?
But to snatch glory from the hands
    of blame—
That is to be, to live, to strive in-
    deed.
A poor Virginia cabin gave the
    seed,
And from its dark and lowly door
    there came
A peer of princes in the world's
    acclaim,
A master spirit for the nation's
    need.
Strong, silent, purposeful beyond
    his kind,
    The mark of rugged force on
        brow and lip,
Straight on he goes, nor turns to
    look behind
    Where hot the hounds come
        baying at his hip;
With one idea foremost in his
    mind,
    Like the keen prow of some on-
        forging ship.

THE MONK'S WALK

IN this sombre garden close
What has come and passed, who
    knows?
What red passion, what white
    pain
Haunted this dim walk in vain?

Underneath the ivied wall,
Where the silent shadows fall,

Lies the pathway chill and damp
Where the world-quit dreamers
    tramp.

Just across, where sunlight burns,
Smiling at the mourning ferns,
Stand the roses, side by side,
Nodding in their useless pride.

Ferns and roses, who shall say
What you witness day by day?
Covert smile or dropping eye,
As the monks go pacing by.

Has the novice come to-day
Here beneath the wall to pray?
Has the young monk, lately chid-
    den,
Sung his lyric, sweet, forbidden?

Tell me, roses, did you note
That pale father's throbbing
    throat?
Did you hear him murmur,
    " Love! "
As he kissed a faded glove?

Mourning ferns, pray tell me why
Shook you with that passing sigh?
Is it that you chanced to spy
Something in the Abbot's eye?

Here no dream, nor thought of sin,
Where no worlding enters in;
Here no longing, no desire,
Heat nor flame of earthly fire.

Branches waving green above,
Whisper naught of life nor love;

Softened winds that seem a breath,
Perfumed, bring no fear of death.

Is it living thus to live?
Has life nothing more to give?
Ah, no more of smile or sigh —
Life, the world, and love, good-
    bye.

Gray, and passionless, and dim,
Echoing of the solemn hymn,
Lies the walk, 'twixt fern and rose,
Here within the garden close.

LOVE-SONG

IF Death should claim me for her
    own to-day,
    And softly I should falter from
        your side,
Oh, tell me, loved one, would my
        memory stay,
    And would my image in your
        heart abide?
Or should I be as some forgotten
        dream,
    That lives its little space, then
        fades entire?
Should Time send o'er you its
        relentless stream,
    To cool your heart, and quench
        for aye love's fire?

I would not for the world, love,
        give you pain,
    Or ever compass what would
        cause you grief;

And, oh, how well I know that
  tears are vain!
  But love is sweet, my dear, and
  life is brief;
So if some day before you I should
  go
  Beyond the sound and sight of
  song and sea,
'T would give my spirit stronger
  wings to know
  That you remembered still and
  wept for me.

SLOW THROUGH THE DARK

Slow moves the pageant of a
  climbing race;
  Their footsteps drag far, far be-
  low the height,
  And, unprevailing by their ut-
  most might,
Seem faltering downward from
  each hard won place.
No strange, swift-sprung excep-
  tion we; we trace
  A devious way thro' dim, uncer-
  tain light,—
  Our hope, through the long
  vistaed years, a sight
Of that our Captain's soul sees
  face to face.
  Who, faithless, faltering that
  the road is steep,
Now raiseth up his drear insistent
  cry?

Who stoppeth here to spend a
  while in sleep
Or curseth that the storm obscures
  the sky?
  Heed not the darkness round
  you, dull and deep;
The clouds grow thickest when
  the summit's nigh.

THE MURDERED LOVER

Say a mass for my soul's repose,
  my brother,
  Say a mass for my soul's repose,
  I need it,
Lovingly lived we, the sons of one
  mother,
  Mine was the sin, but I pray
  you not heed it.

Dark were her eyes as the sloe and
  they called me,
  Called me with voice indepen-
  dent of breath.
God! how my heart beat; her
  beauty appalled me,
  Dazed me, and drew to the sea-
  brink of death.

Lithe was her form like a willow.
  She beckoned,
  What could I do save to follow
  and follow,
Nothing of right or result could be
  reckoned;
  Life without her was unworthy
  and hollow.

Ay, but I wronged thee, my
    brother, my brother;
  Ah, but I loved her, thy beauti-
    ful wife.
Shade of our father, and soul of
    our mother,
  Have I not paid for my love
    with my life?

Dark was the night when, re-
    vengeful, I met you,
  Deep in the heart of a desolate
    land.
Warm was the life-blood which
    angrily wet you
  Sharp was the knife that I felt
    from your hand.

Wept you, oh, wept you, alone by
    the river,
  When my stark carcass you
    secretly sank.
Ha, now I see that you tremble
    and shiver;
  'T was but my spirit that passed
    when you shrank!

Weep not, oh, weep not, 't is over,
    't is over;
  Stir the dark weeds with the
    turn of the tide;
Go, thou hast sent me forth, ever
    a rover,
  Rest and the sweet realm of
    heaven denied.

Say a mass for my soul's repose,
    my brother,

Say a mass for my soul, I need
    it.
Sin of mine was it, and sin of no
    other,
  Mine was it all, but I pray you
    not heed it.

PHILOSOPHY

I BEEN t'inkin' 'bout de preachah;
    whut he said de othah
    night,
  'Bout hit bein' people's dooty,
    fu' to keep dey faces bright;
How one ought to live so pleasant
    dat ouah tempah never riles,
  Meetin' evahbody roun' us wid
    ouah very nicest smiles.

Dat 's all right, I ain't a-sputin'
    not a t'ing dat soun's lak
    fac',
  But you don't ketch folks a-grin-
    nin' wid a misery in de
    back;
An' you don't fin' dem a-smilin'
    w'en dey 's hongry ez kin
    be,
  Leastways, dat 's how human
    natur' allus seems to 'pear
    to me.

We is mos' all putty likely fu' to
    have our little cares,
  An' I think we 'se doin' fus' rate
    w'en we jes' go long an'
    bears,

Widout breakin' up ouah faces in
   a sickly so't o' grin,
  W'en we knows dat in ouah in-
    nards we is p'intly mad ez
    sin.

Oh dey 's times fu' bein' pleasant
    an' fu' goin' smilin' roun',
'Cause I don't believe in people
    allus totin' roun' a frown,
But it 's easy 'nough to titter w'en
    de stew is smokin' hot,
  But hit 's mighty ha'd to giggle
    w'en dey 's nuffin' in de
    pot.

A PREFERENCE

MASTAH drink his ol' Made'a,
  Missy drink huh sherry wine,
Ovahseah lak his whiskey,
  But dat othah drink is mine,
    Des' 'lasses an' watah, 'lasses
    an' watah.

W'en you git a steamin' hoe-cake
  On de table, go way, man!
'D ain but one t'ing to go wid it,
  'Sides de gravy in de pan,
    Dat 's 'lasses an' watah, 'lasses
    an' watah.

W'en hit 's 'possum dat you eatin',
  'Simmon beer is moughty sweet;
But fu' evahday consumin'

'D ain't no mo'tal way to beat
  Des' 'lasses an' watah, 'lasses
  an' watah.

W'y de bees is allus busy,
  An' ain' got no time to was'?
Hit 's beca'se dey knows de honey
  Dey 's a makin', gwine to tas'
    Lak 'lasses an' watah, 'lasses
    an' watah.

Oh, hit 's moughty mil' an'
    soothin',
  An' hit don' go to yo' haid;
Dat 's de reason I 's a-backin'
  Up de othah wo'ds I said,
    "Des 'lasses an' watah, 'lasses
    an' watah."

THE DEBT

THIS is the debt I pay
Just for one riotous day,
Years of regret and grief,
Sorrow without relief.

Pay it I will to the end —
Until the grave, my friend,
Gives me a true release —
Gives me the clasp of peace.

Slight was the thing I bought,
Small was the debt I thought,
Poor was the loan at best —
God! but the interest!

ON THE DEDICATION OF DOROTHY HALL

TUSKEGEE, ALA., APRIL 22, 1901.

NOT to the midnight of the gloomy
past,
  Do we revert to-day; we look
    upon
The golden present and the future
  vast
  Whose vistas show us visions of
    the dawn.

Nor shall the sorrows of departed
  years
  The sweetness of our tranquil
    souls annoy,
The sunshine of our hopes dispels
  the tears,
  And clears our eyes to see this
    later joy.

Not ever in the years that God
  hath given
  Have we gone friendless down
    the thorny way,
Always the clouds of pregnant
  black were riven
  By flashes from His own eternal
    day.

The women of a race should be its
  pride;
  We glory in the strength our
    mothers had,
We glory that this strength was
  not denied

To labor bravely, nobly, and be
  glad.

God give to these within this tem-
  ple here,
  Clear vision of the dignity of
    toil,
That virtue in them may its blos-
  soms rear
  Unspotted, fragrant, from the
    lowly soil.

God bless the givers for their noble
  deed,
  Shine on them with the mercy
    of Thy face,
Who come with open hearts to
  help and speed
  The striving women of a strug-
    gling race.

A ROADWAY

LET those who will stride on their
  barren roads
And prick themselves to haste with
  self-made goads,
Unheeding, as they struggle day
  by day,
If flowers be sweet or skies be blue
  or gray:
For me, the lone, cool way by purl-
  ing brooks,
The solemn quiet of the woodland
  nooks,
A song-bird somewhere trilling
  sadly gay,

A pause to pick a flower beside the way.

BY RUGGED WAYS

By rugged ways and thro' the night
We struggle blindly toward the light;
And groping, stumbling, ever pray
For sight of long delaying day.
The cruel thorns beside the road
Stretch eager points our steps to goad,
And from the thickets all about
Detaining hands reach threatening out.

" Deliver us, oh, Lord," we cry,
Our hands uplifted to the sky.
No answer save the thunder's peal,
And onward, onward, still we reel.
" Oh, give us now thy guiding light; "
Our sole reply, the lightning's blight.
" Vain, vain," cries one, " in vain we call; "
But faith serene is over all.

Beside our way the streams are dried,
And famine mates us side by side.
Discouraged and reproachful eyes
Seek once again the frowning skies.
Yet shall there come, spite storm and shock,
A Moses who shall smite the rock,
Call manna from the Giver's hand,
And lead us to the promised land!

The way is dark and cold and steep,
And shapes of horror murder sleep,
And hard the unrelenting years;
But 'twixt our sighs and moans and tears,
We still can smile, we still can sing,
Despite the arduous journeying.
For faith and hope their courage lend,
And rest and light are at the end.

LOVE'S SEASONS

When the bees are humming in the honeysuckle vine
    And the summer days are in their bloom,
Then my love is deepest, oh, dearest heart of mine,
When the bees are humming in the honeysuckle vine.

When the winds are moaning o'er the meadows chill and gray,
    And the land is dim with winter gloom,
Then for thee, my darling, love will have its way,
When the winds are moaning o'er the meadows chill and gray.

In the vernal dawning with the starting of the leaf,

In the merry-chanting time of
  spring,
Love steals all my senses, oh, the
  happy-hearted thief!
In the vernal morning with the
  starting of the leaf.

Always, ever always, even in the
  autumn drear,
  When the days are sighing out
    their grief,
Thou art still my darling, dear-
  est of the dear,
Always, ever always, even in the
  autumn drear.

TO A DEAD FRIEND

It is as if a silver chord
  Were suddenly grown mute,
And life's song with its rhythm
    warred
  Against a silver lute.

It is as if a silence fell
  Where bides the garnered sheaf,
And voices murmuring, " It is
    well,"
  Are stifled by our grief.

It is as if the gloom of night
  Had hid a summer's day,
And willows, sighing at their
    plight,
  Bent low beside the way.

For he was part of all the best
  That Nature loves and gives,

And ever more on Memory's breast
  He lies and laughs and lives.

TO THE SOUTH
ON ITS NEW SLAVERY

Heart of the Southland, heed me
    pleading now,
Who bearest, unashamed, upon
    my brow
The long kiss of the loving tropic
    sun,
And yet, whose veins with thy red
    current run.

Borne on the bitter winds from
    every hand,
Strange tales are flying over all the
    land,
And Condemnation, with his pin-
    ions foul,
Glooms in the place where broods
    the midnight owl.

What art thou, that the world
    should point at thee,
And vaunt and chide the weakness
    that they see?
There was a time they were not
    wont to chide;
Where is thy old, uncompromis-
    ing pride?

Blood-washed, thou shouldst lift
    up thine honored head,
White with the sorrow for thy
    loyal dead

Who lie on every plain, on every
 hill,
And whose high spirit walks the
 Southland still:

Whose infancy our mother's hands
 have nursed.
Thy manhood, gone to battle un-
 accursed,
Our fathers left to till th' re-
 luctant field,
To rape the soil for what she
 would not yield;

Wooing for aye, the cold unam'-
 rous sod,
Whose growth for them still
 meant a master's rod;
Tearing her bosom for the wealth
 that gave
The strength that made the toiler
 still a slave.

Too long we hear the deep im-
 passioned cry
That echoes vainly to the heedless
 sky;
Too long, too long, the Mace-
 donian call
Falls fainting far beyond the out-
 ward wall,

Within whose sweep, beneath the
 shadowing trees,
A slumbering nation takes its
 dangerous ease;
Too long the rumors of thy hatred
 go

For those who loved thee and thy
 children so.

Thou must arise forthwith, and
 strong, thou must
Throw off the smirching of this
 baser dust,
Lay by the practice of this later
 creed,
And be thine honest self again
 indeed.

There was a time when even slav-
 ery's chain
Held in some joys to alternate
 with pain,
Some little light to give the night
 relief,
Some little smiles to take the place
 of grief.

There was a time when, jocund
 as the day,
The toiler hoed his row and sung
 his lay,
Found something gleeful in the
 very air,
And solace for his toiling every-
 where.

Now all is changed, within the
 rude stockade,
A bondsman whom the greed of
 men has made
Almost too brutish to deplore his
 plight,
Toils hopeless on from joyless
 morn till night.

For him no more the cabin's quiet
　　rest,
The homely joys that gave to labor
　　zest;
No more for him the merry banjo's
　　sound,
Nor trip of lightsome dances foot-
　　ing round.

For him no more the lamp shall
　　glow at eve,
Nor chubby children pluck him by
　　the sleeve;
No more for him the master's eyes
　　be bright,—
He has nor freedom's nor a slave's
　　delight.

What, was it all for naught, those
　　awful years
That drenched a groaning land
　　with blood and tears?
Was it to leave this sly convenient
　　hell,
That brother fighting his own
　　brother fell?

When that great struggle held the
　　world in awe,
And all the nations blanched at
　　what they saw,
Did Sanctioned Slavery bow its
　　conquered head
That this unsanctioned crime
　　might rise instead?

Is it for this we all have felt the
　　flame,—
This newer bondage and this
　　deeper shame?
Nay, not for this, a nation's heroes
　　bled,
And North and South with tears
　　beheld their dead.

Oh, Mother South, hast thou for-
　　got thy ways,
Forgot the glory of thine ancient
　　days,
Forgot the honor that once made
　　thee great,
And stooped to this unhallowed
　　estate?

It cannot last, thou wilt come
　　forth in might,
A warrior queen full armored for
　　the fight;
And thou wilt take, e'en with thy
　　spear in rest,
Thy dusky children to thy saving
　　breast.

Till then, no more, no more the
　　gladsome song,
Strike only deeper chords, the
　　notes of wrong;
Till then, the sigh, the tear, the
　　oath, the moan,
Till thou, oh, South, and thine
　　come to thine own.

THE HAUNTED OAK

PRAY why are you so bare, so bare,
  Oh, bough of the old oak-tree;
And why, when I go through the
    shade you throw,
  Runs a shudder over me?

My leaves were green as the best,
    I trow,
  And sap ran free in my veins,
But I saw in the moonlight dim
    and weird
  A guiltless victim's pains.

I bent me down to hear his sigh;
  I shook with his gurgling moan,
And I trembled sore when they
    rode away,
  And left him here alone.

They 'd charged him with the old,
    old crime,
  And set him fast in jail:
Oh, why does the dog howl all
    night long,
  And why does the night wind
    wail?

He prayed his prayer and he swore
    his oath,
  And he raised his hand to the
    sky;
But the beat of hoofs smote on his
    ear,
  And the steady tread drew nigh.

Who is it rides by night, by night,
  Over the moonlit road?

And what is the spur that keeps
    the pace,
  What is the galling goad?

And now they beat at the prison
    door,
  "Ho, keeper, do not stay!
We are friends of him whom you
    hold within,
  And we fain would take him
    away

"From those who ride fast on our
    heels
  With mind to do him wrong;
They have no care for his inno-
    cence,
  And the rope they bear is
    long."

They have fooled the jailer with
    lying words,
  They have fooled the man with
    lies;
The bolts unbar, the locks are
    drawn,
  And the great door open flies.

Now they have taken him from
    the jail,
  And hard and fast they ride,
And the leader laughs low down
    in his throat,
  As they halt my trunk beside.

Oh, the judge, he wore a mask of
    black,
  And the doctor one of white,

And the minister, with his oldest
son,
  Was curiously bedight.

Oh, foolish man, why weep you
now?
  'T is but a little space,
And the time will come when these
shall dread
  The mem'ry of your face.

I feel the rope against my bark,
  And the weight of him in my
grain,
I feel in the throe of his final woe
  The touch of my own last pain.

And never more shall leaves come
forth
  On a bough that bears the ban;
I am burned with dread, I am
dried and dead,
  From the curse of a guiltless
man.

And ever the judge rides by, rides
by,
  And goes to hunt the deer,
And ever another rides his soul
  In the guise of a mortal fear.

And ever the man he rides me
hard,
  And never a night stays he;
For I feel his curse as a haunted
bough,
  On the trunk of a haunted tree.

WELTSCHMERTZ

You ask why I am sad to-day,
I have no cares, no griefs, you say?
Ah, yes, 't is true, I have no
grief —
But — is there not the falling
leaf?

The bare tree there is mourning
left
With all of autumn's gray bereft;
It is not what has happened me,
Think of the bare, dismantled tree.

The birds go South along the sky,
I hear their lingering, long good-
bye.
Who goes reluctant from my
breast?
And yet — the lone and wind-
swept nest.

The mourning, pale-flowered
hearse goes by,
Why does a tear come to my eye?
Is it the March rain blowing
wild?
I have no dead, I know no child.

I am no widow by the bier
Of him I held supremely dear.
I have not seen the choicest one
Sink down as sinks the westering
sun.

Faith unto faith have I beheld,
For me, few solemn notes have
swelled;

Love bekoned me out to the dawn,
And happily I followed on.

And yet my heart goes out to
them
Whose sorrow is their diadem;
The falling leaf, the crying bird,
The voice to be, all lost, un-
heard —

Not mine, not mine, and yet too
much
The thrilling power of human
touch,
While all the world looks on and
scorns
I wear another's crown of thorns.

Count me a priest who under-
stands
The glorious pain of nail-pierced
hands;
Count me a comrade of the thief
Hot driven into late belief.

Oh, mother's tear, oh, father's sigh,
Oh, mourning sweetheart's last
good-bye,
I yet have known no mourning
save
Beside some brother's brother's
grave.

ROBERT GOULD SHAW

WHY was it that the thunder
voice of Fate
Should call thee, studious, from
the classic groves,

Where calm-eyed Pallas with
still footstep roves,
And charge thee seek the turmoil
of the state?
What bade thee hear the voice and
rise elate,
Leave home and kindred and
thy spicy loaves,
To lead th' unlettered and de-
spised droves
To manhood's home and thunder
at the gate?

Far better the slow blaze of Learn-
ing's light,
The cool and quiet of her dearer
fane,
Than this hot terror of a hopeless
fight,
This cold endurance of the final
pain,—
Since thou and those who with
thee died for right
Have died, the Present teaches,
but in vain!

ROSES

OH, wind of the spring-time, oh,
free wind of May,
When blossoms and bird-song
are rife;
Oh, joy for the season, and joy for
the day,
That gave me the roses of life,
of life,
That gave me the roses of life.

Oh, wind of the summer, sing
loud in the night,
    When flutters my heart like a
dove;
One came from thy kingdom, thy
realm of delight,
    And gave me the roses of love,
of love,
    And gave me the roses of love.

Oh, wind of the winter, sigh low
in thy grief,
    I hear thy compassionate breath;
I wither, I fall, like the autumn-
kissed leaf,
      He gave me the roses of death,
of death,
      He gave me the roses of death.

A LOVE SONG

Ah, love, my love is like a cry in
the night,
A long, loud cry to the empty sky,
The cry of a man alone in the
desert,
With hands uplifted, with parch-
ing lips,

Oh, rescue me, rescue me,
Thy form to mine arms,
The dew of thy lips to my mouth,
Dost thou hear me?— my call
thro' the night?

Darling, I hear thee and answer,
Thy fountain am I,

All of the love of my soul will I
bring to thee,
All of the pains of my being shall
wring to thee,
Deep and forever the song of my
loving shall sing to thee,
Ever and ever thro' day and thro'
night shall I cling to thee.
Hearest thou the answer?
Darling, I come, I come.

ITCHING HEELS

Fu' de peace o' my eachin' heels,
set down;
    Don' fiddle dat chune no mo'.
Don' you see how dat melody stuhs
me up
    An' baigs me to tek to de flo'?
You knows I's a Christian, good
an' strong;
    I wusship f'om June to June;
My pra'ahs dey ah loud an' my
hymns ah long:
    I baig you don' fiddle dat chune.

I's a crick in my back an' a mis-
ery hyeah
    Whaih de j'ints 's gittin' ol' an'
stiff,
But hit seems lak you brings me
de bref o' my youf;
    W'y, I's suttain I noticed a
w'iff.
Don' fiddle dat chune no mo', my
chile,
    Don' fiddle dat chune no mo';

I 'll git up an' taih up dis groun'
  fu' a mile,
  An' den I 'll be chu'ched fu' it,
  sho'.

Oh, fiddle dat chune some mo', I
  say,
  An' fiddle it loud an' fas':
I 's a youngstah ergin in de mi'st
  o' my sin;
  De p'esent 's gone back to de
  pas'.
I 'll dance to dat chune, so des fid-
  dle erway;
  I knows how de backslidah
  feels;
So fiddle it on 'twell de break o'
  de day
  Fu' de sake o' my eachin' heels.

TO AN INGRATE

This is to-day, a golden summer's
  day
  And yet — and yet
  My vengeful soul will not for-
  get
The past, forever now forgot, you
  say.

From that half height where I had
  sadly climbed,
  I stretched my hand,
  I lone in all that land,
Down there, where, helpless, you
  were limed.

Our fingers clasped, and dragging
  me a pace,
  You struggled up.
  It is a bitter Cup,
That now for naught, you turn
  away your face.

I shall remember this for aye and
  aye.
  Whate'er may come,
  Although my lips are dumb,
My spirit holds you to that yester-
  day.

IN THE TENTS OF AKBAR

In the tents of Akbar
  Are dole and grief to-day,
For the flower of all the Indies
  Has gone the silent way.

In the tents of Akbar
  Are emptiness and gloom,
And where the dancers gather,
  The silence of the tomb.

Across the yellow desert,
  Across the burning sands,
Old Akbar wanders madly,
  And wrings his fevered hands.

And ever makes his moaning
  To the unanswering sky,
For Sutna, lovely Sutna,
  Who was so fair to die.

For Sutna danced at morning,
  And Sutna danced at eve;

Her dusky eyes half hidden
  Behind her silken sleeve.

Her pearly teeth out-glancing
  Between her coral lips,
The tremulous rhythm of passion
  Marked by her quivering hips.

As lovely as a jewel
  Of fire and dewdrop blent,
So danced the maiden Sutna
  In gallant Akbar's tent.

And one who saw her dancing,
  Saw her bosom's fall and rise
Put all his body's yearning
  Into his lovelit eyes.

Then Akbar came and drove
  him —
A jackal — from his door,
And bade him wander far and look
  On Sutna's face no more.

Some day the sea disgorges,
  The wilderness gives back,
Those half-dead who have wan-
    dered,
  Aimless, across its track.

And he returned — the lover,
  Haggard of brow and spent;
He found fair Sutna standing
  Before her master's tent.

" Not mine, nor Akbar's, Sutna! "
  He cried and closely pressed,
And drove his craven dagger
  Straight to the maiden's breast.

Oh, weep, oh, weep, for Sutna,
  So young, so dear, so fair,
Her face is gray and silent
  Beneath her dusky hair.

And wail, oh, wail, for Akbar,
  Who walks the desert sands,
Crying aloud for Sutna,
  Wringing his fevered hands.

In the tents of Akbar
  The tears of sorrow run,
But the corpse of Sutna's slayer,
  Lies rotting in the sun.

THE FOUNT OF TEARS

ALL hot and grimy from the road,
  Dust gray from arduous years,
I sat me down and eased my load
  Beside the Fount of Tears.

The waters sparkled to my eye,
  Calm, crystal-like, and cool,
And breathing there a restful sigh,
  I bent me to the pool.

When, lo! a voice cried: " Pilgrim,
  rise,
  Harsh tho' the sentence be,
And on to other lands and skies —
  This fount is not for thee.

" Pass on, but calm thy needless
  fears,
  Some may not love or sin,
An angel guards the Fount of
  Tears;
  All may not bathe therein."

Then with my burden on my back
I turned to gaze awhile,
First at the uninviting track,
Then at the water's smile.

And so I go upon my way,
Thro'out the sultry years,
But pause no more, by night, by
day,
Beside the Fount of Tears.

LIFE'S TRAGEDY

It may be misery not to sing at all
And to go silent through the
brimming day.
It may be sorrow never to be
loved,
But deeper griefs than these
beset the way.

To have come near to sing the
perfect song
And only by a half-tone lost
the key,
There is the potent sorrow, there
the grief,
The pale, sad staring of life's
tragedy.

To have just missed the perfect
love,
Not the hot passion of untem-
pered youth,
But that which lays aside its vanity
And gives thee, for thy trusting
worship, truth —

This, this it is to be accursed in-
deed;
For if we mortals love, or if we
sing,
We count our joys not by the
things we have,
But by what kept us from the
perfect thing.

DE WAY T'INGS COME

De way t'ings come, hit seems to
me,
Is des' one monst'ous mystery;
De way hit seem to strike a man,
Dey ain't no sense, dey ain't no
plan;
Ef trouble sta'ts a pilin' down,
It ain't no use to rage er frown,
It ain't no use to strive er pray,
Hit 's mortal boun' to come dat
way.

Now, ef you 's hongry, an' yo' plate
Des' keep on sayin' to you,
" Wait,"
Don't mek no diffunce how you
feel,
'T won't do no good to hunt a
meal,
Fu' dat ah meal des' boun' to hide
Ontwell de devil 's satisfied,
An' 'twell dey 's some'p'n by to
cyave
You 's got to ease yo'se'f an' sta've.

But ef dey 's co'n meal on de she'f
You need n't bothah 'roun' yo'se'f,

Somebody 's boun' to amble in
An' 'vite you to dey co'n meal bin;
An' ef you 's stuffed up to be froat
Wid co'n er middlin', fowl er
    shoat,
Des' look out an' you 'll see fu'
    sho
A 'possum faint befo' yo' do'.

De way t'ings happen, huhuh,
    chile,
Dis worl' 's done puzzled me one
    w'ile;
I 's mighty skeered I 'll fall in
    doubt,
I des' won't try to reason out
De reason why folks strive an'
    plan
A dinnah fu' a full-fed man,
An' shet de do' an' cross de street
F'om one dat raaly needs to eat.

NOON

Shadder in de valley
Sunlight on de hill,
Sut'ny wish dat locus'
Knowed how to be still.
Don't de heat already
Mek a body hum,
'Dout dat insec' sayin'
Hottah days to come?

Fiel' 's a shinin' yaller
Wid de bendin' grain,
Guinea hen a callin',
Now 's de time fu' rain;

Shet yo' mouf, you rascal,
Wha' 's de use to cry?
You do' see no rain clouds
Up dah in de sky.

Dis hyeah sweat 's been po'in'
Down my face sence dawn;
Ain't hit time we 's hyeahin'
Dat ah dinnah ho'n?
Go on, Ben an' Jaspah,
Lif' yo' feet an' fly,
Hit out fu' de shadder
Fo' I drap an' die.

Hongry, lawd a' mussy,
Hongry as a baih,
Seems lak I hyeah dinnah
Callin' evahwhaih;
Daih 's de ho'n a blowin'!
Let dat cradle swing,
One mo' sweep, den da'kies,
Beat me to de spring!

AT THE TAVERN

A lilt and a swing,
And a ditty to sing,
Or ever the night grow old;
    The wine is within,
    And I 'm sure 't were a sin
For a soldier to choose to be cold,
    my dear,
For a soldier to choose to be cold.

We 're right for a spell,
But the fever is — well,
No thing to be braved, at least;

So bring me the wine;
No low fever in mine,
For a drink is more kind than a
     priest, my dear,
For a drink is more kind than a
     priest.

DEATH

STORM and strife and stress,
Lost in a wilderness,
Groping to find a way,
Forth to the haunts of day

Sudden a vista peeps,
Out of the tangled deeps,
Only a point — the ray
But at the end is day.

Dark is the dawn and chill,
Daylight is on the hill,
Night is the flitting breath,
Day rides the hills of death.

NIGHT, DIM NIGHT

Night, dim night, and it rains, my
     love, it rains,
   (Art thou dreaming of me, I
     wonder)
The trees are sad, and the wind
     complains,
   Outside the rolling of the thun-
     der,
And the beat against the panes.

Heart, my heart, thou art mourn-
     ful in the rain,
   (Are thy redolent lips a-
     quiver?)
My soul seeks thine, doth it seek
     in vain?
   My love goes surging like a
     river,
Shall its tide bear naught save
     pain?

Lyrics of
Love and Sorrow

I

Love is the light of the world, my dear,
  Heigho, but the world is gloomy;
The light has failed and the lamp down hurled,
  Leaves only darkness to me.

Love is the light of the world, my dear,
  Ah me, but the world is dreary;
The night is down, and my curtain furled
  But I cannot sleep, though weary.

Love is the light of the world, my dear,
  Alas for a hopeless hoping,
When the flame went out in the breeze that swirled,
  And a soul went blindly groping.

II

The light was on the golden sands,
  A glimmer on the sea;
My soul spoke clearly to thy soul,
  Thy spirit answered me.

Since then the light that gilds the sands,
  And glimmers on the sea,
But vainly struggles to reflect
  The radiant soul of thee.

III

The sea speaks to me of you
  All the day long;
Still as I sit by its side
  You are its song.

The sea sings to me of you
  Loud on the reef;
Always it moans as it sings,
  Voicing my grief.

IV

My dear love died last night;
  Shall I clothe her in white?
My passionate love is dead,
  Shall I robe her in red?
But nay, she was all untrue,
  She shall not go drest in blue;
Still my desolate love was brave,
  Unrobed let her go to her grave.

V

There are brilliant heights of sorrow
  That only the few may know;
And the lesser woes of the world, like waves,
  Break noiselessly, far below.
I hold for my own possessing,
  A mount that is lone and still —
The great high place of a hopeless grief,

And I call it my " Heart-break
Hill."
And once on a winter's midnight
I found its highest crown,
And there in the gloom, my soul
and I,
Weeping, we sat us down.

But now when I seek that summit
We are two ghosts that go;
Only two shades of a thing that
died,
Once in the long ago.
So I sit me down in the silence,
And say to my soul, " Be still,"
So the world may not know we
died that night,
From weeping on " Heart-break
Hill."

Lyrics of
Sunshine and Shadow

A BOY'S SUMMER SONG

'Tis fine to play
In the fragrant hay,
And romp on the golden load;
To ride old Jack
To the barn and back,
Or tramp by a shady road.
To pause and drink,
At a mossy brink;
Ah, that is the best of joy,
And so I say
On a summer's day,
What's so fine as being a boy?
Ha, Ha!

With line and hook
By a babbling brook,
The fisherman's sport we ply;
And list the song
Of the feathered throng
That flit in the branches nigh.
At last we strip
For a quiet dip;
Ah, that is the best of joy.
For this I say
On a summer's day,
What's so fine as being a boy?
Ha, Ha!

THE SAND-MAN

I know a man
With face of tan,
But who is ever kind;
Whom girls and boys
Leaves games and toys
Each eventide to find.

When day grows dim,
They watch for him,
He comes to place his claim;
He wears the crown
Of Dreaming-town;
The sand-man is his name.

When sparkling eyes
Troop sleepywise
And busy lips grow dumb;
When little heads
Nod toward the beds,
We know the sand-man's come.

JOHNNY SPEAKS

The sand-man he's a jolly old
fellow,
His face is kind and his voice is
mellow,
But he makes your eyelids as heavy
as lead,
And then you got to go off to bed;
I don't think I like the sand-
man.

But I've been playing this live-
long day;
It does make a fellow so tired to
play!
Oh, my, I'm a-yawning right here
before ma,

I'm the sleepiest fellow that ever
you saw.
I think I do like the sand-man.

WINTER-SONG

OH, who would be sad tho' the
sky be a-graying,
And meadow and woodlands are
empty and bare;
For softly and merrily now there
come playing,
The little white birds thro' the
winter-kissed air.

The squirrel's enjoying the rest
of the thrifty,
He munches his store in the old
hollow tree;
Tho' cold is the blast and the
snow-flakes are drifty
He fears the white flock not a
whit more than we.

Chorus:

Then heigho for the flying snow!
Over the whitened roads we go,
With pulses that tingle,
And sleigh-bells a-jingle
For winter's white birds here's a
cheery heigho!

A CHRISTMAS FOLKSONG

DE win' is blowin' wahmah,
An hit's blowin' f'om de bay;
Dey's a so't o' mist a-risin'
All erlong de meddah way;

Dey ain't a hint o' frostin'
On de groun' ner in de sky,
An' dey ain't no use in hopin'
Dat de snow'll 'mence to fly.
It's goin' to be a green Christ-
mas,
An' sad de day fu' me.
I wish dis was de las' one
Dat evah I should see.

Dey's dancin' in de cabin,
Dey's spahkin' by de tree;
But dancin' times an' spahkin'
Are all done pas' fur me.
Dey's feastin' in de big house,
Wid all de windahs wide —
Is dat de way fu' people
To meet de Christmas-tide?
It's goin' to be a green Christ-
mas,
No mattah what you say.
Dey's us dat will remembah
An' grieve de comin' day.

Dey's des a bref o' dampness
A-clingin' to my cheek;
De aih's been dahk an' heavy
An' threatenin' fu' a week,
But not wid signs o' wintah,
Dough wintah'd seem so deah —
De wintah's out o' season,
An' Christmas eve is heah.
It's goin' to be a green Christ-
mas,
An' oh, how sad de day!
Go ax de hongry chu'chya'd,
An' see what hit will say

Dey's Allen on de hillside,
　An' Marfy in de plain;
Fu' Christmas was like springtime,
　An' come wid sun an' rain.
Dey's Ca'line, John, an' Susie,
　Wid only dis one lef':
An' now de curse is comin'
　Wid murder in hits bref.
　　It's goin' to be a green Christ-
　　　　mas —
　　　　Des hyeah my words an'
　　　　　see:
　　　　Befo' de summah beckons
　　　　　Dey's many 'll weep wid
　　　　　me.

THE FOREST GREETING

GOOD hunting! — aye, good hunt-
　　ing,
　Wherever the forests call;
But ever a heart beats hot with
　　fear,
　And what of the birds that fall?

Good hunting! — aye, good hunt-
　　ing,
　Wherever the north winds
　　blow;
But what of the stag that calls for
　　his mate?
　And what of the wounded doe?

Good hunting! — aye, good hunt-
　　ing;
　And ah! we are bold and strong;

But our triumph call through the
　　forest hall
　Is a brother's funeral song.

For we are brothers ever,
　Panther and bird and bear;
Man and the weakest that fear his
　　face,
　Born to the nest or lair.

Yes, brothers, and who shall judge
　　us?
　Hunters and game are we;
But who gave the right for me to
　　smite?
　Who boasts when he smiteth me?

Good hunting! — aye, good hunt-
　　ing,
　And dim is the forest track;
But the sportsman Death comes
　　striding on:
　Brothers, the way is black.

THE LILY OF THE VALLEY

SWEETEST of the flowers a-bloom-
　　ing
　In the fragrant vernal days
Is the Lily of the Valley
　With its soft, retiring ways.

Well, you chose this humble blos-
　　som
　As the nurse's emblem flower,
Who grows more like her ideal
　Every day and every hour.

Like the Lily of the Valley
  In her honesty and worth,
Ah, she blooms in truth and virtue
  In the quiet nooks of earth.

Tho' she stands erect in honor
  When the heart of mankind
    bleeds,
Still she hides her own deserving
  In the beauty of her deeds.

In the silence of the darkness
  Where no eye may see and know,
There her footsteps shod with
    mercy,
  And fleet kindness come and go.

Not amid the sounds of plaudits,
  Nor before the garish day,
Does she shed her soul's sweet per-
    fume,
  Does she take her gentle way.

But alike her ideal flower,
  With its honey-laden breath,
Still her heart blooms forth its
    beauty
  In the valley shades of death.

ENCOURAGED

Because you love me I have
  much achieved,
Had you despised me then I must
  have failed,
  But since I knew you trusted
  and believed,

I could not disappoint you and so
  prevailed.

TO J. Q.

What are the things that make
  life bright?
  A star gleam in the night.
What hearts us for the coming
  fray?
  The dawn tints of the day.
What helps to speed the weary
  mile?
  A brother's friendly smile.
What turns o' gold the evening
  gray?
  A flower beside the way.

DIPLOMACY

Tell your love where the roses
  blow,
  And the hearts of the lilies
    quiver,
Not in the city's gleam and glow,
  But down by a half-sunned river.
Not in the crowded ball-room's
  glare,
  That would be fatal, Marie,
    Marie,
How can she answer you then and
  there?
  So come then and stroll with me,
  my dear,
  Down where the birds call,
  Marie, Marie.

SCAMP

Ain't it nice to have a mammy
  W'en you kin' o' tiahed out
Wid a-playin' in de meddah,
  An' a-runnin' roun' about
Till hit's made you mighty hongry,
  An' yo' nose hit gits to know
What de smell means dat's a-
      comin'
  F'om de open cabin do'?
    She wash yo' face,
    An' mek yo' place,
  You's hongry as a tramp;
Den hit's eat you suppah right
      away,
  You sta'vin' little scamp.

W'en you's full o' braid an' bacon,
  An' dey ain't no mo' to eat,
An' de lasses dat's a-stickin'
  On yo' face ta'se kin' o' sweet,
Don' you t'ink hit's kin' o' pleasin'
  Fu' to have som'body neah
Dat'll wipe yo' han's an' kiss you
  Fo' dey lif' you f'om you' cheah?
    To smile so sweet,
    An' wash yo' feet,
  An' leave 'em co'l an' damp;
Den hit's come let me undress
      you, now
  You lazy little scamp.

Don' yo' eyes git awful heavy,
  An' yo' lip git awful slack,
Ain't dey som'p'n' kin' o' weak-
    nin'
  In de backbone of yo' back?

Don' yo' knees feel kin' o' trimbly,
  An' yo' head go bobbin' roun',
W'en you says yo' "Now I lay
    me,"
  An' is sno'in on de "down"?
    She kiss yo' nose,
    She kiss yo' toes,
  An' den tu'n out de lamp,
Den hit's creep into yo' trunnel
      baid,
  You sleepy little scamp.

WADIN' IN DE CRICK

Days git wa'm an' wa'mah,
  School gits mighty dull,
Seems lak dese hyeah teachahs
  Mus' feel mussiful.
Hookey's wrong, I know it
  Ain't no gent'man's trick;
But de aih's a-callin',
  "Come on to de crick."

Dah de watah's gu'glin'
  Ovah shiny stones,
Des hit's ve'y singin'
  Seems to soothe yo' bones.
W'at's de use o' waitin'
  Go on good an' quick:
Dain't no fun lak dis hyeah
  Wadin' in de crick.

W'at dat jay-b'ud sayin'?
  Bettah shet yo' haid,
Fus' t'ing dat you fin' out,
  You'll be layin' daid.

Jay-bu'ds sich a tattlah,
  Des seem lak his trick
Fu' to tell on folkses
  Wadin' in de crick.

Willer boughs a-bendin'
  Hidin' of de sky,
Wavin' kin' o' frien'ly
  Ez de win' go by,
Elum trees a-shinin',
  Dahk an' green an' thick,
Seem to say, " I see yo'
  Wadin' in de crick."

But de trees don' chattah,
  Dey des look an' sigh
Lak hit's kin' o' peaceful
  Des a-bein' nigh,
An' yo' t'ank yo' Mastah
  Dat dey trunks is thick
W'en yo' mammy fin's you
  Wadin' in de crick.

Den yo' run behin' dem
  Lak yo' scaihed to def,
Mammy come a-flyin',
  Mos' nigh out o' bref;
But she set down gentle
  An' she drap huh stick,—
An' fus' t'ing, dey's mammy
  Wadin' in de crick.

THE QUILTING

DOLLY sits a-quilting by her
  mother, stich by stitch,
Gracious, how my pulses throb,
  how my fingers itch,
While I note her dainty waist and
  her slender hand,
As she matches this and that, she
  stitches strand by strand.
And I long to tell her Life's a
  quilt and I'm a patch;
Love will do the stitching if she'll
  only be my match.

PARTED

SHE wrapped her soul in a lace of
  lies,
  With a prime deceit to pin it;
And I thought I was gaining a
  fearsome prize,
  So I staked my soul to win it.

We wed and parted on her com-
  plaint,
  And both were a bit of barter,
Tho' I'll confess that I'm no saint,
  I'll swear that she's no martyr.

FOREVER

I HAD not known before
  Forever was so long a word.
The slow stroke of the clock of
  time
  I had not heard.

'Tis hard to learn so late;
  It seems no sad heart really
  learns,
But hopes and trusts and doubt
  and fears,
  And bleeds and burns.

The night is not all dark,
  Nor is the day all it seems,
But each may bring me this re-
      lief —
  My dreams and dreams.

I had not known before
  That Never was so sad a word,
So wrap me in forgetfulness —
  I have not heard.

THE PLANTATION CHILD'S LULLABY

WINTAH time hit comin'
  Stealin' thoo de night;
Wake up in the mo'nin'
  Evah t'ing is white;
Cabin lookin' lonesome
  Stannin' in de snow,
Meks you kin' o' nervous,
  W'en de win' hit blow.

Trompin' back from feedin',
  Col' an' wet an' blue,
Homespun jacket ragged,
  Win' a-blowin' thoo.
Cabin lookin' cheerful,
  Unnerneaf de do',
Yet you kin' o' keerful
  W'en de win' hit blow.

Hickory log a-blazin'
  Light a-lookin' red,
Faith o' eyes o' peepin'
  'Rom a trun'le bed,
Little feet a-patterin'
  Cleak across de flo';

Bettah had be keerful
  W'en de win' hit blow.

Suppah done an' ovah,
  Evah t'ing is still;
Listen to de snowman
  Slippin' down de hill.
Ashes on de fiah,
  Keep it wa'm but low.
What's de use o' keerin'
  Ef de win' do blow?

Smoke house full o' bacon,
  Brown an' sweet an' good;
Taters in de cellah,
  'Possum roam de wood;
Little baby snoozin'
  Des ez ef he know.
What's de use o' keerin'
  Ef de win' do blow?

TWILIGHT

'TWIXT a smile and a tear,
  'Twixt a song and a sigh,
'Twixt the day and the dark,
  When the night draweth nigh.

Ah, sunshine may fade
  From the heavens above,
No twilight have we
  To the day of our love.

CURIOSITY

MAMMY's in de kitchen, an' de
    do' is shet;
All de pickaninnies climb an' tug
    an' sweat,

Gittin' to de winder, stickin' dah
    lak flies,
Evah one ermong us des all nose
    an' eyes.

" Whut's she cookin', Isaac? "
    " Whut's she cookin', Jake? "
" Is it sweet pertaters? Is hit pie
    er cake? "
But we couldn't mek out even
    whah we stood
Whut was mammy cookin' dat
    could smell so good.

Mammy spread de winder, an'
    she frown an' frown,
How de pickaninnies come a-tum-
    blin' down!
Den she say: " Ef you-all keeps
    a-peepin' in,
How I'se gwine to whup you, my!
    't 'ill be a sin!
Need n' come a-sniffin' an' a-nosin'
    hyeah,
'Ca'se I knows my business, nevah
    feah."
Won't somebody tell us — how I
    wish dey would! —
Whut is mammy cookin' dat it
    smells so good?

We know she means business, an'
    we dassent stay,
Dough it's mighty tryin' fuh to
    go erway;
But we goes a-troopin' down de
    ol' wood-track

'Twell dat steamin' kitchen brings
    us stealin' back,
Climbin' an' a-peepin' so's to see
    inside.
Whut on earf kin mammy be so
    sha'p to hide?
I'd des up an' tell folks w'en I
    knowed I could,
Ef I was a-cookin' t'ings dat smelt
    so good.

Mammy in de oven, an' I see huh
    smile;
Moufs mus' be a-wat'rin' roun'
    hyeah fuh a mile;
Den we almos' hollah ez we hu'ie
    down,
'Ca'se hit's apple dumplin's, big an'
    fat an' brown!
W'en de do' is opened, solemn lak
    an' slow,
Wisht you see us settin' all dah
    in a row
Innercent an' p'opah, des lak chil'-
    un should
W'en dey mammy's cookin' t'ings
    dat smell so good.

OPPORTUNITY

GRANNY's gone a-visitin',
    Seen huh git huh shawl
W'en I was a-hidin' down
    Hime de gyahden wall.
Seen huh put her bonnet on,
    Seen huh tie de strings,
An' I'se gone to dreamin' now
    'Bout dem cakes an' t'ings.

On de she'f behime de do'—
  Mussy, what a feas'!
Soon ez she gits out o' sight,
  I kin eat in peace.
I bin watchin' fu' a week
  Des fu' dis hycah chance.
Mussy, w'en I gits in daih,
  I'll des sholy dance.

Lemon pie an' gingah-cake,
  Let me set an' t'ink —
Vinegah an' sugah, too,
  Dat'll mek a drink;
Ef dey's one t'ing dat I loves
  Mos' pu'ticlahly,
It is eatin' sweet t'ings an'
  A-drinkin' Sangaree.

Lawdy, won' po' granny raih
  W'en she see de she'f;
W'en I t'ink erbout huh face,
  I's mos' 'shamed myse'f.
Well, she gone, an 'hyeah I is,
  Back behime de do'—
Look hyeah! gran' 's done 'spected
    me,
  Dain't no sweets no mo'.

Evah sweet is hid erway,
  Job des done up brown;
Pusson t'ink dat someun t'ought
  Dey was t'eves erroun';
Dat des breaks my heart in two,
  Oh how bad I feel!
Des to t'ink my own gramma
  B'lieved dat I 'u'd steal!

PUTTIN' THE BABY
AWAY

EIGHT of 'em hyeah all tol' an' yet
Dese eyes o' mine is wringin' wet;
My haht's a-achin' ha'd an' so',
De way hit nevah ached befo';
My soul's a-pleadin', " Lawd, give
    back
Dis little lonesome baby black,
Dis one, dis las' po' he'pless one
Whose little race was too soon
    run."

Po' Little Jim, des fo' yeahs ol'
A-layin' down so still an' col'.
Somehow hit don' seem ha'dly
    faih,
To have my baby lyin' daih
Wi'dout a smile upon his face,
Wi'dout a look erbout de place;
He ust to be so full o' fun
Hit don' seem right dat all's done,
    done.

Des eight in all but I don' caih,
Dey wa'nt a single one to spaih;
De worl' was big, so was my haht,
An' dis hyeah baby owned hit's
    paht;
De house was po', dey clothes was
    rough,
But daih was meat an' meal
    enough;
An' daih was room fu' little Jim;
Oh! Lawd, what made you call fu'
    him?

It do seem monst'ous ha'd to-day,
To lay dis baby boy away;
I'd learned to love his teasin'
    smile,
He mought o' des been lef' er-
    while;
You wouldn't t'ought wid all de
    folks,
Dat's roun' hyeah mixin' teahs an'
    jokes,
De Lawd u'd had de time to see
Dis chile an' tek him 'way f'om
    me.

But let it go, I reckon Jim,
'Ll des go right straight up to
    Him
Dat took him f'om his mammy's
    nest
An' lef' dis achin' in my breas',
An' lookin' in dat fathah's face
An' 'memberin' dis lone sorrerin'
    place,
He'll say, " Good Lawd, you ought
    to had
Do sumpin' fu' to comfo't dad ! "

THE FISHER CHILD'S LUL-
LABY

THE wind is out in its rage to-
    night,
    And your father is far at sea.
The rime on the window is hard
    and white
    But dear, you are near to me.

Heave ho, weave low,
    Waves of the briny deep;
Seethe low and breathe low,
    But sleep you, my little one,
        sleep, sleep.

The little boat rocks in the cove no
    more,
    But the flying sea-gulls wail;
I peer through the darkness that
    wraps the shore,
    For sight of a home set sail.
    Heave ho, weave low,
        Waves of the briny deep;
    Seethe low and breathe low,
        But sleep you, my little one,
            sleep, sleep.

Ay, lad of mine, thy father may
    die
    In the gale that rides the sea,
But we'll not believe it, not you
    and I,
    Who mind us of Galilee.
    Heave ho, weave low,
        Waves of the briny deep;
    Seethe low and breathe low,
        But sleep you, my little one,
            sleep, sleep.

FAITH

I's a-gittin' weary of de way dat
    people do,
De folks dat's got dey 'ligion in
    dey fiah-place an' flue;
Dey's allus somep'n comin' so de
    spit'll have to turn,

An' hit tain't no p'oposition fu' to
    mek de hickory bu'n.
Ef de sweet pertater fails us an' de
    go'geous yallah yam,
We kin tek a bit o' comfo't f'om
    ouah sto' o' summah jam.
W'en de snow hit git to flyin',
    dat's de Mastah's own desiah,
De Lawd'll run de wintah an' yo'
    mammy'll run de fiah.

I ain' skeered because de win' hit
    staht to raih and blow,
I ain't bothahed w'en he come er
    rattlin' at de do',
Let him taih hisse'f an' shout, let
    him blow an' bawl,

Dat's de time de branches shek an'
    bresh-wood 'mence to fall.
W'en de sto'm er railin' an' de
    shettahs blowin' 'bout,
Dat de time de fiah-place crack
    hits welcome out.
Tain' my livin' business fu' to
    trouble ner enquiah,
De Lawd'll min' de wintah an' my
    mammy'll min' de fiah.

Ash-cake allus gits ez brown w'en
    February's hyeah
Ez it does in bakin' any othah time
    o' yeah.
De bacon smell ez callin'-like, de
    kittle rock an' sing,
De same way in de wintah dat dey
    do it in de spring;

Dey ain't no use in mopin' 'round
    an' lookin' mad an' glum
Erbout de wintah season, fu' hit's
    des plumb boun' to come;

An' ef it comes to runnin' t'ings
    I's willin' to retiah,
De Lawd'll min' de wintah an'
    my mammy'll min' de fiah.

THE FARM CHILD'S LULLABY

Oh, the little bird is rocking in
    the cradle of the wind,
    And it's bye, my little wee one,
      bye;
The harvest all is gathered and
    the pippins all are binned;
    Bye, my little wee one, bye;
The little rabbit's hiding in the
    golden shock of corn,
The thrifty squirrel's laughing
    bunny's idleness to scorn;
You are smiling with the angels
    in your slumber, smile till
    morn;
    So it's bye, my little wee one,
      bye.

There'll be plenty in the cellar,
    there'll be plenty on the
    shelf;
    Bye, my little wee one, bye;
There'll be goodly store of sweet-
    ings for a dainty little elf;
    Bye, my little wee one, bye.

The snow may be a-flying o'er the
    meadow and the hill,
The ice has checked the chatter of
    the little laughing rill,
But in your cosey cradle you are
    warm and happy still;
    So bye, my little wee one, bye.

Why, the Bob White thinks the
    snowflake is a brother to his
    song;
    Bye, my little wee one, bye;
And the chimney sings the sweeter
    when the wind is blowing
    strong;
    Bye, my little wee one, bye;
The granary's overflowing, full is
    cellar, crib, and bin,
The wood has paid its tribute and
    the ax has ceased its din;
The winter may not harm you
    when you're sheltered safe
    within;
    So bye, my little wee one, bye.

THE PLACE WHERE THE RAINBOW ENDS

THERE'S a fabulous story
Full of splendor and glory,
    That Arabian legends trans-
    cends;
Of the wealth without measure,
The coffers of treasure,
    At the place where the rainbow
    ends.

Oh, many have sought it,
And all would have bought it,
    With the blood we so recklessly
    spend;
But none has uncovered,
The gold, nor discovered
    The spot at the rainbow's end.

They have sought it in battle,
And e'en where the rattle
    Of dice with man's blasphemy
    blends;
But howe'er persuasive,
It still proves evasive,
    This place where the rainbow
    ends.

I own for my pleasure,
I yearn not for treasure,
    Though gold has a power it
    lends;
And I have a notion,
To find without motion,
    The place where the rainbow
    ends.

The pot may hold pottage,
The place be a cottage,
    That a humble contentment de-
    fends,
Only joy fills its coffer,
But spite of the scoffer,
    There's the place where the rain
    bow ends.

Where care shall be quiet,
And love shall run riot,

And I shall find wealth in my
    friends;
Then truce to the story,
Of riches and glory;
    There's the place where the rain-
      bow ends.

HOPE

DE dog go howlin' 'long de road,
    De night come shiverin' down;
My back is tiahed of its load,
    I cain't be fu' f'om town.
No mattah ef de way is long,
My haht is swellin' wid a song,
    No mattah 'bout de frownin'
      skies,
    I'll soon be home to see my Lize.

My shadder staggah on de way,
    It's monstous col' to-night;
But I kin hyeah my honey say
    "W'y bless me if de sight
O' you ain't good fu' my so'
    eyes."
(Dat talk's dis lak my lady Lize)
    I's so'y case de way was long
    But Lawd you bring me love
      an' song.

No mattah ef de way is long,
    An' ef I trimbles so'
knows de fiah's burnin' strong,
    Behime my Lizy's do'.
An' daih my res' an' joy shell be,
Whaih my ol' wife's awaitin'
    me —

Why what I keer fu' stingin'
    blas',
I see huh windah light at las'.

APPRECIATION

MY muvver's ist the nicest one
    'At ever lived wiz folks;
She lets you have ze mostes' fun,
    An' laffs at all your jokes.

I got a ol' maid auntie, too,
    The worst you ever saw;
Her eyes ist bore you through and
      through,—
    She ain't a bit like ma.

She's ist as slim as slim can be,
    An' when you want to slide
Down on ze balusters, w'y she
    Says 'at she's harrified.

She ain't as nice as Uncle Ben,
    What says 'at little boys
Won't never grow to be big men
    Unless they're fond of noise.

But muvver's nicer zan 'em all,
    She calls you, "precious lamb,"
An' let's you roll your ten-pin ball,
    An' spreads your bread wiz jam.

An' when you're bad, she ist looks
    sad,
    You fink she's goin' to cry;
An' when she don't you're awful
    glad,
    An' den you're good, Oh, my!

At night, she takes ze softest
    hand,
  An' lays it on your head,
An' says " Be off to Sleepy-Land
  By way o' trundle-bed."

So when you fink what muvver
    knows
  An' aunts an' uncle tan't,
It skeers a feller; ist suppose
  His muvver 'd been a aunt.

A SONG

On a summer's day as I sat by a
    stream,
  A dainty maid came by,
And she blessed my sight like a
    rosy dream,
    And left me there to sigh, to
      sigh,
    And left me there to sigh, to
      sigh.

On another day as I sat by the
    stream,
  This maiden paused a while,
Then I made me bold as I told
    my dream,
    She heard it with a smile, a
      smile,
    She heard it with a smile, a
      smile.

Oh, the months have fled and the
    autumn's red,
  The maid no more goes by;

For my dream came true and the
    maid I wed,
    And now no more I sigh, I
      sigh,
    And now no more I sigh.

DAY

The gray dawn on the mountain
    top
  Is slow to pass away.
Still lays him by in sluggish
    dreams,
  The golden God of day.

And then a light along the hills,
  Your laughter silvery gay;
The Sun God wakes, a bluebird
    trills,
  You come and it is day.

TO DAN

Step me now a bridal measure,
Work give way to love and leisure,
Hearts be free and hearts be gay —
Doctor Dan doth wed to-day.

Diagnosis, cease your squalling —
Check that scalpel's senseless bawl-
    ing,
Put that ugly knife away —
Doctor Dan doth wed to-day.

'Tis no time for things unsightly
Life's the day and life goes lightly
Science lays aside her sway —
Love rules Dr. Dan to-day.

Gather, gentlemen and ladies,
For the nuptial feast now made
      is,
Swing your garlands, chant your
      lay
For the pair who wed to-day.

Wish them happy days and many,
Troubles few and griefs not any,
Lift your brimming cups and say
God bless them who wed to-day.

Then a cup to Cupid daring,
Who for conquest ever faring,
With his arrows dares assail
E'en a doctor's coat of mail.

So with blithe and happy hymning
And with harmless goblets brim-
      ming,
Dance a step — musicians play —
Doctor Dan doth wed to-day.

WHAT'S THE USE

WHAT'S the use o' folks a-frownin'
      When the way's a little rough?
Frowns lay out the road fur smil-
      in'
      You'll be wrinkled soon enough.
            What's the use?

What's the use o' folks a-sighin'?
      It's an awful waste o' breath,
An' a body can't stand wastin'
      What he needs so bad in death.
            What's the use?

What's the use o' even weepin'?
      Might as well go long an' smile.
Life, our longest, strongest arrow,
      Only lasts a little while.
            What's the use?

A LAZY DAY

THE trees bend down along the
      stream,
      Where anchored swings my tiny
            boat.
The day is one to drowse and
      dream
      And list the thrush's throttling
            note.
When music from his bosom bleeds
Among the river's rustling reeds.

No ripple stirs the placid pool,
      When my adventurous line is
            cast,
A truce to sport, while clear and
      cool,
      The mirrored clouds slide softly
            past.
The sky gives back a blue divine,
And all the world's wide wealth
      is mine.

A pickerel leaps, a bow of light,
The minnows shine from side to
      side.
The first faint breeze comes up
      the tide —
I pause with half uplifted oar,
While night drifts down to claim
      the shore.

ADVICE

W'en you full o' worry
  'Bout yo' wo'k an' sich,
W'en you kind o' bothered
  Case you can't get rich,
An' yo' neighboh p'ospah
  Past his jest desu'ts,
An' de sneer of comerds
  Stuhes yo' heaht an' hu'ts,
Des don' pet yo' worries,
  Lay 'em on de she'f,
Tek a little trouble
  Brothah, wid yo'se'f.

Ef a frien' comes mou'nin'
  'Bout his awful case,
You know you don' grieve him
  Wid a gloomy face,
But you wrassle wid him,
  Try to tek him in;
Dough hit cracks yo' features,
  Law, you smile lak sin,
Ain't you good ez he is?
  Don' you pine to def;
Tek a little trouble
  Brothah, wid yo'se'f.

Ef de chillun pestahs,
  An' de baby's bad,
Ef yo' wife gits narvous,
  An' you're gettin' mad,
Des you grab yo' boot-strops,
  Hol' yo' body down,
Stop a-tinkin' cuss-w'rds,
  Chase away de frown,
Knock de haid o' worry,
  Twell dey ain' none lef';

Tek a little trouble,
  Brothah, wid yo'se'f.

LIMITATIONS

Ef you's only got de powah fe' to
  blow a little whistle,
    Keep ermong de people wid de
    whistles.
Ef you don't, you'll fin' out sho'tly
  dat you's th'owed yo' fines'
  feelin'
    In a place dat's all a bed o' this-
    tles.
'Tain't no use a-goin' now, ez
  sho's you bo'n,
A-squeakin' of yo' whistle 'g'inst
  a gread big ho'n.

Ef you ain't got but a teenchy bit
  o' victuals on de table,
    Whut' de use a-claimin' hit's a
    feas'?
Fe' de folks is mighty 'spicious,
  an' dey's ap' to come a-
  peerin',
    Lookin' fe' de scraps you lef'
    at leas'.
W'en de meal's a-hidin' f'om de
  meal-bin's top,
You needn't talk to hide it; ef you
  sta'ts, des stop.

Ef yo' min' kin only carry half a
  pint o' common idees,
    Don' go roun' a-sayin' hit's a
    bar'l;

'Ca'se de people gwine to test you,
    an' dey'll fin' out you's
    a-lyin',
  Den dey'll twis' yo' sayin's in a
    snarl.
Wuss t'ing in de country dat I
  evah hyahed —
A crow dot sat a-squawkin', " I's
  a mockin'-bird."

A GOLDEN DAY

I FOUND you and I lost you,
  All on a gleaming day.
The day was filled with sunshine,
  And the land was full of May.

A golden bird was singing
  Its melody divine,
I found you and I loved you,
  And all the world was mine.

I found you and I lost you,
  All on a golden day,
But when I dream of you, dear,
  It is always brimming May.

THE UNLUCKY APPLE

'Twas the apple that in Eden
  Caused our father's primal fall;
And the Trojan War, remember —
  'Twas an apple caused it all.
So for weeks I've hesitated,
  You can guess the reason why,
For I want to tell my darling
  She's the apple of my eye.

THE DISCOVERY

THESE are the days of elfs and
  fays:
Who says that with the dreams of
  myth,
These imps and elves disport them-
  selves?
Ah no, along the paths of song
Do all the tiny folk belong.

Round all our homes,
Kobolds and gnomes do daily cling,
Then nightly fling their lanterns
  out.
And shout on shout, they join the
  rout,
And sing, and sing, within the
  sweet enchanted ring.

Where gleamed the guile of moon-
  light's smile,
Once paused I, listening for a
  while,
And heard the lay, unknown by
  day,—
The fairies' dancing roundelay.

Queen Mab was there, her shim-
  mering hair
Each fairy prince's heart's despair.
She smiled to see their sparkling
  glee,
And once I ween, she smiled at me.

Since when, you may by night or
  day,
Dispute the sway of elf-folk gay;
But, hear me, stay!

I've learned the way to find Queen
  Mab and elf and fay.

Where e'er by streams, the moon-
    light gleams,
Or on a meadow softly beams,
There, footing round on dew-lit
    ground,
The fairy folk may all be found.

MORNING

THE mist has left the greening
    plain,
The dew-drops shine like fairy
    rain,
The coquette rose awakes again
  Her lovely self adorning.
The Wind is hiding in the trees,
A sighing, soothing, laughing
    tease,
Until the rose says "Kiss me,
    please,"
  'Tis morning, 'tis morning.

With staff in hand and careless-
    free,
The wanderer fares right jauntily,
For towns and houses are, thinks
    he,
  For scorning, for scorning.
My soul is swift upon the wing,
And in its deeps a song I bring;
Come, Love, and we together sing,
  " 'Tis morning, 'tis morning."

THE AWAKENING

I DID not know that life could be
    so sweet,
I did not know the hours could
    speed so fleet,
Till I knew you, and life was sweet
    again.
The days grew brief with love
    and lack of pain —

I was a slave a few short days
    ago,
The powers of Kings and Princes
    now I know;
I would not be again in bondage,
    save
I had your smile, the liberty I
    crave.

LOVE'S DRAFT

THE draft of love was cool and
    sweet
  You gave me in the cup,
But, ah, love's fire is keen and
    fleet,
  And I am burning up.

Unless the tears I shed for you
  Shall quench this burning flame
It will consume me through and
    through,
  And leave but ash—a name.

A MUSICAL

OUTSIDE the rain upon the street,
   The sky all grim of hue,
Inside, the music-painful sweet,
   And yet I heard but you.

As is a thrilling violin,
   So is your voice to me,
And still above the other strains,
   It sang in ecstasy.

TWELL DE NIGHT IS PAS'

ALL de night long twell de moon
     goes down,
   Lovin' I set at huh feet,
Den fu' de long jou'ney back
     f'om de town,
   Ha'd, but de dreams mek it
     sweet.

All de night long twell de break of
     de day,
   Dreamin' agin in my sleep,
Mandy comes drivin' my sorrers
     away,
   Axin' me, " Wha' fu' you
     weep?"

All de day long twell de sun goes
     down,
   Smilin', I ben' to my hoe,
Fu' dough de weddah git nasty an'
     frown,
   One place I know I kin go.

All my life long twell de night has
     pas'
   Let de wo'k come ez it will,
So dat I fin' you, my honey, at las',
   Somewhaih des ovah de hill.

BLUE

STANDIN' at de winder,
   Feelin' kind o' glum,
Listenin' to de raindrops
   Play de kettle drum,
Lookin' crost de medders
   Swimmin' lak a sea;
Lawd 'a' mussy on us,
   What's de good o' me?

Can't go out a-hoein',
   Wouldn't ef I could;
Groun' too wet fu' huntin',
   Fishin' ain't no good.
Too much noise fo' sleepin',
   No one hyeah to chat;
Des mus' stan' an' listen
   To dat pit-a-pat.

Hills is gittin' misty,
   Valley's gittin' dahk;
Watch-dog's 'mence a-howlin',
   Rathah have 'em ba'k
Dan a-moanin' solemn
   Somewhaih out o' sight;
Rain-crow des a-chucklin'—
   Dis is his delight.

Mandy, bring my banjo,
   Bring de chillen in,

Come in f'om de kitchen,
  I feel sick ez sin.
Call in Uncle Isaac,
  Call Aunt Hannah, too,
Tain't no use in talkin',
  Chile, I's sholy blue.

DREAMIN' TOWN

COME away to dreamin' town,
  Mandy Lou, Mandy Lou,
Whaih de skies don' nevah frown,
    Mandy Lou;
Whaih he streets is paved with
    gol',
Whaih de days is nevah col',
An' no sheep strays f'om de fol',
    Mandy Lou.

Ain't you tiahed of every day,
  Mandy Lou, Mandy Lou,
Tek my han' an' come away,
    Mandy Lou,
To the place whaih dreams is
    King,
Whaih my heart hol's everything,
An' my soul can allus sing,
    Mandy Lou.

Come away to dream wid me,
  Mandy Lou, Mandy Lou,
Whaih our hands an' hea'ts are
    free,
    Mandy Lou;
Whaih de sands is shinin' white,
Whaih de rivahs glistens bright,
    Mandy Lou.

Come away to dreamland town,
  Mandy Lou, Mandy Lou,
Whaih de fruit is bendin' down
  Des fu' you.
Smooth your brow of lovin' brown
An' my love will be its crown;
Come away to dreamin' town,
    Mandy Lou.

AT NIGHT

WHUT time 'd dat clock strike?
    Nine? No — eight;
  I didn't think hit was so late.
Aer chew! I must 'a' got a cough
  I raally b'lieve I did doze off —
Hit's mighty soothin' to de tiah,
  A-dozin' dis way by de fiah;
Oo oom — hit feels so good t
    stretch
  I sutny is one weary wretch!

Look hyeah, dat boy done gone t
    sleep!
  He des ain't wo'th his boa'd ar
    keep;
I des don't b'lieve he'd bat h
    eyes
    If Gab'el called him fo'm d
    skies!
But sleepin's good dey ain't n
    doubt —
  Dis pipe o' mine is done gor
    out.
Don't bu'n a minute, bless my sou
  Des please to han' me dat a
    coal.

You 'Lias git up now, my son,
  Seems lak my nap is des begun;
You sutny mus' ma'k down de day
  W'en I treats comp'ny dis away!
W'y, Brother Jones, dat drowse
    come on,
  An' laws! I dremp dat you was
    gone!
You 'Lias, whaih yo' mannahs,
    suh,
  To hyeah me call an' nevah
    stuh!

To-morrer mo'nin' w'en I call
  Dat boy'll be sleepin' to beat all,
Don't mek no diffunce how I roah,
  He'll des lay up an' sno' and
    sno'.
Now boy, you done hyeahed whut
  I said,
  You bettah tek yo'se'f yo baid,
Case ef you gits me good an'
    wrong
  I'll mek dat sno' a diffunt song.

Dis wood fiah is invitin' dho',
  Hit seems to wa'm de ve'y flo'—
An' nuffin' ain't a whit ez sweet,
  Ez settin' toastin' of yo' feet.
Hit mek you drowsy, too, but La!
  Hyeah, 'Lias, don't you hyeah
    yo' ma?
Ef I gits sta'ted f'om dis cheah
  I' lay, you scamp, I'll mek you
    heah!

To-morrer mo'nin' I kin bawl
  Twell all de neighbohs hyeah
    me call;
An' you'll be snoozin' des ez deep
  Ez if de day was made fu' sleep;
Hit's funny when you got a cough
  Somehow yo' voice seems too fu'
    off —
Can't wake dat boy fu' all I say,
  I reckon he'll sleep daih twell
    day!

KIDNAPED

I HELD my heart so far from harm,
  I let it wander far and free
In mead and mart, without alarm,
  Assured it must come back to
    me.

And all went well till on a day,
  Learned Dr. Cupid wandered
    by
A search along our sylvan way
  For some peculiar butterfly.

A flash of wings, a hurried dive,
  A flutter and a short-lived flit;
This Scientist, as I am alive
  Had seen my heart and captured
    it.

Right tightly now 'tis held among
  The specimens that he has
    trapped,
And sings (Oh, love is ever
    young),
  'Tis passing sweet to be kid-
    naped.

COMPENSATION

BECAUSE I had loved so deeply,
  Because I had loved so long,
God in His great compassion
  Gave me the gift of song.

Because I have loved so vainly,
  And sung with such faltering
    breath,
The Master in infinite mercy
  Offers the boon of Death.

WINTER'S APPROACH

DE sun hit shine an' de win' hit
    blow,
Ol' Brer Rabbit be a-layin' low,
  He know dat de wintah time
    a-comin',
De huntah man he walk an' wait,
He walk right by Brer Rabbit's
    gate —
  He know —

De dog he lick his sliverin' chop,
An' he tongue 'gin' his mouf go
    flop, flop —
  He —
He rub his nose fu' to clah his
    scent
So's to tell w'ich way dat cotton-
    tail went,
  He —

De huntah's wife she set an' spin
A good wahm coat fu' to wrop him
    in
  She —

She look at de skillet an' she smile,
    oh my!
An' ol' Brer Rabbit got to sholy
    fly.
  Dey know.

ANCHORED

IF thro' the sea of night which
    here surrounds me,
  I could swim out beyond the
    farthest star,
Break every barrier of circumstance
    that bounds me,
  And greet the Sun of sweeter
    life afar,

Tho' near you there is passion,
    grief, and sorrow,
  And out there rest and joy and
    peace and all,
I should renounce that beckoning
    for to-morrow,
  I could not choose to go beyond
    your call.

THE VETERAN

UNDERNEATH the autumn sky,
Haltingly, the lines go by.
Ah, would steps were blithe and
    gay,
As when first they marched away,
Smile on lip and curl on brow,—
Only white-faced gray-beards now,
Standing on life's outer verge,
E'en the marches sound a dirge.

Blow, you bugles, play, you fife,
Rattle, drums, for dearest life.
Let the flags wave freely so,
As the marching legions go,
Shout, hurrah and laugh and jest,
This is memory at its best.
(Did you notice at your quip,
That old comrade's quivering lip?)

Ah, I see them as they come,
Stumbling with the rumbling drum;
But a sight more sad to me
E'en than these ranks could be
Was that one with cane upraised
Who stood by and gazed and gazed,
Trembling, solemn, lips compressed,
Longing to be with the rest.

Did he dream of old alarms,
As he stood, " presented arms " ?
Did he think of field and camp
And the unremitting tramp
Mile on mile — the lonely guard
When he kept his midnight ward?
Did he dream of wounds and scars
In that bitter war of wars?

What of that? He stood and stands
In my memory — trembling hands,
Whitened beard and cane and all
As if waiting for the call
Once again: " To arms, my sons,"
And his ears hear far-off guns,
Roll of cannon and the tread
Of the legions of the Dead!

YESTERDAY AND TO-MORROW

YESTERDAY I held your hand,
Reverently I pressed it,
And its gentle yieldingness
From my soul I blessed it.

But to-day I sit alone,
Sad and sore repining;
Must our gold forever know
Flames for the refining?

Yesterday I walked with you,
Could a day be sweeter?
Life was all a lyric song
Set to tricksy meter.

Ah, to-day is like a dirge,—
Place my arms around you,
Let me feel the same dear joy
As when first I found you.

Let me once retrace my steps,
From these roads unpleasant,
Let my heart and mind and soul
All ignore the present.

Yesterday the iron seared
And to-day means sorrow.
Pause, my soul, arise, arise,
Look where gleams the morrow.

THE CHANGE

Love used to carry a bow, you
know,
But now he carries a taper;
It is either a length of wax aglow,
Or a twist of lighted paper.

I pondered a little about the scamp,
And then I decided to follow
His wandering journey to field and
camp,
Up hill, down dale or hollow.

I dogged the rollicking, gay, young
blade
In every species of weather;
Till, leading me straight to the
home of a maid
He left us there together.

And then I saw it, oh, sweet sur-
prise,
The taper it set a-burning
The love-light brimming my lady's
eyes,
And my heart with the fire of
yearning.

THE CHASE

The wind told the little leaves to
hurry,
And chased them down the way,
While the mother tree laughed
loud in glee,
For she thought her babes at
play.

The cruel wind and the rain
laughed loudly,
We'll bury them deep, they said,
And the old tree grieves, and the
little leaves
Lie low, all chilled and dead.

SUPPOSE

If 'twere fair to suppose
That your heart were not taken,
That the dew from the rose
Petals still were not shaken,
I should pluck you,
Howe'er you should thorn me
and scorn me,
And wear you for life as the green
of the bower.

If 'twere fair to suppose
That that road was for va-
grants,
That the wind and the rose,
Counted all in their fragrance;
Oh, my dear one,
By love, I should take you and
make you,
The green of my life from the
scintillant hour.

THE DEATH OF THE
FIRST BORN

Cover him over with daisies white
And eke with the poppies red,
Sit with me here by his couch to-
night,

For the First-Born, Love, is
dead.

Poor little fellow, he seemed so
    fair
As he lay in my jealous arms;
Silent and cold he is lying there
    Stripped of his darling charms.

Lusty and strong he had grown
    forsooth,
    Sweet with an infinite grace,
Proud in the force of his conquer-
    ing youth,
    Laughter alight in his face.

Oh, but the blast, it was cruel and
    keen,
    And ah, but the chill it was rare;
The look of the winter-kissed
    flow'r you've seen
    When meadows and fields were
    bare.

Can you not wake from this white,
    cold sleep
    And speak to me once again?
True that your slumber is deep,
    so deep,
    But deeper by far is my pain.

Cover him over with daisies white,
    And eke with the poppies red,
Sit with me here by his couch to-
    night,
    For the First-Born, Love, is
    dead.

BEIN' BACK HOME

HOME agin, an' home to stay —
Yes, it's nice to be away.
Plenty things to do an' see,
But the old place seems to me
Jest about the proper thing.
Mebbe 'ts 'cause the mem'ries
    cling
Closer 'round yore place o' birth
'N ary other spot on earth.

W'y it's nice jest settin' here,
Lookin' out an' seein' clear,
'Thout no smoke, ner dust, ner
    haze
In these sweet October days.
What's as good as that there lane,
Kind o' browned from last night's
    rain?
'Pears like home has got the start
When the goal's a feller's heart.

What's as good as that there jay
Screechin' up'ards towards the
    gray
Skies? An' tell me, what's as fine
As that full-leafed pumpkin vine?
Tow'rin' buildin's — yes, they're
    good;
But in sight o' field and wood,
Then a feller understan's
'Bout the house not made with
    han's.

Let the others rant an' roam
When they git away from home;
Jest gi' me my old settee

An' my pipe beneath a tree;
Sight o' medders green an' still,
Now and then a gentle hill,
Apple orchards, full o' fruit,
Nigh a cider press to boot —

That's the thing jest done up
    brown;
D'want to be too nigh to town;
Want to have the smells an' sights,
An' the dreams o' long still nights,
With the friends you used to know
In the keerless long ago —
Same old cronies, same old folks,
Same old cider, same old jokes.

Say, it's nice a-gittin' back,
When yore pulse is growin' slack,
An' yore breath begins to wheeze
Like a fair-set valley breeze;
Kind o' nice to set aroun'
On the old familiar groun',
Knowin' that when Death does
    come,
That he'll find you right at home.

THE OLD CABIN

In de dead of night I sometimes,
    Git to t'inkin' of de pas'
An' de days w'en slavery helt me
    In my mis'ry — ha'd an' fas'.
Dough de time was mighty tryin',
    In dese houahs somehow hit
        seem
Dat a brightah light come slippin'
    Thoo de kivahs of my dream.

An' my min' fu'gits de whuppins
    Draps de feah o' block an' lash
An' flies straight to somep'n' joy-
        ful
    In a secon's lightnin' flash.
Den hit seems I see a vision
    Of a dearah long ago
Of de childern tumblin' roun' me
    By my rough ol' cabin do'.

Talk about yo' go'geous mansions
    An' yo' big house great an'
        gran',
Des bring up de fines' palace
    Dat you know in all de lan'.
But dey's somep'n' dearah to me,
    Somep'n' faihah to my eyes
In dat cabin, less you bring me
    To yo' mansion in de skies.

I kin see de light a-shinin'
    Thoo de chinks atween de logs,
I kin hyeah de way-off bayin'
    Of my mastah's huntin' dogs,
An' de neighin' of de hosses
    Stampin' on de ol' bahn flo',
But above dese soun's de laughin'
    At my deah ol' cabin do'.

We would gethah daih at evenin',
    All my frien's 'ud come erroun'
An' hit wan't no time, twell, bless
        you,
    You could hyeah de banjo's
        soun'.
You could see de dahkies dancin'
    Pigeon wing an' heel an' toe —

Joyous times I tell you people
Roun' dat same ol' cabin do'.

But at times my t'oughts gits sad-
dah,
Ez I riccolec' de folks,
An' dey frolickin' an' talkin'
Wid dey laughin' an dey jokes.
An' hit hu'ts me w'en I membahs
Dat I 'll nevah see no mo'
Dem ah faces gethered smilin'
Roun' dat po' ol' cabin do'.

DESPAIR

Let me close the eyes of my soul
That I may not see
What stands between thee and me.

Let me shut the ears of my heart
That I may not hear
A voice that drowns yours, my
dear.

Let me cut the cords of my life,
Of my desolate being,
Since cursed is my hearing and see-
ing.

CIRCUMSTANCES ALTER
CASES

Tim Murphy's gon' walkin' wid
Maggie O'Neill,
O chone!
If I was her muther, I 'd frown
on sich foolin',
O chone!

I'm sure it's unmutherlike, darin'
an' wrong
To let a gyrul hear tell the sass an'
the song
Of every young felly that happens
along,
O chone!

An' Murphy, the things that's
be'n sed of his doin',
O chone!
'Tis a cud that no dacent folks
wants to be chewin',
O chone!
If he came to my door wid his
cane on a twirl,
Fur to thry to make love to you,
Biddy, my girl,
Ah, wouldn't I send him away
wid a whirl,
O chone!

They say the gossoon is indecent
and dirty,
O chone!
In spite of his dressin' so.
O chone!
Let him dress up ez foine ez a
king or a queen,
Let him put on more wrinkles
than ever was seen,
You'll be sure he's no match for
my little colleen,
O chone!

Faith the two is comin' back an'
their walk is all over,
O chone!

'Twas a pretty short walk fur to
    take wid a lover,
      O chone!
Why, I believe that Tim Mur-
    phy's a kumin' this way,
Ah, Biddy jest look at him steppin'
    so gay,
I'd niver belave what the gos-
    sipers say,
      O chone!

He's turned in the gate an' he's
    coming a-caperin',
      O chone!
Go, Biddy, go quick an' put on a
    ciane apern,
      O chone!
Be quick as ye kin fur he's right at
    the dure;
Come in, master Tim, fur ye're
    welcome I'm shure.
We were talkin' o' ye jest a minute
    before.
      O chone!

TILL THE WIND GETS RIGHT

OH the breeze is blowin' balmy
    An the sun is in a haze;
There's a cloud jest givin' coolness
    To the laziest of days.
There are crowds upon the lake-
    side,
    But the fish refuse to bite,
So I'll wait and go a-fishin'
    When the wind gets right.

Now my boat tugs at her anchor,
    Eager now to kiss the spray,
While the little waves are callin'
    Drowsy sailor come away,
There's a harbor for the happy,
    And its sheen is just in sight,
But I won't set sail to get there,
    Till the wind gets right.

That's my trouble, too, I reckon.
    I've been waitin' all too long,
Tho' the days were always
    Still the wind is always wrong.
An' when Gabriel blows his trum-
    pet,
    In the day o' in the night,
I will still be found waitin',
    Till the wind gets right.

A SUMMER NIGHT

SUMMAH is de lovin' time —
    Do' keer what you say.
Night is allus peart an' prime,
    Bettah dan de day.
Do de day is sweet an' good,
    Birds a-singin' fine,
Pines a-smellin' in de wood,—
    But de night is mine.

Rivah whisperin' " howdy do,"
    Ez it pass you by —
Moon a-lookin' down at you,
    Winkin' on de sly.
Frogs a-croakin' f'om de pon',
    Singin' bass dey fill,
An' you listen way beyon'
    Ol' man whippo'will.

Hush up, honey, tek my han',
  Mck yo' footsteps light;
Somep'n' kin' o' hol's de lan'
  On a summah night.
Somep'n' dat you nevah sees
  An' you nevah hyeahs,
But you feels it in de breeze,
  Somep'n' nigh to teahs.

Somep'n' nigh to teahs? dat's so;
  But hit's nigh to smiles.
An' you feels it ez you go
  Down de shinin' miles.
Tek my han', my little dove;
  Hush an' come erway —
Summah is de time fu' love,
  Night-time beats de day!

AT SUNSET TIME

Adown the west a golden glow
  Sinks burning in the sea,
And all the dreams of long ago
  Come flooding back to me.
The past has writ a story strange
  Upon my aching heart,
But time has wrought a subtle
    change,
  My wounds have ceased to
    smart.

No more the quick delight of
    youth,
  No more the sudden pain,
I look no more for trust or truth
  Where greed may compass gain.

What, was it I who bared my
    heart
  Through unrelenting years,
And knew the sting of misery's
    dart,
  The tang of sorrow's tears?

'Tis better now, I do not weep,
  I do not laugh nor care;
My soul and spirit half asleep
  Drift aimless everywhere.
We float upon a sluggish stream,
  We ride no rapids mad,
While life is all a tempered dream
  And every joy half sad.

NIGHT

Silence, and whirling worlds afar
  Through all encircling skies.
What floods come o'er the spirit's
    bar,
  What wondrous thoughts arise.

The earth, a mantle falls away,
  And, winged, we leave the sod;
Where shines in its eternal sway
  The majesty of God.

AT LOAFING-HOLT

Since I left the city's heat
For this sylvan, cool retreat,
High upon the hill-side here
Where the air is clean and clear,
I have lost the urban ways.

Mine are calm and tranquil days,
Sloping lawns of green are mine,
Clustered treasures of the vine;
Long forgotten plants I know,
Where the best wild berries grow,
Where the greens and grasses
    sprout,
When the elders blossom out.
Now I am grown weather-wise
With the lore of winds and skies.
Mine the song whose soft refrain
Is the sigh of summer rain.
Seek you where the woods are cool,
Would you know the shady pool
Where, throughout the lazy day,
Speckled beauties drowse or play?
Would you find in rest or peace
Sorrow's permanent release? —
Leave the city, grim and gray,
Come with me, ah, come away.
Do you fear the winter chill,
Deeps of snow upon the hill?
'Tis a mantle, kind and warm,
Shielding tender shoots from harm.
Do you dread the ice-clad
    streams,—
They are mirrors for your dreams.
Here's a rouse, when summer's
    past
To the raging winter's blast.
Let him roar and let him rout,
We are armored for the bout.
How the logs are glowing, see!
Who sings louder, they or he?
Could the city be more gay?
Burn your bridges! Come away!

WHEN A FELLER'S ITCHIN' TO BE SPANKED

W'EN us fellers stomp around,
    makin' lots o' noise,
Gramma says, "There's certain
    times come to little boys
W'en they need a shingle or the
    soft side of a plank;"
She says "we're a-itchin' for a
    right good spank."
    An' she says, "Now thes you
        wait,
    It's a-comin'— soon or late,
W'en a feller's itchin' fer a spank."

W'en a feller's out o' school, you
    know how he feels,
Gramma says we wriggle 'roun'
    like a lot o' eels.
W'y it's like a man that's thes
    home from out o' jail.
What's the use o' scoldin' if we
    pull Tray's tail?
    Gramma says, tho', "Thes you
        wait,
    It's a-comin'— soon or late,
You'se the boys that's itchin' to
    be spanked."

Cats is funny creatures an' I like
    to make 'em yowl,
Gramma alwus looks at me with
    a awful scowl
An' she says, "Young gentlemen,
    mamma should be thanked
Ef you'd get your knickerbocker
    right well spanked."

An' she says, " Now thes you
wait,
It's a-comin'— soon or late,"
W'en a feller's itchin' to be
spanked.

Ef you fin' the days is gettin'
awful hot in school
An' you know a swimmin' place
where it's nice and cool,
Er you know a cat-fish hole brim-
min' full o' fish,
Whose a-goin' to set around school
and wish?
'Tain't no use to hide your bait,
It's a-comin,— soon or late,
W'en a feller's itchin' to be
spanked.

Ol' folks know most ever'thing
'bout the world, I guess,
Gramma does, we wish she knowed
thes a little less,
But I alwus kind o' think it 'ud be
as well
Ef they wouldn't alwus have to
up an' tell;
We kids wish 'at they'd thes
wait,
It's a-comin'— soon or late,
W'en a feller's itchin' to be
spanked.

THE RIVER OF RUIN

ALONG by the river of ruin
They dally — the thoughtless ones,
They dance and they dream

By the side of the stream,
As long as the river runs.

It seems all so pleasant and
cheery —
No thought of the morrow is
theirs,
And their faces are bright
With the sun of delight,
And they dream of no night-
brooding cares.

The women wear garlanded
tresses,
The men have rings on their
hands,
And they sing in their glee,
For they think they are free —
They that know not the treacher-
ous sands.

Ah, but this be a venturesome jour-
ney,
Forever those sands are ashift,
And a step to one side
Means a grasp of the tide,
And the current is fearful and
swift.

For once in the river of ruin,
What boots it, to do or to dare,
For down we must go
In the turbulent flow,
To the desolate sea of Despair.

TO HER

YOUR presence like a benison to
    me
    Wakes my sick soul to dreamful
      ecstasy,
I fancy that some old Arabian
    night
Saw you my houri and my heart's
    delight.

And wandering forth beneath the
    passionate moon,
    Your love-strung zither and my
    soul in tune,
We knew the joy, the haunting of
    the pain
    That like a flame thrills
    through me now again.

To-night we sit where sweet the
    spice winds blow,
    A wind the northland lacks and
    ne'er shall know,
With clasped hands and spirits all
    aglow
    As in Arabia in the long ago.

A LOVE LETTER

OH, I des received a letter f'om de
    sweetest little gal;
    Oh, my; oh, my.
She's my lovely little sweetheart
    an' her name is Sal:
    Oh, my; oh, my.

She writes me dat she loves me an'
    she loves me true,
    She wonders ef I'll tell huh dat
    I loves huh, too;
An' my heaht's so full o' music dat
    I do' know what to do;
    Oh, my; oh, my.

I got a man to read it an' he read
    it fine;
    Oh, my; oh, my.
Dey ain' no use denying dat her
    love is mine;
    Oh, my; oh, my.
But hyeah's de t'ing dat's puttin
    me in such a awful plight,
I t'ink of huh at mornin' an'
    dream of huh at night;
But how's I gwine to cou't huh
    w'en I do' know how t
    write?
    Oh, my; oh, my.

My heaht is bubblin' ovah wid d
    t'ings I want to say;
    Oh, my; oh, my.
An' dey's lots of folks to cop
    what I tell 'em fu' de pay
    Oh, my; oh, my.
But dey's t'ings dat I's a-t'inki
    dat is only fu' huh ears,
An' I couldn't lu'n to write 'em
    I took a dozen years;
So to go down daih an' tell hu
    is de only way, it 'pears;
    Oh, my; oh, my.

AFTER MANY DAYS

I've always been a faithful man
  An' tried to live for duty,
But the stringent mode of life
  Has somewhat lost its beauty.

The story of the generous bread
  He sent upon the waters,
Which after many days returns
  To trusting sons and daughters,

Had oft impressed me, so I want
  My soul influenced by it,
And bought a loaf of bread and
      sought
  A stream where I could try it.

I cast my bread upon the waves
  And fancied then to await it;
It had not floated far away
  When a fish came up and ate it.

And if I want both fish and bread,
  And surely both I'm wanting,
About the only way I see
  Is for me to go fishing.

LIZA MAY

Little brown face full of smiles,
And a baby's guileless wiles,
      Liza May, Liza May.

Eyes a-peeping thro' the fence
With an interest intense,
      Liza May.

Ah, the gate is just ajar,
And the meadow is not far,
      Liza May, Liza May.

And the road feels very sweet,
To your little toddling feet,
      Liza May.

Ah, you roguish runaway,
What will toiling mother say,
      Liza May, Liza May?

What care you who smile to greet
Everyone you chance to meet,
      Liza May?

Soft the mill-race sings its song,
Just a little way along,
      Liza May, Liza May.

But the song is full of guile,
Turn, ah turn, your steps the
      while,
      Liza May.

You have caught the gleam and
      glow
Where the darkling waters flow,
      Liza May, Liza May.

Flash of ripple, bend of bough,
Where are all the angels now?
      Liza May.

Now a mother's eyes intense
Gazing o'er a shabby fence,
      Liza May, Liza May.

Then a mother's anguished face
Peering all around the place,
  Liza May.

Hear the agonizing call
For a mother's all in all,
  Liza May, Liza May.

Hear a mother's maddened prayer
To the calm unanswering air,
  Liza May.

What's become of — Liza May?
What has darkened all the day?
  Liza May, Liza May.

Ask the waters dark and fleet,
If they know the smiling, sweet
  Liza May.

Call her, call her as you will,
On the meadow, on the hill,
  Liza May, Liza May.

Through the brush or beaten track
Echo only gives you back,
  Liza May.

Ah, but you were loving — sweet,
On your little toddling feet,
  Liza May, Liza May.

But through all the coming years,
Must a mother breathe with tears,
  Liza May.

THE MASTERS

Oh, who is the Lord of the land of
    life,
  When hotly goes the fray?
When, fierce we smile in the midst
    of strife
  Then whom shall we obey?

Oh, Love is the Lord of the land
    of life
  Who holds a monarch's sway;
He wends with wish of maid and
    wife,
  And him you must obey.

Then who is the Lord of the land
    of life,
  At setting of the sun?
Whose word shall sway when
    Peace is rife
  And all the fray is done?

Then Death is the Lord of the
    land of life,
  When your hot race is run.
Meet then his scythe and pruning-
    knife
  When the fray is lost or won.

TROUBLE IN DE KITCHEN

Dey was oncet a awful quoil
    'twixt de skillet an' de pot;
De pot was des a-bilin' an' de skil-
    let sho' was hot.
Dey slurred each othah's colah an'
    dey called each othah names,

W'ile de coal-oil can des gu-gled,
  po'in oil erpon de flames.

De pot, hit called de skillet des a
  flat, disfiggered t'ing,
An' de skillet 'plied dat all de pot
  could do was set an' sing,
An' he 'lowed dat dey was 'lusions
  dat he wouldn't stoop to mek
'Case he reckernize his juty, an' he
  had too much at steak.

Well, at dis de pot biled ovah, case
  his tempah gittin' highah,
An' de skillet got to sputterin',
  den de fat was in de fiah.
Mistah fiah lay daih smokin' an'
  a-t'inkin' to hisse'f,
W'ile de peppah-box us nudgin' of
  de gingah on de she'f.

Den dey all des lef' hit to 'im,
  'bout de trouble an' de talk;
An' howevah he decided, w'y dey
  bofe 'u'd walk de chalk;
But de fiah uz so 'sgusted how dey
  quoil an' dey shout
Dat he cooled 'em off, I reckon,
  w'en he puffed an' des went
  out.

CHRISTMAS

Step wid de banjo an' glide wid
  de fiddle,
  Dis ain' no time fu' to pottah
  an' piddle;

Fu' Christmas is comin', it's right
  on de way,
  An' dey's houahs to dance 'fo'
  de break o' day.

What if de win' is taihin' an'
  whistlin'?
  Look at dat fiah how hit 's
  spittin' an' bristlin'!
Heat in de ashes an' heat in de
  cindahs,
  Ol' mistah Fros' kin des look
  thoo de windahs.

Heat up de toddy an' pas' de wa'm
  glasses,
  Don' stop to shivah at blowin's
  an' blas'es,
Keep on de kittle an' keep it a-
  hummin',
  Eat all an' drink all, dey's lots
  mo' a-comin'.
Look hyeah, Maria, don't open
  dat oven,
  Want all dese people a-pushin'
  an' shovin'?

Res' f'om de dance? Yes, you
  done cotch dat odah,
  Mammy done cotch it, an' law!
  hit nigh flo'd huh;
'Possum is monst'ous fu' mekin'
  folks fin' it!
  Come, draw yo' cheers up, I 's
  sho' I do' min' it.
Eat up dem critters, you men folks
  an' wimmens,
  'Possums ain' skace w'en dey's
  lots o' pu'simmons.

ROSES AND PEARLS

Your spoken words are roses fine
    and sweet,
The songs you sing are perfect
    pearls of sound.
How lavish nature is about your
    feet,
To scatter flowers and jewels both
    around.

Blushing the stream of petal beauty
    flows,
Softly the white strings trickle
    down and shine.
Oh! speak to me, my love, I crave
    a rose.
Sing me a song, for I would pearls
    were mine.

RAIN-SONGS

The rain streams down like harp-
    strings from the sky;
    The wind, that world-old
        harpist sitteth by;
And ever as he sings his low re-
    frain,
    He plays upon the harp-strings
        of the rain.

A LOST DREAM

Ah, I have changed, I do not
    know
Why lonely hours affect me so.

In days of yore, this were not wont,
No loneliness my soul could daunt.

For me too serious for my age,
The weighty tome of hoary sage,
Until with puzzled heart astir,
One God-giv'n night, I dreamed
    of her.

I loved no woman, hardly knew
More of the sex that strong men
    woo
Than cloistered monk within his
    cell;
But now the dream is lost, and hell

Holds me her captive tight and
    fast
Who prays and struggles for the
    past.
No living maid has charmed my
    eyes,
But now, my soul is wonder-wise.

For I have dreamed of her and
    seen
Her red-brown tresses' ruddy
    sheen,
Have known her sweetness, lip to
    lip,
The joy of her companionship.

When days were bleak and winds
    were rude,
She shared my smiling solitude,
And all the bare hills walked with
    me
To hearken winter's melody.

And when the spring came o'er the
   land
We fared together hand in hand
Beneath the linden's leafy screen
That waved above us faintly
   green.

In summer, by the river-side,
Our souls were kindred with the
   tide
That floated onward to the sea
As we swept toward Eternity.

The bird's call and the water's
   drone
Were all for us and us alone.
The water-fall that sang all night
Was her companion, my delight,

And e'en the squirrel, as he sped
Along the branches overhead,
Half kindly and half envious,
Would chatter at the joy of us.

Twas but a dream, her face, her
   hair,
The spring-time sweet, the winter
   bare,
The summer when the woods we
   ranged,—
Twas but a dream, but all is
   changed.

Yes, all is changed and all has
   fled,
The dream is broken, shattered,
   dead.
And yet, sometimes, I pray to know
How just a dream could hold me
   so.

A SONG

Thou art the soul of a summer's
   day,
Thou art the breath of the rose.
   But the summer is fled
   And the rose is dead
Where are they gone, who knows,
   who knows?

Thou art the blood of my heart o'
   hearts,
Thou art my soul's repose,
   But my heart grows numb
   And my soul is dumb
Where art thou, love, who knows,
   who knows?

Thou art the hope of my after
   years —
Sun for my winter snows
   But the years go by
   'Neath a clouded sky.
Where shall we meet, who knows,
   who knows?

Miscellaneous

THE CAPTURE

DUCK come switchin' 'cross de lot
    Hi, oh, Miss Lady!
Hurry up an' hide de pot
    Hi, oh, Miss Lady!
Duck's a mighty 'spicious fowl,
Slick as snake an' wise as owl;
Hol' dat dog, don't let him yowl!
    Hi, oh, Miss Lady!

Th'ow dat co'n out kind o' slow
    Hi, oh, Miss Lady!
Keep yo'se'f behin' de do'
    Hi, oh, Miss Lady!
Lots o' food'll kill his feah,
Co'n is cheap but fowls is deah —
"Come, good ducky, come on
    heah."
    Hi, oh, Miss Lady!

Ain't he fat and ain't he fine,
    Hi, oh, Miss Lady!
Des can't wait to make him
    mine.
    Hi, oh, Miss Lady!
See him waddle when he walk,
Sh! keep still and don't you talk!
Got you! Don't you daih to
    squawk!
    Hi, oh, Miss Lady!

WHEN WINTER DARKEN-ING ALL AROUND

WHEN winter covering all the
    ground
    Hides every sign of Spring, sir.
However you may look around,
    Pray what will then you sing,
    sir?

The Spring was here last year I
    know,
    And many bards did flute, sir;
I shall not fear a little snow
    Forbid me from my lute, sir.

If words grow dull and rhymes
    grow rare,
    I'll sing of Spring's farewell, sir.
For every season steals an air,
    Which has a Springtime smell,
    sir.

But if upon the other side,
    With passionate longing burn-
    ing,
Will seek the half unjeweled tide,
    And sing of Spring's returning.

FROM THE PORCH AT RUNNYMEDE

I STAND above the city's rush and
    din,
    And gaze far down with calm
    and undimmed eyes,

To where the misty smoke wreath
    grey and dim
  Above the myriad roofs and
    spires rise;

Still is my heart and vacant is my
    breath —
  This lovely view is breath and
    life to me,
Why I could charm the icy soul
    of death
  With such a sight as this I stand
    and see.

I hear no sound of labor's din or
    stir,
  I feel no weight of worldly
    cares or fears,
Sweet song of birds, of wings the
    soothing whirr,
  These sounds alone assail my
    listening ears.

Unwhipt of conscience here I
    stand alone,
  The breezes humbly kiss my gar-
    ment's hem;
I am a king — the whole world is
    my throne,
  The blue grey sky my royal
    diadem.

EQUIPMENT

WITH what thou gavest me, O
    Master,
  I have wrought.

Such chances, such abilities,
  To see the end was not for my
    poor eyes,
Thine was the impulse, thine the
    forming thought.

Ah, I have wrought,
  And these sad hands have right
    to tell their story,
It was no hard up striving after
    glory,
  Catching and losing, gaining
    and failing,
Raging me back at the world's
    raucous railing.
  Simply and humbly from stone
    and from wood,
Wrought I the things that to thee
    might seem good.

If they are little, ah God! but the
    cost,
  Who but thou knowest the all
    that is lost!
If they are few, is the workman-
    ship true?
  Try them and weigh me, what-
    e'er be my due!

EVENING

THE moon begins her stately ride
  Across the summer sky;
The happy wavelets lash the
    shore,—
  The tide is rising high.

Beneath some friendly blade of
  grass
The lazy beetle cowers;
The coffers of the air are filled
With offerings from the flow-
  ers.

And slowly buzzing o'er my head
  A swallow wings her flight;
I hear the weary plowman sing
  As falls the restful night.

TO PFRIMMER

(Lines on reading " Driftwood.")

DRIFTWOOD gathered here and
  there
Along the beach of time;
Now and then a chip of truth
'Mid boards and boughs of rhyme;
Driftwood gathered day by day,—
The cypress and the oak,—
Twigs that in some former time
From sturdy home trees broke.
Did this wood come floating thick
All along down " Injin Crik?"
Or did kind tides bring it thee
From the past's receding sea
Down the stream of memory?

TO THE MIAMI

Kiss me, Miami, thou most con-
  stant one!
  I love thee more for that thou
    changest not.

When Winter comes with frigid
  blast,
Or when the blithesome Spring
  is past
  And Summer's here with sun-
    shine hot,
Or in sere Autumn, thou has
  still the pow'r
To charm alike, whate'er the hour.

Kiss me, Miami, with thy dewy
  lips;
  Throbs fast my heart e'en as
    thine own breast beats.
My soul doth rise as rise thy
  waves,
As each on each the dark shore
  laves
  And breaks in ripples and re-
    treats.
There is a poem in thine every
  phase;
Thou still has sung through all
  thy days.

Tell me, Miami, how it was with
  thee
  When years ago Tecumseh in
    his prime
His birch boat o'er thy waters
  sent,
And pitched upon thy banks his
  tent.
  In that long-gone, poetic time,
Did some bronze bard thy flowing
  stream sit by
And sing thy praises, e'en as I?

Did some bronze lover 'neath this
   dark old tree
   Whisper of love unto his Indian
      maid?
And didst thou list his murmurs
   deep,
And in thy bosom safely keep
   The many raging vows they
      said?
Or didst thou tell to fish and frog
   and bird
The raptured scenes that there
   occurred?

But, O dear stream, what volumes
   thou couldst tell
   To all who know thy language
      as I do,
Of life and love and jealous hate!
But now to tattle were too late,—
   Thou who hast ever been so
      true.
Tell not to every passing idler
   here
All those sweet tales that reached
   thine ear.

But, silent stream, speak out and
   tell me this:
   I say that men and things are
      still the same;
Were men as bold to do and dare?
Were women then as true and
   fair?
   Did poets seek celestial flame,
The hero die to gain a laureled
   brow,
And women suffer, then as now?

CHRISTMAS CAROL

RING out, ye bells!
All Nature swells
With gladness at the wondrous
   story,—
   The world was lorn,
   But Christ is born
To change our sadness into glory

Sing, earthlings, sing!
To-night a King
Hath come from heaven's high
   throne to bless us.
   The outstretched hand
   O'er all the land
Is raised in pity to caress us.

Come at his call;
Be joyful all;
Away with mourning and with
   sadness!
   The heavenly choir
   With holy fire
Their voices raise in songs of glad
   ness.

The darkness breaks
And Dawn awakes,
Her cheeks suffused with youthful
   blushes.
   The rocks and stones
   In holy tones
Are singing sweeter than the
   thrushes.

Then why should we
In silence be,

When Nature lends her voice to
    praises;
    When heaven and earth
    Proclaim the truth
Of Him for whom that lone star
    blazes?

    No, be not still,
    But with a will
Strike all your harps and set them
    ringing;
    On hill and heath
    Let every breath
Throw all its power into singing!

A SUMMER PASTORAL

It's hot to-day. The bees is
    buzzin'
    Kinder don't-keer-like aroun'
An' fur off the warm air dances
    O'er the parchin' roofs in town.
In the brook the cows is standin';
    Childern hidin' in the hay;
Can't keep none of 'em a workin',
    'Cause it's hot to-day.

It's hot to-day. The sun is
    blazin'
    Like a great big ball o' fire;
Seems as ef instead o' settin'
    It keeps mountin' higher an'
    higher.
I'm as triflin' as the children,
    Though I blame them lots an'
    scold;
I keep slippin' to the spring-house,
    Where the milk is rich an' cold.

The very air within its shadder
    Smells o' cool an' restful things,
An' a roguish little robin
    Sits above the place an' sings.
I don't mean to be a shirkin',
    But I linger by the way
Longer, mebbe, than is needful,
    'Cause it's hot to-day.

It's hot to-day. The horses stum-
    ble
    Half asleep across the fiel's;
An' a host o' teasin' fancies
    O'er my burnin' senses steals,—
Dreams o' cool rooms, curtains
    lowered,
    An' a sofy's temptin' look;
Patter o' composin' raindrops
    Or the ripple of a brook.

I strike a stump! That wakes
    me sudden;
    Dreams all vanish into air.
Lordy! how I chew my whiskers;
    'Twouldn't do fur me to swear.
But I have to be so keerful
    'Bout my thoughts an' what I
    say;
Somethin' might slip out unheeded,
    'Cause it's hot to-day.

Git up, there, Suke! you, Sal, git
    over!
    Sakes alive! how I do sweat.
Every stitch that I've got on me,
Bet a cent, is wringin' wet.
If this keeps up, I'll lose my tem-
    per.

Gee there, Sal, you lazy brute!
Wonder who on airth this weather
    Could 'a' be'n got up to suit?

You, Sam, go bring a tin o' water;
    Dash it all, don't be so slow!
'Pears as ef you tuk an hour
    'Tween each step to stop an'
      blow.
Think I want to stand a meltin'
    Out here in this b'ilin' sun,
While you stop to think about it?
    Lift them feet o' your'n an' run.

It ain't no use; I'm plumb fe-
    taggled.
    Come an' put this team away.
I won't plow another furrer;
    It's too mortal hot to-day.
I ain't weak, nor I ain't lazy,
    But I'll stand this half day's loss
'Fore I let the devil make me
    Lose my patience an' git cross.

IN SUMMER TIME

WHEN summer time has come, and all
The world is in the magic thrall
Of perfumed airs that lull each
    sense
To fits of drowsy indolence;
When skies are deepest blue above,
And flow'rs aflush,— then most I
    love
To start, while early dews are
    damp,
And wend my way in woodland
    tramp
Where forests rustle, tree on tree,
And sing their silent songs to me;
Where pathways meet and path
    ways part,—
To walk with Nature heart by
    heart,
Till wearied out at last I lie
Where some sweet stream steals
    singing by
A mossy bank; where violets vie
In color with the summer sky,—
Or take my rod and line and hook,
And wander to some darkling
    brook,
Where all day long the willows
    dream,
And idly droop to kiss the stream,
And there to loll from morn till
    night —
Unheeding nibble, run, or bite —
Just for the joy of being there
And drinking in the summer air,
The summer sounds, and summer
    sights,
That set a restless mind to rights
When grief and pain and raging
    doubt
Of men and creeds have worn it
    out;
The birds' song and the water's
    drone,
The humming bees' low monotone,
The murmur of the passing breeze,
And all the sounds akin to these,
That make a man in summer time

Feel only fit for rest and rhyme.
Joy springs all radiant in my
breast;
Though pauper poor, than king
more blest,
The tide beats in my soul so strong
That happiness breaks forth in
song,
And rings aloud the welkin blue
With all the songs I ever knew.
O time of rapture! time of song!
How swiftly glide thy days along
Adown the current of the years,
Above the rocks of grief and tears!
'Tis wealth enough of joy for me
In summer time to simply be

A THANKSGIVING POEM

THE sun hath shed its kindly
light,
Our harvesting is gladly o'er
Our fields have felt no killing
blight,
Our bins are filled with goodly
store.

From pestilence, fire, flood, and
sword
We have been spared by thy de-
cree,
And now with humble hearts, O
Lord,
We come to pay our thanks to
thee.

We feel that had our merits been
The measure of thy gifts to us,

We erring children, born of sin,
Might not now be rejoicing
thus.

No deed of ours hath brought us
grace;
When thou were nigh our sight
was dull,
We hid in trembling from thy
face,
But thou, O God, wert merci-
ful.

Thy mighty hand o'er all the land
Hath still been open to bestow
Those blessings which our wants
demand
From heaven, whence all bless-
ings flow.

Thou hast, with ever watchful eye,
Looked down on us with holy
care,
And from thy storehouse in the
sky
Hast scattered plenty every-
where.

Then lift we up our songs of
praise
To thee, O Father, good and
kind;
To thee we consecrate our days;
Be thine the temple of each
mind.

With incense sweet our thanks
ascend;

Before thy works our powers
 pall;
Though we should strive years
 without end,
  We could not thank thee for
  them all.

NUTTING SONG

THE November sun invites me,
And although the chill wind smites
 me,
I will wander to the woodland
 Where the laden trees await;
And with loud and joyful singing
I will set the forest ringing,
As if I were king of Autumn,
  And Dame Nature were my
  mate,—

While the squirrel in his gambols
Fearless round about me ambles,
As if he were bent on showing
 In my kingdom he'd a share;
While my warm blood leaps and
 dashes,
And my eye with freedom flashes,
As my soul drinks deep and deeper
 Of the magic in the air.

There's a pleasure found in nut-
 ting,
All life's cares and griefs outshut-
 ting,
That is fuller far and better
 Than what prouder sports im-
 part.

Who could help a carol trilling
As he sees the baskets filling?
Why, the flow of song keeps run-
 ning
O'er the high walls of the heart.

So when I am home returning,
When the sun is lowly burning,
I will once more wake the echoes
 With a happy song of praise,—
For the golden sunlight blessing,
And the breezes' soft caressing,
And the precious boon of living
 In the sweet November days.

LOVE'S PICTURES

LIKE the blush upon the rose
 When the wooing south wind
  speaks,
Kissing soft its petals,
 Are thy cheeks.

Tender, soft, beseeching, true,
 Like the stars that deck the skies
Through the ether sparkling,
 Are thine eyes.

Like the song of happy birds,
 When the woods with spring re-
  joice,
In their blithe awak'ning,
 Is thy voice.

Like soft threads of clustered silk
 O'er thy face so pure and fair,
Sweet in its profusion,
 Is thy hair.

Like a fair but fragile vase,
  Triumph of the carver's art,
Graceful formed and slender,—
  Thus thou art.

Ah, thy cheek, thine eyes, thy
    voice,
  And thy hair's delightful wave
Make me, I'll confess it,
  Thy poor slave!

THE OLD HOMESTEAD

'Tis an old deserted homestead
  On the outskirts of the town,
Where the roof is all moss-cov-
    ered,
  And the walls are tumbling
      down;
But around that little cottage
  Do my brightest mem'ries cling,
For 'twas there I spent the mo-
    ments
  Of my youth,— life's happy
      spring.

I remember how I used to
  Swing upon the old front gate,
While the robin in the tree tops
  Sung a night song to his mate;
And how later in the evening,
  As the beaux were wont to do,
Mr. Perkins, in the parlor,
  Sat and sparked my sister Sue.

There my mother — heaven bless
    her! —
  Kissed or spanked as was our
      need,
And by smile or stroke implanted
  In our hearts fair virtue's seed;
While my father, man of wisdom,
  Lawyer keen, and farmer stout,
Argued long with neighbor Dob-
    bins
  How the corn crops would turn
      out.

Then the quiltings and the
    dances —
  How my feet were wont to fly,
While the moon peeped through
    the barn chinks
  From her stately place on high.
Oh, those days, so sweet, so happy,
  Ever backward o'er me roll;
Still the music of that farm life
  Rings an echo in my soul.

Now the old place is deserted,
  And the walls are falling down;
All who made the home life cheer-
    ful,
  Now have died or moved to
      town.
But about that dear old cottage
  Shall my mem'ries ever cling,
For 'twas there I spent the mo-
    ments
  Of my youth,— life's happy
      spring.

ON THE DEATH OF W. C.

THOU arrant robber, Death!
Couldst thou not find
Some lesser one than he
To rob of breath,—
Some poorer mind
Thy prey to be?

His mind was like the sky,—
    As pure and free;
His heart was broad and open
    As the sea.
His soul shone purely through his
        face,
And Love made him her dwelling
        place.

Not less the scholar than the
        friend,
    Not less a friend than man;
The manly life did shorter end
    Because so broad it ran.

Weep not for him, unhappy Muse!
His merits found a grander use
Some other-where. God wisely
        sees
The place that needs his qualities.
Weep not for him, for when Death
        lowers
O'er youth's ambrosia-scented bow-
        ers
He only plucks the choicest flow-
        ers.

AN OLD MEMORY

How sweet the music sounded
    That summer long ago,
When you were by my side, love,
    To list its gentle flow.

I saw your eyes a-shining,
    I felt your rippling hair,
I kissed your pearly cheek, love,
    And had no thought of care.

And gay or sad the music,
    With subtle charm replete;
I found in after years, love
    'Twas you that made it sweet.

For standing where we heard it,
    I hear again the strain;
It wakes my heart, but thrills it
    With sad, mysterious pain.

It pulses not so joyous
    As when you stood with me,
And hand in hand we listened
    To that low melody.

Oh, could the years turn back
        love!
    Oh, could events be changed
To what they were that time, love
    Before we were estranged;

Wert thou once more a maiden
    Whose smile was gold to me
Were I once more the lover
    Whose word was life to thee,—

O God! could all be altered,
  The pain, the grief, the strife,
And wert thou — as thou shouldst
    be —
  My true and loyal wife!

But all my tears are idle,
  And all my wishes vain.
What once you were to me, love,
  You may not be again.

For I, alas! like others,
  Have missed my dearest aim.
I asked for love. Oh, mockery!
  Fate comes to me with fame!

A CAREER

" BREAK me my bounds, and let
    me fly
To regions vast of boundless sky;
Nor I, like piteous Daphne, be
Root-bound. Ah, no! I would
    be free
As yon same bird that in its flight
Outstrips the range of mortal
    sight;
Free as the mountain streams that
    gush
From bubbling springs, and down-
    ward rush
Across the serrate mountain's
    side,—
The rocks o'erwhelmed, their
    banks defied,—
And like the passions in the soul,
Swell into torrents as they roll.

Oh, circumscribe me not by rules
That serve to lead the minds of
    fools!
But give me pow'r to work my
    will,
And at my deeds the world shall
    thrill.
My words shall rouse the slumb'r-
    ing zest
That hardly stirs in manhood's
    breast;
And as the sun feeds lesser lights,
As planets have their satellites,
So round about me will I bind
The men who prize a master
    mind!"

He lived a silent life alone,
And laid him down when it was
    done;
And at his head was placed a
    stone
On which was carved a name un-
    known!

ON THE RIVER

THE sun is low,
The waters flow,
My boat is dancing to and fro.
The eve is still,
Yet from the hill
The killdeer echoes loud and shrill.

The paddles plash,
The wavelets dash,
We see the summer lightning flash;

While now and then,
In marsh and fen
Too muddy for the feet of men,

Where neither bird
Nor beast has stirred,
The spotted bullfrog's croak is
heard.
The wind is high,
The grasses sigh,
The sluggish stream goes sobbing
by.

And far away
The dying day
Has cast its last effulgent ray;
While on the land
The shadows stand
Proclaiming that the eve's at hand.

POOR WITHERED ROSE

A Song

Poor withered rose, she gave it me,
Half in revenge and half in glee;
Its petals not so pink by half
As are her lips when curled to
laugh,
As are her cheeks when dimples
gay
In merry mischief o'er them play.

Chorus

Forgive, forgive, it seems un-
kind
To cast thy petals to the
wind;

But it is right, and lest I err
So scatter I all thought of her.

Poor withered rose, so like my
heart,
That wilts at sorrow's cruel dart.
Who hath not felt the winter's
blight
When every hope seemed warm
and bright?
Who doth not know love unre-
turned,
E'en when the heart most wildly
burned?

Poor withered rose, thou liest
dead;
Too soon thy beauty's bloom hath
fled.
'Tis not without a tearful ruth
I watch decay thy blushing routh;
And though thy life goes out in
dole,
Thy perfume lingers in my soul.

WORN OUT

You bid me hold my peace
And dry my fruitless tears,
Forgetting that I bear
A pain beyond my years.

You say that I should smile
And drive the gloom away;
I would, but sun and smiles
Have left my life's dark day.

All time seems cold and void,
  And naught but tears remain;
Life's music beats for me
  A melancholy strain.

I used at first to hope,
  But hope is past and gone;
And now without a ray
  My cheerless life drags on.

Like to an ash-stained hearth
  When all its fires are spent;
Like to an autumn wood
  By storm winds rudely shent,—

So sadly goes my heart,
  Unclothed of hope and peace;
It asks not joy again,
  But only seeks release.

JAMES WHITCOMB RILEY

(From a Westerner's Point of View.)

No matter what you call it,
  Whether genius, or art,
He sings the simple songs that come
  The closest to your heart.
Fur trim an' skillful phrases,
  I do not keer a jot;
'Tain't the words alone, but feelin's,
  That tech the tender spot.
An' that's jest why I love him,—
  Why, he's got sech human feelin',
An' in ev'ry song he gives us,
  You kin see it creepin', stealin',

Through the core the tears go tricklin',
  But the edge is bright an' smiley;
I never saw a poet
  Like that poet Whitcomb Riley.

His heart keeps beatin' time with our'n
  In measures fast or slow;
He tells us jest the same ol' things
  Our souls have learned to know.
He paints our joys an' sorrers
  In a way so stric'ly true,
That a body can't help knowin'
  That he has felt them too.
If there's a lesson to be taught,
  He never fears to teach it,
An' he puts the food so good an' low
  That the humblest one kin reach it.
Now in our time, when poets rhyme
  For money, fun, or fashion,
'Tis good to hear one voice so clear
  That thrills with honest passion.
So let the others build their songs,
  An' strive to polish highly,—
There's none of them kin tech the heart
  Like our own Whitcomb Riley.

A MADRIGAL

DREAM days of fond delight and hours
  As rosy-hued as dawn, are mine.

Love's drowsy wine,
Brewed from the heart of Passion
    flowers,
  Flows softly o'er my lips
And save thee, all the world is
    in eclipse.

There were no light if thou wert
    not;
  The sun would be too sad to
    shine,
  And all the line
Of hours from dawn would be a
    blot;
  And Night would haunt the
    skies,
  An unlaid ghost with staring
    dark-ringed eyes.

Oh, love, if thou wert not my love,
  And I perchance not thine —
    what then?
  Could gift of men
Or favor of the God above,
  Plant aught in this bare heart
  Or teach this tongue the sing-
    er's soulful art?

Ah, no! 'Tis love, and love alone
  That spurs my soul so surely on;
  Turns night to dawn,
And thorns to roses fairest blown;
  And winter drear to spring —
  Oh, were it not for love I could
    not sing!

A STARRY NIGHT

A CLOUD fell down from the heav-
    ens,
  And broke on the mountain's
    brow;
It scattered the dusky fragments
  All over the vale below.

The moon and the stars were anx-
    ious
  To know what its fate might be;
So they rushed to the azure op'n-
    ing,
  And all peered down to see.

A LYRIC

MY lady love lives far away,
And oh my heart is sad by day,
And ah my tears fall fast by night,
What may I do in such a plight.

Why, miles grow few when love is
    fleet,
And love, you know, hath flying
    feet;
Break off thy sighs and witness
    this,
How poor a thing mere distance is.

My love knows not I love her so,
And would she scorn me, did she
    know?
How may the tale I would impart
Attract her ear and storm her
    heart?

Calm thou the tempest in my
    breast,
Who loves in silence loves the
    best,
But bide thy time, she will awake,
No night so dark but morn will
    break.

But though my heart so strongly
    yearn,
My lady loves me not in turn,
How may I win the blest reply
That my void heart shall satisfy.

Love breedeth love, be thou but
    true,
And soon thy love shall love thee,
    too;
If Fate hath meant you heart for
    heart,
There's naught may keep you
    twain apart.

HOW SHALL I WOO THEE

How shall I woo thee to win thee,
    mine own?
    Say in what tongue shall I tell
      of my love.
who was fearless so timid have
    grown,

All that was eagle has turned
    into dove.
The path from the meadow that
    leads to the bars
Is more to me now than the path
    of the stars.

How shall I woo thee to win thee,
    mine own,
    Thou who art fair and as far as
      the moon?
Had I the strength of the torrent's
    wild tone,
    Had I the sweetness of warblers
      in June;
The strength and the sweetness
    might charm and persuade,
But neither have I my petition to
    aid.

How shall I woo thee to win thee,
    mine own?
    How shall I traverse the dis-
      tance between
My humble cot and your glorious
    throne?
    How shall a clown gain the ear
      of a queen?
Oh teach me the tongue that shall
    please thee the best,
For till I have won thee my heart
    may not rest.